Managing Import and Export Opportunities and Risks
An Insider's Guide for the Busy Executive

Business Education Edition

Third Edition

International Trade Publishing
an imprint of
Shayne Law Group, P.C.

DISCLAIMER

This book is provided for educational purposes and, therefore, judgments are made as to what materials, authorities, and points to include and/or exclude. Neither the publisher nor authors assume any liability for actions taken in reliance upon any materials or opinions expressed in this book.

Every Importer and Exporter is unique as are their products and transactions. While the materials are intended to help you identify some of the issues that might affect you, your product, and/or transaction, a more thorough examination of the facts and circumstances, as well as a review of the current laws, rules and decisions, should be made before taking any action. Whether the review is conducted in-house or by an experienced trade attorney, what is important is that you base your decision upon a more complete review and not solely upon materials provided in this book for educational purposes.

ATTRIBUTION

"K" LINE AMERICA, INC. for the photographs of one of their containerships along with the loading of containers.

NEW YORK PUBLIC LIBRARY for the print of cargo loading in the 19th Century.

PORT OF SEATTLE for the photographs of the loading of a container sized crate in 1912.

PORT OF SEATTLE for the photographs of the loading of containers in the 1950s.

U.S. CUSTOMS AND BORDER PROTECTION for the cargo inspection photographs.

INCOTERMS® is the registered trademark of the International Chamber of Commerce (Chambre De Commerce Internationale Association).

INCOTERMS® FOR AMERICANS® is the registered trademark of Frank Reynolds.

ATLAS HAULING A CONTAINER is the registered trademark of William Shayne.

For permissions, contact William Shayne, Shayne Law Group, P.C., 64 Fulton Street, Suite 1000, New York, NY 10038, email: wshayne@shaynelawgroup.com.

Third Edition. Published 2017 by International Trade Publishing Co., New York, NY. International Trade Publishing Co. is an imprint of Shayne Law Group, P.C.

Second Edition. Published 2014 by International Trade Publishing Co., New York, NY. International Trade Publishing Co. is an imprint of Shayne Law Group, P.C.

First Edition. As Managing Opportunity and Risk in International Trade, Published 1995 by Unz & Co., Middlesex, NJ.

ISBN-13: 978-0-9842086-3-0

Library of Congress Control Number: 2016997383

INTRODUCTION TO THE BUSINESS EDUCATION EDITION

International Trade is, at the business and legal level, a term which covers a wide and diverse set of concepts and laws involving international and domestic business, as well as compliance issues.

The reality is that most businesses, even if not directly involved with international trade as a buyer, seller or service provider, are nonetheless affected by it, through the use of foreign made products and materials, or by competition.

Legal issues are an unavoidable part of business. Managing *Import and Export Opportunities and Risks* seeks to place those issues in the context of business practicalities.

This edition addresses business implications in the context of domestic and international laws, treaties and established commercial trade practices.

The goal of the Business Education Edition of *Managing Import and Export Opportunities and Risks*, is to provide a rich understanding of the issues affecting international trade today and to help you appreciate, and more importantly, identify the opportunities and risks affecting your business transactions.

OUTLINE

– Page intentionally left blank –

FOREWORD

I have been actively involved in international trade and Customs issues for more than 44 years, with experience in both the public and private sector. I started my Government career as an Import Specialist with U.S. Customs in the port of Baltimore and ended it as the Commissioner of Customs in 1997. In between, I served as an Attorney-Advisor at the U.S. International Trade Commission and as Staff Director of the House Ways and Means Trade Subcommittee, where I was proud to have led the effort to enact The Customs Modernization Act in 1993.

Throughout my Government career, I have strived to work with the business community to foster a partnership with Government to facilitate trade and compliance in a safe, secure and efficient manner. For the past 19 years I have worked in the private sector with a broad range of clients to accomplish the same goals. There is no question that this goal has become more challenging in the post-9/11 world, where security has become such a priority for Customs and the volume and complexity of trade has increased exponentially.

The risks faced by companies moving goods globally have expanded as well, and the need for international traders to be on top of their game has never been more critical. Where there may have been an opportunity to hide behind a lack of operational knowledge in the past, the introduction of the concept of "Informed Compliance" in the Customs Modernization Act ended such opportunity years ago. Understanding what needs to be done, or can be done to effect the process of international trade, is essential to avoiding corporate and personal liability. Conversely, understanding these rules enables one to take advantage of the many opportunities strewn throughout the law.

Over my career I have had the opportunity to view international trade from various perspectives. From my perspective, as both a Commissioner of Customs and an Import Specialist, where our primary focus was compliance and enforcement, the failure of importers and exporters to know their obligations was a perennial problem. In private practice, I have found that most client problems arise from a failure to understand the rules and obligations and, at a more basic level, a failure to ask questions before acting.

The authors of Managing Import and Export Opportunities and Risks have found a balance between understanding the legal requirements and business practicalities of international trade. It is not a legal treatise on Trade Law or a documentation manual, nor was it intended to be either. It is exactly what it says it is - a guide for busy executives, aimed at putting international trade and compliance in context of business realities.

It is the product of Bill and Mel's practical and legal experience, presented in an easy to read and useful format that showcases their experience in educating business professionals. The language is clear and uncharacteristically brief for lawyers, concepts are explained plainly in business terms, and are made readily accessible for both quick reference and in-depth review.

There will always be questions to ask, but Managing Import and Export Opportunities and Risks is a good resource for answers and, more importantly, the understanding you need in order to ask the right questions.

George J. Weise - Ocean View, Delaware, April 2016

PREFACE

When I first started teaching professionals about international trade I was met by audiences with experience ranging from beginner to those with over 30 years in international trade. Despite my practical and legal experience, I was skeptical of my ability to impart knowledge to professionals who had more years of experience in international trade than I had years of age. I was just waiting for one of those seasoned professionals to try to take the floor and show me up. It never happened.

It only took me five minutes to identify those seasoned professionals. None of them had ever told me how many years of experience they had nor had I asked. It wasn't their grey hair that tipped me off either. It was apparent because they were the ones taking notes. They were the ones who knew enough to understand that they didn't know everything. The approach to this book is rooted in that observation.

When I first started preparing Customs Entries my father asked me what I should do first. I immediately started discussing the valuation laws. He stopped me cold. He said, "The first thing you do is take out the staple." He explained that every transaction contains a story and that you couldn't make decisions about it unless you first understand that story. The same applies to managing your international trade transactions; you need to know the full story.

My classes routinely included professionals ranging from documentation clerks to licensed customs brokers, freight forwarders, accountants, attorneys, to corporate officers and owners, but it was clear that, in the context of international trade, they couldn't see the whole story.

Executives have a particular problem in that these stories are conveyed to them by others. You can't, however, assume the messengers know enough to see the whole picture and convey the whole story. From a supervisory standpoint you need to be able to discern that there is a missing part of the story.

The First Edition of this book was not written purely from my intellectual experience. It was written from my teaching experience and working with professionals, the questions that they were asking, the context in which those questions arose, and observations as to shortfalls in their knowledge. For 5 years I videotaped every one of my classes, including questions and discussions, as a vehicle for refining my praxis and transcribing the *best of* or at least most effective presentations.

Stylistically it follows the style of Harvey B. Mackay who wrote "Swim with the Sharks Without Being Eaten Alive" who said what he needed to say and then had the wisdom and courage to stop talking even if it meant having a chapter of only one-half page.

Meanwhile, my co-author Mel Lazar had been teaching adults at New York University in their Continuing Education School. Together, we added additional materials that we thought would provide further insight.

The 3rd Edition is, exactly what the subtitle says it is, an Insider's Guide for the Busy Executive which balances the legal and practical. **We presume that a busy executive will not read the entire book**. The Executive Briefings found at the beginning of each chapter are intended to provide you with a good foundation on what issues might affect your opportunities and risks, even if you have not read a particular section in its entirety. Sidebar notes add insights.

Timing is everything in life and this 3rd Edition includes important changes introduced in the Trade Facilitation and Enforcement Act of 2015, rules which became effective July 1st 2016 and the January 23rd 2017 trade initiatives of President Donald Trump.

William (Billie) Shayne, New York, NY, January 2017

ABOUT THE AUTHORS

The authors are attorneys with extensive practical and legal experience in the areas of Customs, International Trade and Transportation. For most of their careers they have each been teaching the subject to businesses.

William C. Shayne

William Shayne (Billie) started his career working in Customs Brokerage where he performed every task from messenger to post-entry problem resolution to designing and programming automated systems for Customs and Transportation related activities.

Shifting to the legal side, he has been practicing for over 30 years in the areas of Customs, International Trade and Transportation law, representing Importers, Exporters, Multi-National Businesses, Freight Forwarders, Non-Vessel Operating Common Carriers, Customs Brokers, and others involved in International Trade.

He is a principal in Shayne Law Group, P.C. and Schrier, Shayne, Koenig, Samberg & Ryne, P.C. where he is the Managing Attorney of their International Trade practice. He is admitted to practice before various courts including the Court of International Trade, Court of Appeals for the Federal Circuit, United States District Courts for the Southern and Eastern Districts of New York, Northern District of Illinois, and the Court of Appeals for the Second Circuit.

He has been teaching international trade to industry professionals, including management, in-house counsel, and accountants for over 35 years.

He holds a Bachelor degree from Ithaca College, a Master's degree in Adult Education from Fordham University, and a Juris Doctor degree from Quinnipiac University School of Law.

This book originated from his years of experience in teaching the trade, and his observation of the risks and opportunities of which even seasoned professionals were unaware.

He is also the author of several other books on International Trade including:

Managing Risk and Opportunity in International Trade -An Introduction to Risk Management for Importers and Exporters (Shayne)

NAFTA Rules of Origin (Shayne)

The *U.S. – Canada Free Trade Agreement (Lande and Shayne)*

The *Customs Brokers' Act of 1984 (Shayne)*

He is also the creator of Trade-ID.com which is the only identity verification application specifically designed for use in international trade by Customs Brokers seeking to protect their clients from the risks of Identity Theft.

Melvin E. Lazar

Mel Lazar was, for almost 30 years an Associate Professor in the Finance, Law & Tax Department at NYU's School of Professional Studies. He taught various courses including International Trade Law and Regulation, Principles of International Trade, and Fundamentals of Business Law.

He holds a B.S. Degree in Commerce & Economics from the University of Vermont, an MBA Degree from the NYU Graduate School of Business, and a Juris Doctor Degree from NYU School of Law.

His extensive professional experience in the field of International Trade has been in both the public and private sectors. He served as Senior Attorney in the Office of Chief Counsel U.S. Customs Service in New York. He also served as Assistant Regional Counsel in the Office of Regional Counsel, U.S. Customs Service in New York.

He is presently Of Counsel to Shayne Law Group, P.C. focusing on Customs, International Trade, and Transportation matters. He is admitted to practice before various Federal Courts, including the U.S. Court of International Trade and the U.S. Supreme Court.

The authors can be contacted at:

SHAYNE
LAW GROUP, P.C.

64 Fulton Street
Suite 1000
New York, NY 10038

212 566-4949

William Shayne - wshayne@shaynelawgroup.com

Melvin Lazar - mlazar@shaynelawgroup.com

– Balance of page intentionally left blank –

SPECIAL THANKS

(In Alphabetical Order)

A book like this does not get written without the input of many people, either as part of intellectual conversation or reviews of early drafts. We therefore wish to express our profound appreciation to the following:

MICHAEL BARATTA, for his assistance in locating samples of various Customs documents and for preparing a 2016 rendition of an 1826 Entry. Michael is President of Corbett International, Inc., which is believed to be the second oldest Customs Brokerage firm in the United States.

ERNEST CHAMBRE, who was a Conservator for U. S. Customs and my mentor in collecting historical documents.

DEANNA CLARK-ESPOSITO, who was a senior attorney at Shayne Law Group, P.C. for her assistance in researching and authoring various sections of the book.

ELLEN A. DILAPI, for contributing much of the research required for updating the book. Ellen is an attorney at Shayne Law Group, P.C. and an associate of mine at other firms over the years. She has been practicing Customs Law for 15 years. She was also Assistant Director of Programs at the Practicing Law Institute where she designed and coordinated continuing legal educations programs and publications.

JOEL DITKOWSKY, for his ability to locate the most elusive resources. Joel has been a Customs Broker for over 50 years. He is the past President of the J.F.K. Airport Customs Brokers Association and an industry representative to KAAMCO (Kennedy Airport Airline Management Council). He has been an instructor on Trade and Security issues to personnel from various government agencies at the Merchant Marine Academy at Kings Point and has been program coordinator for the Long Island Importers and Exporters Association, Inc. for the last 10 years. Joel currently runs the problem resolution desk for Freight Brokers Global Services Inc. and is a Principal Consultant with EXIMDO Trade Services, handling C-TPAT and other related supply chain security matters.

SEAN DOHERTY, for his comments, suggestions and updates on forthcoming changes affecting international traffic. Sean retired from U.S. Customs and Border Protection after 35 years of service. He served in numerous key managerial positions in both New York and Washington, DC and was the first Field Director of the New York C-TPAT Field Office. Sean is currently an Advisory Executive with BSI Supply Chain Solutions, providing guidance and training in maintaining government certification programs in supply chain security, including C-TPAT, Partners in Protection, and Authorized Economic Operators.

AUDREY DRILLICH, for her invaluable insight into reader perspective, extensive research, and countless other efforts that were key in bringing this book together. She has over 20 years of experience working for importers and has been my Paralegal and Executive Assistant at various Customs and International Trade law firms for the last 16 years.

CJ ERICKSON, for his assistance in locating sample documents. CJ is a former partner of mine and is currently a partner in the Intellectual Property firm of Cowan, Liebowitz & Latman, P.C.

BETA BROKERS is a fictitious Customs Broker used in specimen documents.

RICHARD AND KRISTIN HANEL of H.W. St. John Company, a New York based Customs Broker founded in 1902, for providing me with specimen documents on so many occasions.

KATHLEEN KING, PHD, the head of the Master's Program in Adult Education at Fordham University, now at the University of Central Florida, for inspiration and the language and knowledge to support and enhance my teaching skills.

ANTHONY LAFORTEZA, for sharing his export logistic experience. Anthony has been involved in Transportation and Export Logistics for over 50 years. Tony has been teaching Air and Ocean Freight Shipping and International Trade Logistics for 15 years at The World Trade Institute, Pace University, Baruch College Continuing and Professional Studies, and NYU School of Professional Studies.

MARTIN MARGULIES, Professor of Law, now Professor Emeritus, at Quinnipiac University School of Law for encouraging me to continually delve into alternatives; a good practice in any endeavor, but particularly in International Trade where alternatives are where the opportunities can be found.

JOSEPH MATTERA, for proving invaluable research. Joe is principal of International Trade Information Resources, former librarian for U.S. Customs and now in private practice providing intelligence research for importers and exporters.

FRANK REYNOLDS, for his comments, suggestions and insights. Frank is the President of International Projects, Inc. and author of *Incoterms® for Americans®*, a mainstay in Incoterms education, and has over 50 years of experience in International Trade. In addition to the previous editions of *Incoterms® for Americans®*, Frank has written nine books on trade related topics, including the *A to Z of International Trade* dictionary for the International Chamber of Commerce. He has also co-authored five books and written hundreds of trade-related columns for the *Journal of Commerce, The Exporter, Managing Exports* and the ICC's *Documentary Credit Insight.*

RON VAN DYCK for his review and comments in the context of management operations. Ron has been with Reliable Automatic Sprinkler, Inc. for over 20 years and is Vice President for Purchasing.

JAMES ROBERTS, of J.M. Rodgers Co., Inc. for his updates on current entry practices. James has been involved in International Trade for over 40 years, 30 of which as a Customs Broker, and has been involved in both Customs and C-TPAT Compliance.

JEFFREY SHAYNE for his extensive editing and copywriting assistance and for graphic design work on some of the more complex graphics used in the book, including Atlas Hauling a Container, which is used in the cover page artwork. Jeffrey is an aspiring copywriter, musician, and graphic designer working towards a career in marketing and advertising.

KEN SHAYNE who ran the export side of the family business and from whom I received a never ending line of stories of the scams that he saw being perpetrated against U.S. exporters.

MICHAEL SHAYNE for his graphic design work and illustrations. Michael is a freelance graphic designer, web designer and developer, and filmmaker.

LEONARD SHAYNE, my father and my teacher, the former President of Leading Forwarders, Inc., President of the National Customs Brokers & Forwarders Association of America, Inc., President of the New York Customs Brokers and Freight Forwarders Association. My dad taught me the business, as he put it, the way he wished that he had been taught; not solely intellectually, but experientially; performing every task associated with importing and exporting, from lodging documents with carriers, to devanning containers, traffic, to entry, to post entry, and business accounting and management. Much of the practical incite in my teaching and this book is the result of the way he taught me the trade.

Author of *Not All Importers-Exporters are Crooks,* an examination of his experiences with importer problems with Customs and still available at LuLu.com. (Interestingly, decades later, with all the changes in enforcement, in many aspects the stories are still the same – only the product and names have changed –sometimes not even the products.)

CAREN SHAYNE for her patience with all the stacks of research and drafts cluttering our apartment.

GEORGE WEISE for the Foreword to this edition of "Managing Import and Export Opportunities and Risks". Rarely, in recent times, has someone come to the position of Commissioner of Customs with the wealth of relevant knowledge as George did, and it showed in what was accomplished during his term. Mel and I are exceedingly gratified that he agreed to write the Foreword. I have been in this field for over 40 years, all in the private sector. I only regret that I never had the opportunity to work with George while he was Commissioner.

KENNEY WHITMAN for his review and comments with respect to ocean transportation. Kenney has been involved in ocean transportation for over 35 years and is the President of Oceanic Container Line Inc., a Non-Vessel Operating Common Carrier (NVO).

TABLE OF CONTENTS

– Balance of page intentionally left blank –

ILLUSTRATIONS

– Balance of page intentionally left blank –

1. INTRODUCTION

From the time this book was first published in 1995, the nature of international trade has changed, not so much in the business environment, and not even so much as it relates to the laws, rules and regulations which we have to deal with but more in terms of *when* we have to deal with them. Terrorist activities, especially the events of 9-11-2001, have forced us to look at activities beyond our physical borders and that has had a major impact on compliance timeframes, pushing them back from arrival in the U.S. to before the shipment leaves the port of export.

Add to that, significant health and safety issues, both at the federal and state levels, which have pushed obligations back even further: in many instances, all the way back to the manufacturing level.

Generally not thought about in the context of business is the rising risk of identity theft. Identity theft has been on the rise with respect to both imports and exports. Identity theft in international trade is more often theft of corporate identity than of personal identity. However, in both instances, it is the theft of one's good reputation. In the case of international trade, identity theft could jeopardize your good record with Customs which could, in turn, result in an increase in shipment inspections, document reviews, delays, and imposition of erroneous penalties.

This is not a traditional text on international trade or importing and/or exporting. This book was designed to examine the international transaction in order to expose both its risks and opportunities; to explain the legal requirements, not for their own sake but as they relate to practical consequences, so they can either be followed, or in some instances, avoided or modified. As in prior editions, the goal is not to make you an expert on importing or exporting procedures, but to give you a clear understanding of the major risks and how to avoid them, and to point out often overlooked opportunities and pitfalls.

Customs duties are taxes that are paid upon importation of merchandise. In the same way that a company may legally take advantage of the opportunities under the internal revenue law to design a transaction to minimize taxes, an import transaction can also be legally designed to minimize Customs Duties.

Penalties are best thought of as unexpected expenses that arise either, from a legal standpoint, the failure to comply with the law, or, from a commercial standpoint, a variety of logistical complications. The problem today is that, very often, the penalties alone can amount to more than the Customs duties, and sometimes as much as the cost of the goods themselves.

Even those that once saw themselves as merely service providers, middleman or trading companies, have seen these liabilities pushed onto their plate, either as a result of government rules or the expectations of their clients.

Knowledge and planning can help maximize opportunity and almost simultaneously control risks.

> Like any other tax, an importer is obligated to pay only the lowest tax that is legally due. There is no requirement to pay more, although generally, no government will complain if that is what you want to do.
>
> It is obvious that a false statement as to value of description in the United States would violate U.S. law and lead to penalties.
>
> What is not so obvious is that a false statement intended to help someone in another country avoid government charges and entanglements, can, independent of the problems it may create for them in the foreign country, also constitute a violation, for you, of U.S. Law.

1.1. WHO SHOULD READ THIS BOOK

This book is designed for management directly or indirectly involved in international trade. It is not designed or intended to be either a clerk's guide on filling in forms, or an all-inclusive legal dissertation.

As lawyers who practice primarily in the areas of law involving Customs, related government agencies, transportation, and international trade, and as professionals with work experience in the customs brokerage, freight forwarding and NVOCC industries, it has been our aim in this text to try to combine the precision of a lawyer with the practicality of a businessman. As a consequence, this text does not cover every area or every issue; many of the details would bore even the authors to tears.

This book covers what we believe that a person responsible for imports and/or exports, either at the planning or management level, needs to know to make effective decisions.

Importers all too often rely upon the foreign exporter's knowledge of what is required to import goods into the United States. This is dangerous because it is the importer who is liable to the importing country for what the foreign exporter does or doesn't do.

While the obligations and rules may be couched in terms of exporters and importers, the reality today, is that from a business management standpoint, all businesses, both exporting and importing, are merely the opposite side of the same transaction, which means that to service a customer's needs, you really have to think as both. And if you are merely providing services such as Freight Forwarding, Carriage or Customs Brokerage, the only way to service them effectively is to understand both aspects of their transaction.

> Regardless of which side of a transaction you may be on, you cannot effectively manage the transaction unless you understand the transaction from both sides.

1.2. WHY READ THIS BOOK

This book is written for management. It is intended to educate executives on the trade issues their businesses face in order to more effectively manage their Opportunities and Risks.

This is not a how-to-book. Many other books are available which address operational details and provide do-it-yourself forms.

> ***The best defense against risk is knowledge.***

What this book will do:

- ✓ Translate trade and legal complexities into management practicalities,
- ✓ Help you convert the appearance of good practice into the reality of compliance, and
- ✓ Highlight opportunities and risks that too often get lost in the mire of legalisms.

Over the last few decades there has been a substantial change in the laws governing International Trade and, as a result of a series of reorganized priorities, "***You don't want to be found doing things improperly***"[1]. Under a notion termed '***Informed Compliance***' there has been a significant increase in the responsibility imposed upon importers and others involved in International Trade to exercise '***reasonable care.***' Informed Compliance puts businesses under an ***affirmative obligation*** to take steps to determine how to comply with the law[2], not just to avoid violating it overtly.

Customs and Border Protection (CBP), formerly known as U.S. Customs Service (USCS), is responsible for enforcement of both U.S. import and export laws, now offers an incentive for compliance with those laws. An importer who plays by the "importing rules" will be rewarded with easier entry procedures. Conversely, Customs has reassured the trade community that it will assess stiff penalties against importers who don't comply.

While there is generally less regulation from the U.S. side on exports than on imports, exporters should not take this to mean that their activities are without risk. Today, considerable emphasis is placed on enforcement of the export trade regulations and filings. Exporters should expect to be held to the same standards of Informed Compliance as importers.

In the U.S. the primary security focus has been directed towards imports. However, with the advent of worldwide mutual recognition on cargo security, caution should be used when exporting as well.

What constitutes opportunity may be easy to comprehend, but the nature and scope of risk may be less obvious and ever changing. Many of the more controllable risks are the result of routine business practices that have not kept up with the times but, having never been called into question, were accepted as compliant. All too often importers and exporters only find out their practices were deficient when a problem arises. What they saw as evidence of good practices was really just good fortune.

Trade Trivia

U.S. Customs was, for over 200 years, primarily a revenue agency. And, until 1913 when the personal income tax was enacted, was the main source of government revenues; in some years as much as 90%. Today, Customs duties, while still the second largest source of federal revenues, represent only a small fraction of federal revenue.

As duties became less important as a source of revenue, the focus has moved toward regulatory enforcement.

In 2003, Customs was merged into the Department of Homeland Security, because of its broad obligations to protect U.S. borders.

Managing Import and Export Opportunities and Risks is intended to make the importance of opportunities and risks clear so that you can better evaluate which are, or might be, important to your business.

Having been written with the busy executive in mind, it also takes into account that you will likely read only what you perceive as important.

1.3. HOW TO USE THIS BOOK

Where possible, we have included Executive Briefings at the beginning of each chapter. They are, of necessity, abbreviated, but generally provide a glimpse into what we believe is important. While we know that you will benefit from reading our entire tome, we appreciate that management needs to prioritize its time and it is hoped that these Executive Briefings will help you focus your time on what is important to you and your business.

DON'T READ EVERYTHING.

READ WHAT IS IMPORTANT

WHEN IT IS IMPORTANT.

Through Executive Briefings and Side Bar Comments we will help you understand what is important in a subject. Side Bar Comments like this one, point out areas of particular importance or what would otherwise be considered a tidbit of valuable information.

Executive Briefing

Executive Briefings such as this provide a business summary of what the authors believe is important in the section that follows so that you can decide whether it is important to you.

Some sections need Executive Briefings for individual topics. Some have none because the importance of the subject is self-evident.

Insights are provided to help you identify points that are often overlooked.

They can be found anywhere within the text and are always in a Sidebar Comment.

Side Bar Comments point out things that are of special interest or would otherwise be considered a tidbit of valuable information.

As you get started, if you do nothing else, we suggest that you

COPY

The Table of Contents, and
Best Practices, §22 at 211

READ

The Executive Briefings, and
The Sidebar Comments.

1.4. LINKS TO ONLINE MATERIALS

Current versions of Customs Laws, Regulations, Harmonized Tariff, and Rulings are available on line.

Harmonized Tariff Schedules of the United States (HSTUS)
By Chapter:
https://hts.usitc.gov/current

Customs Laws - Tariff Act of 1930, 19 as amended (19 U.S.C.)
Sections 1202 - 1683g:
http://www.gpo.gov/fdsys/granule/USCODE-2010-title19/USCODE-2010-title19-chap4

Customs Regulations (19 C.F.R.):

http://www.ecfr.gov/cgi-bin/text-idx?tpl=/ecfrbrowse/Title19/19tab_02.tpl

Customs Rulings on Classification, Value, and Marking:

http://rulings.cbp.gov

Consolidated Export Sanctions List Search including OFAC and SDN as well as various other programs:

http://apps.export.gov/csl-search#/csl-search

Customs has issued numerous Informed Compliance Guides under the title **What Every Member of the Trade Community Should Know About.**

A number of these guides cover the basic concepts of valuation, classification, and compliance, however, most are product specific. At the time of printing there were over 75 product specific Informed Compliance guides available.

At times, new guides are published and existing ones updated. It is therefore good practice to periodically review the list of Informed Compliance Publications for guides that might impact your product line and transactions.

You will see an Informed Compliance Publication cover page at various times in this book as a means of letting you know that publication related to this topic is available on Customs website.

www.cbp.gov/trade/rulings/informed-compliance-publications

1.5. ATTENTION TO DETAILS – AN AUTHOR'S CAUTION

Trying to translate the mass of laws, regulations, government and commercial practices, all written in legalese, into business practicalities of necessity means that judgments have been made in writing this book as to the level of detail we addressed.

Every business and transaction is unique so while you gain knowledge and insight from Managing Import and Export Opportunities and Risks, any decisions and actions you take should still be based upon a review of your unique facts and circumstances to ensure that important details affecting your opportunity and risk are not overlooked or not taken into account.

---

[1]Director of International Trade, Compliance Division, United States Customs Service, quoted in "Customs Aims to Be Customer-Friendly", Women's Wear Daily, November 2, 1994

[2]House Ways and Means Committee Report, H.R. Rep. No 3450, 103d Cong., First Sess. 120. (1993)

– Balance of page intentionally left blank –

2. PUSHING BACK THE BORDER

Executive Briefing

It used to be that once a purchase was made, importing was a matter of logistics, and compliance was only addressed once goods arrived in the United States.

Today, the reality is that many requirements must be met before the goods can even be shipped to the U.S. Safety, security, and even environmental issues now require advance documentation and filings. Issues that were once solely the province of the Traffic Department are now as much the concern of the Design and Purchasing Departments.

Importers and Exporters have always had an:

- ✓ Obligation to make sure that goods they ordered were produced in conformity with U.S. laws,
- ✓ Opportunity to design their product and their transactions to minimize their duty/tax liabilities, and
- ✓ Incentive to formulate best practices to avoid financial risks.

What has changed is:

- What they are required to do,
- By when it has to be done,
- How much government intervention they have to deal with, and
- The impact of a failure of manufacturing quality control has on cost.

Most importers still consider that the involvement of the U.S. Government, and especially Customs, is triggered only when goods are arriving in the United States with the intent that they will stay here.

And that's the way it was for almost 200 years. Until as recently as the 1960s, all vessel cargo was loose and it was laden and unloaded by hand or by hoists and nets. The volume of cargo was much smaller, enforcement activities were essentially manual, 100% of the Customs Entries were examined and cargo was visually inspected by Customs prior to release.

- Continued on next page –

Port of New York, 18th Century [3]
Loading loose cargo by hoists

Port of Seattle 1912
Loading cargo by crane

The appearance of the containership in the 1960s, coupled with substantial increase in the volume of shipments, along with the automated link between Customs Brokers (the entry filer) and Customs, changed the way Customs handled enforcement and inspection of both entries and shipments.

Birth of containerization, Late 1950's
Loaded as though it was loose cargo.[4]

Present Date
Loading of full container[5]

Present Day
K-Line Humber Bridge
8,212 TEU or about 4,100 40ft Containers

Early container ships carried only a few hundred containers. Today's larger container ships carry up to 4,600 TEUs (2300 40ft containers) and it is expected that the next generations of vessels will carry from 13,000 to 30,000 TEUs (6,500 to 15,000 40ft containers). Those containers, which have been a boon for commercial traffic, are also a boon for smugglers.

Sealed Container[6]

Container being inspected[7]

Breaking the seal[8]

Sealed cargo containers, while offering security and efficiency, are also ideal for hiding the true nature of prohibited goods, including counterfeits, contraband, and weapons of mass destruction.

Drugs concealed in container floor.[9]

The increase in terrorism against the United States in the 1990's, culminating with the attacks of 9-11-2001, shifted risk perception from the importation of illicit goods and those not conforming to regulatory requirements, to the importation of Weapons of Mass Destruction. Adding to that the importations of contaminated foods and lead paint on toys, made change a necessity.

As a practical matter, from an International Trade perspective, the term border refers to a much a larger area than a map would show. Our protective borders have been pushed back to a point before cargo is loaded onto carriers bound for the U.S., before the point the cargo is packed and stowed for transport, and even back to the point of manufacturer.

– Balance of page intentionally left blank –

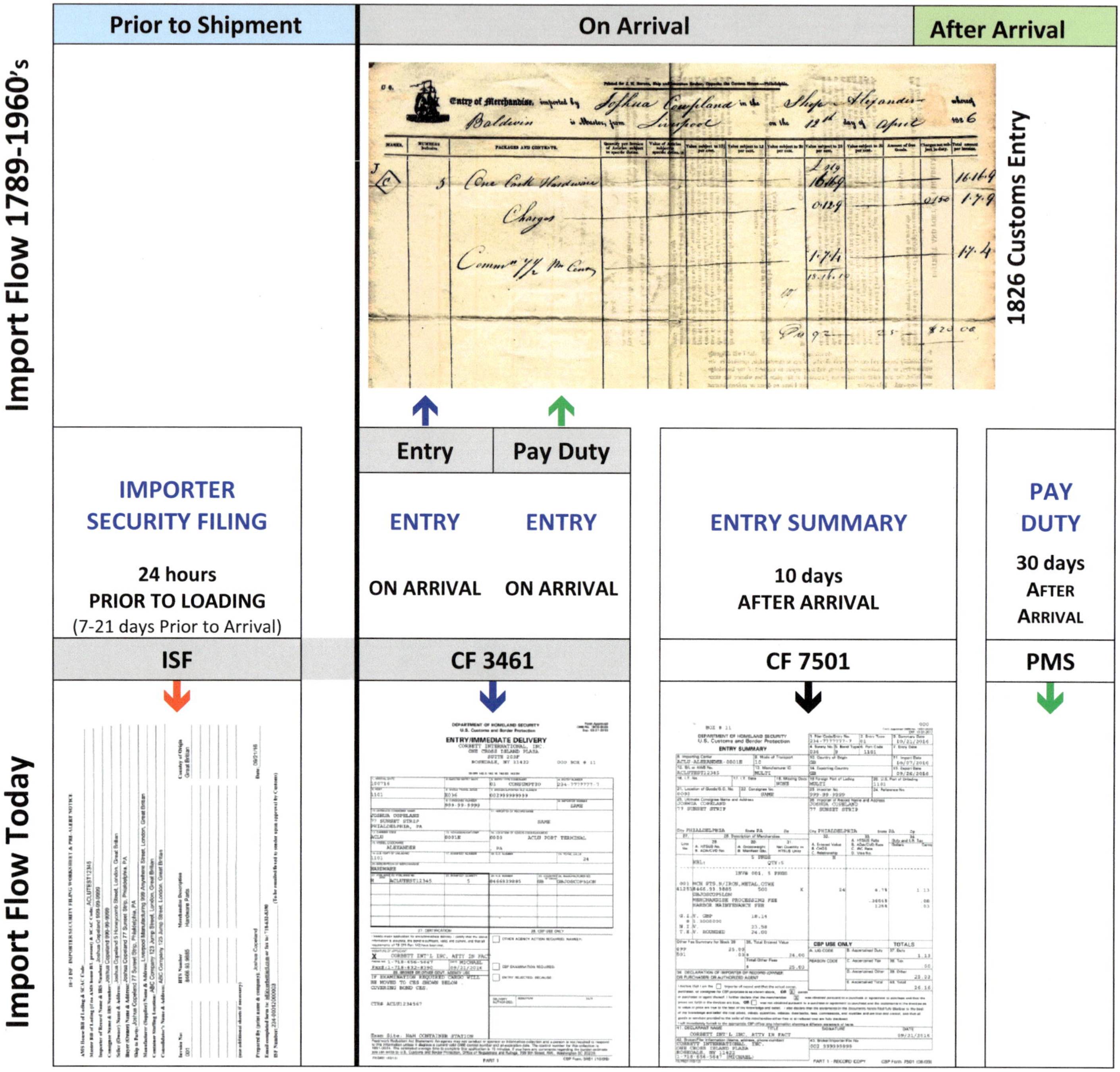

The term "Arrival" is used for illustrative purposes. Arrival is a conceptual approximation (+/- 5 days).

Figure 1 - Entry Flow – Pushing the Borders Back

As a result, since 2001, a series of new initiatives were undertaken to increase security, all of which have imposed increased burden on commerce:

- The creation of the Customs-Trade Partnership against Terrorism (C-TPAT), which provides importers with the opportunity for reduced inspections in exchange for implementation of verifiable, enhanced supply chain security procedures. (2001)
- The "24-hour rule", which requires advance information filing and a clearance by Customs to even load the container on board a U.S. bound vessel. (2006)[10]

- Container Security Initiative (CSI), which among other things, put U.S. Customs Officers in foreign ports. (2002)
- The World Customs Organization's (WCO) adoption of the SAFE Framework of Standards to Secure and Facilitate Global Trade (SAFE Framework), which set out a common security schema for all member countries to follow and a provision for Mutual Recognition between international programs. (2005)[11]
- U.S. Safe Ports Act (2006) requires 100% inbound cargo screened for radiation.
- The Importer Security Filing (ISF), also known as "10+2," provides additional shipment details not previously required under the 24-hour rule and allows Customs to make a better evaluation of risk earlier on in the shipment process. (2009)

These systems, while born out of a need for security, also serve to improve enforcement of the rules, regulations and practices that affect every importer – except that now the government review starts weeks earlier, before the cargo is dispatched to the United States.

> In order to enhance detection of illicit shipments, information about current shipments are compared to a historical profile of the parties, ports, origin, and other relevant information.

Today, only about 4% of the cargo is physically inspected after arrival in the United States. But, 100% of the shipments are screened and evaluated for risk, based upon the information filed with Customs under both the 24-hour rule and Importer Security Filing programs, starting even before the cargo is loaded on to a U.S. bound vessel.

> Importing and Exporting is not just about buying and selling goods.
>
> Imports and exports are merely the opposite sides of the same transaction and what each party does affects the other.

Initially, other countries saw heightened cargo security post 9-11-2011 as being primarily a U.S. concern. In the years since, all major countries have come to realize the same concerns, and have similarly pushed back their borders under internationally common Security Framework of the World Customs Organization (WCO).

Consequently, other countries now expect that each security measure imposed upon them to secure U.S. bound cargo should be equally applied with respect to cargo being shipped to their own country - hardly an unreasonable expectation.

One aspect of the heightened interest in supply chain security has been to impose on importers and exporters the obligation to implement *best practices* for cargo security.

For the importer, risk infers the possibility of paying anything more than needed or required. That applies equally to the cost of merchandise, cost of shipping, Customs duties or taxes and an assortment of penalties, damages or losses, including unnecessary legal expenses.

For the exporter, risk refers to all the potential importing problems of its clients, penalties and/or seizure upon exportation as well as an inability to get paid.

For service providers, risk refers to an inability to effectively service your client and any suit by them claiming that you failed to perform services, either:

- In a workman like fashion according to industry standards, or
- In accordance with the terms of service to which you had agreed.

[3] Downloaded from: http://www.historypreserved.com/View_Draughts_Photos.htm

[4] Downloaded from: http://www.portseattle100.org/map-and-timeline/1950-1959

[5] Downloaded from: http://www.cbp.gov/newsroom/photo-gallery/photo/2013/12/trade-container-loading-red-hook-jd

[6] Downloaded from: https://www.flickr.com/photos/cbpphotos/15155405768/in/photolist-9MqnRC-9MqnSW-dqDkdV-dqDkgn-dqDtM3-dqDtPN-fDAahX-fDSJf3-fDA9wr-fDSGV7-fDSHBd-p6er6E-p6eq8s-p6eELz-9vGdnR-9vGdfD-pnGczL-doMF16-f4EfpF-aA4Zsj-4pm635-pkGGDU-p6exFV-9WcVsC-9WcVff-p6fw8w-p6eW41-pkGLwU-9sbQGi-bqbq5D-9WcUYW-6udHef-drJe42-dUfRJz-5AU5hn-drJec6-drJdZ2-drJe7M-drJdCv-drJnWy-drJdUk-drJdNT-htPivF-8ZzLFn-7fhy1U-f4GjHX-htPiHp-drKdHw-6a85UC-TtSuy

[7] Downloaded from: https://www.flickr.com/photos/cbpphotos/5765142282/in/photolist-9MrRWS-9MrRKw-9MrRA3-9Mp2YP-9Mp4Gt-9fnuWA-9fjo2K-9fjvvM-9fjqe4-puxasZ-puvoBq-pd2Zk2-pd42Aa-9Mp2U4-9fjp9g-9fjp3r-9fnwgw-9fnvZ3-9fnvTL-9fjpor-9fnwj3-9Mp1wp-8XG3pV-9MrPf1-9MrPY1-9MrPH1-9MrQ8S-9MrQk3-9Mp2G6-9MrQrY-9Mp1U2-9Mp1tp-dUfNGk-bqYZoT-bqYZfK-byPHfD-bqYZmX-9MoYUr-dUfTy8-bqYZbc-dUmuWL-dUmuSL-bZ46S3-dUmwfJ-dUfRVB-eazhpQ-jen7fz-eatBta-eazgYf-eazh9G

[8] Downloaded from: https://www.flickr.com/photos/cbpphotos/15155455017/in/photolist-9MqnRC-9MqnSW-dqDkdV-dqDkgn-dqDtM3-dqDtPN-fDAahX-fDSJf3-fDA9wr-fDSGV7-fDSHBd-p6er6E-p6eq8s-p6eELz-9vGdnR-9vGdfD-pnGczL-doMF16-f4EfpF-aA4Zsj-4pm635-pkGGDU-p6exFV-9WcVsC-9WcVff-p6fw8w-p6eW41-pkGLwU-9sbQGi-bqbq5D-9WcUYW-6udHef-drJe42-dUfRJz-5AU5hn-drJec6-drJdZ2-drJe7M-drJdCv-drJnWy-drJdUk-drJdNT-htPivF-8ZzLFn-7fhy1U-f4GjHX-htPiHp-drKdHw-6a85UC-TtSuy

[9] Downloaded from Customs and Border Protection: http:// link missing

[10] SECURITY AND ACCOUNTABILITY FOR EVERY PORT ACT OF 2006 commonly referred to as Safe Ports Act, Public Law 109-347, 109th Congress, 120 STAT. 1884

[11] http://www.wcoomd.org/en/topics/research/activities-and-programmes/~/media/44CC67F66E7C48FC9834F3504F9D7C19.ashx
http://www.wcoomd.org/en/topics/facilitation/instrument-and-tools/tools/safe_package.aspx

3. EXPORTER'S RESPONSIBILITIES

Executive Briefing

As the world becomes ever smaller, the differences between the concerns of the importer and exporter also become smaller. The exporter and importer are simply the opposite sides of the same transaction.

The substantial number of international conventions, the standardization of many international rules with respect to documentation and even classification and value, are causing the few remaining differences to shrink at an ever-increasing pace.

Today, the only way to be a good exporter is, in reality, to know as much as a knowledgeable importer, so that the client's needs can be anticipated.

While taxes are not a primary issue for exporters, export licensing is. Every article exported must be licensed for export. Most licenses are executed by the exporter, and often by its forwarder. Of concern is that many articles that are generally not considered particularly sophisticated are, nevertheless, considered 'high tech,' or otherwise restricted, and require a special form of government issued license. Exporters have an obligation to obtain the necessary export licenses and to comply with various restrictions that may still exist with respect to which countries they may sell certain goods. (*See* "U.S. Export Licenses" §3.3 at 17.) The failure to meet this obligation can result in seizure of the shipment along with substantial penalties.

Figure 2 - Confederate Currency - Export Duties

Trade Trivia

Until the imposition of income taxes, Customs Duties were the primary source of government revenue.

During the U.S. Civil War, the North (United States of America) continued to impose duties on imports but not exports.

The South (Confederate States of America) taxed exports and not imports. Because of their need for foreign exchange, Confederate currency was not accepted by the Confederacy in payment of those taxes.

Exports may also require a completion of certain export declarations. Those declarations can be country specific.

Customs and Border Protection, which is primarily responsible for enforcement of import laws, is also charged with enforcement of the export laws, and programs such as "Operation Exodus," and later "Shield America," have been very successful. Moreover, the new 'Informed Compliance' standard imposed by U.S. Customs on importers to exercise 'reasonable care' should be viewed by the prudent exporter as equally applicable to exports. (*See* "U.S. Export Licenses" §3.3 at 17 and "Informed Compliance" §22.1 at 212.)

The Commerce Department also requires that certain products to be exported must be subject to export licenses. These are complex and detailed rules and, depending on the product, will vary.

> Exporters, however, are now starting to feel the pinch of delays and costs associated with inspections, something importers have long since come to accept as part of the cost of doing business.

The exporter also has the obvious responsibility of producing goods which conform to the buyer's specifications. All too often, importers rely upon the exporter's knowledge of the importing country's laws and requirements, which can include knowledge of the specifications and standards for the product itself. (*See* "Restrictions on Domestically Produced Goods & Re-imported Goods" §16 at 151.) What may very well be of even greater significance, and less obvious, is the expectation that the exporter will know what documentation is required by the importing country. As a practical matter, if not contractually, the exporter has the responsibility to provide complete and accurate documentation with respect to the entire transaction.

> All too often Exporter mentality seems to be that the purchaser knows what they need and a seller's responsibility is limited to booking of the order and collecting payment.

If the exporter fails to live up to these expectations, the importer will bear the brunt, ranging from aggravation to an inability to import the goods. The additional costs may include storage charges or even the imposition of a variety of penalties ranging in the U.S. of up to three times the value of the goods.

3.1. ELECTRONIC EXPORT INFORMATION AND PRINCIPAL PARTY IN INTEREST

The paper version of what was known as the Shipper's Export Declaration (SED) has been replaced by the electronic version known as the Electronic Export Information or EEI. Along with the change in format came changes in the information required to be filed, and the person who is required to provide the information and maintain supporting documentations.

U.S. Census imposes different requirements depending upon the nature of the export transaction, distinguishing between those where the U.S. seller is the exporter and those where a foreign entity has taken control of the shipment domestically and acts as the exporter.

The Electronic Export Information filing incorporates 27 pieces of information, many of which are dependent on knowledge of other agency laws. While legally you can file your own EEI through the AES Direct http://aesdirect.census.gov/[12], most exporters find it more prudent to engage an Agent, usually a Freight Forwarder, to do this for them.

3.1.1. U.S. PRINCIPLE PARTY IN INTEREST (USPPI)

If you are the U.S. seller of goods sold for export you are likely the "U.S. Principal Party in Interest" in the transaction, and responsible for both the accuracy of the information about the transaction, as well as the filing of the Electronic Export Information (EEI).

> There is an exemption to filing Electronic Export Information for shipments valued under $2,500.
>
> However, since there are so many exceptions to the exemption, care should be taken if choosing not to file EEI.

The U.S. Principal Party in Interest is generally the person in the United States that receives the primary monetary benefit or other benefit of the export transaction and can include:

- U.S. Seller (wholesaler/distributor) of the merchandise for export.
- U.S. Manufacturer if selling the merchandise for export.
- U.S. Order Party - Party who directly negotiated between the U.S. seller and foreign buyer and received the order for the export of the merchandise.
- Foreign Entity if in the U.S. when items are purchased or obtained for export.

As a USPPI in a normal export transaction you are required to:

- Prepare the Electronic Export Information (EEI) OR authorize forwarding or other agent to prepare and file the EEI (Power of Attorney, Shipper's Letter of Instruction, or other written authorization.)
- Provide all required information to the Export Agent/Freight Forwarder so they can complete and file the EEI.
- Maintain documentation to support the information reported on the EEI.

While a forwarder may be required to provide the Seller (USPPI) with evidence of the proper filing of the information they provided, a forwarder's confidentiality obligation to its client, the Buyer (FPPI), would generally preclude them from sharing shipping details with the USPPI.

As the seller, getting your client's forwarder to actually provide the proof of filing can sometimes be difficult, if not impossible.

A good practice is, therefore, to annually make a request to Census for a record of all AES transactions filed under your EIN. (*See* "Free From the Authors" §23 at 241.)

3.1.2. FOREIGN PRINCIPAL PARTY IN INTEREST (FPPI)

Where the buyer takes delivery **prior to export** and makes its own arrangements for shipment in what is termed a "Routed Shipment," your purchaser will generally be considered a "Foreign Principle Party in Interest."

The Foreign Principal Party in Interest (FPPI) is generally the party shown on the transportation document to whom final delivery will be made or the "ultimate consignee,"[13] who will make use of the goods, whether their name appears on the shipping documents or not.

From a liability standpoint this is good for the U.S. seller since your responsibility is essentially reduced to providing accurate details about their sale.

Most of the basic information about the goods to be shipped has to be provided by the seller / USPPI.

The fundamental differences are:

- Who selects and designates the Authorized Agent or Freight Forwarder,
- Who provides the routing and destination details, and

- Who pays the Forwarder.

Since, as the USPPI, you are required to maintain copies of the documentation and information you supplied to the Freight Forwarder, you have a direct interest in ensuring that the filed Electronic Export Information accurately reflects the information you provided.

3.2. SOLAS GROSS WEIGHT VERIFICATION FILING

The Safety of Life at Sea or SOLAS[14] is an international treaty that requires ocean carriers to have a verified gross mass or weight for all cargo loaded on board their vessels.

> **CAUTION**
>
> Under SOLAS, cargo without a Verified Gross Mass (VGM) statement on file will not be loaded onboard the ship. The cost of delays, including demurrage, detention and additional drayage, will all be borne by the shipper.

It may be the carrier's obligation to maintain the Verified Gross Mass certification, but it is left to the shipper to provide it to the carrier.

The Verified Gross Mass (VGM) is the sum of the weight of the goods, the empty container (Tare Weight) in addition to pallets, dunnage and bracing.

VGWs may be signed by the shipper, or its agent, either electronically or on paper.

There are no uniform practices as to how cargo arriving at a carrier terminal, WITHOUT a pre-filed VGM, is to be handled. The last thing you want as a shipper is to find that the terminal will not accept your container because the VGM has not been pre-filed or that your cargo has to be rolled to another voyage because the VFG was not available in time.

There are two basic methods for obtaining a Verified Gross Mass. Both require the use of scales that are certified as accurate.

One method involves adding up the values of each of the materials stuffed into the container, including packaging, pallets, dunnage, and bracing to the Tare Weight (empty weight) of the container. When a container is stuffed at the factory, obtaining the information necessary to calculate the VGM is not expected to create a problem. Essentially, the weights provided by the factory serves as the Gross Weight on the Bill of Lading and that is added to the Tare Weight provided by the carrier and/or as printed on the container. Consequently, filing of the VGM prior to the delivery of the container to a terminal should not have any significant impact on operations.

> SOLAS went into effect on July 1, 2016. It will take time for it to become routine practice, so, at least until the end of 2016, asking in advance of your shipment about local practices would be prudent.

If you are shipping Less than a Container Load (LCL), you will not be the shipper on the Master Bill of Lading and the consolidator will arrange for the VGM on behalf of the NVO.

Otherwise, the only other means of obtaining the gross weight is to have the container weighed. This applies in particular to project type goods, household goods or personal effects, for which true weights are not known.

The problem for you as the shipper is that the timing, method, and availability of third-party services for obtaining the VGM are governed by a bewildering combination of rules imposed by the exporting country, the carriers, and the terminals which may not be uniform.

3.3. U.S. EXPORT LICENSES

While the United States does not impose duties on exports, it does control them.

3.3.1. COMMERCE DEPARTMENT

The Commerce Department requires an export license for certain classes of goods. The goods subject to the license requirement are organized by Export Control Classification Numbers (ECCN) and Export Administration Regulations (EAR). The types of goods covered generally include:

1. Nuclear & Miscellaneous
2. Materials, Chemicals, Microorganisms and Toxins
3. Materials Processing
4. Electronics
5. Computers
6. Telecommunications
7. Information Security
8. Sensors and Lasers
9. Navigation and Avionics
10. Marine
11. Aerospace and Propulsion

> Not every product in these groups is covered by the licensing requirement. Each product has to be analyzed and examined in detail to determine if it falls within the ECCN.

If the product does not fall into one of the above ECCNs that are listed on the Commerce Control List, it falls into the basket provision of EAR 99 and generally does not require a license.

> **CAUTION**
>
> Even if goods are EAR 99, when they are to be shipped to an embargoed country, to an end user of concern, or in support of a prohibited end use, a license may still be required.

There are numerous other laws that can impact your right to import or export a particular product. They are not all termed licenses, but since the consequence of failing to have a registration or document can result in an inability to move a shipment or to its seizure, from a practical standpoint it is all the same. It is not practical to list all restrictions that exist. Determining which might affect you or your transaction is more than a clerical activity and this is where working with a knowledgeable professional, be it your Customs Broker, Freight Forwarder or other logistics provider, government office, or Customs Counsel, can be the difference between success and failure. See Sources of Assistance, §22.6 at 233.

3.4. SUPPLY CHAIN SECURITY

Supply chain security programs were originally conceived as applying only to importers. But the reality is that Exports and Imports are merely the opposite ends of the supply chain. Just as under C-TPAT an importer is responsible for ensuring the security of their cargo from foreign origin to domestic destination, the same applies to many export customers under their local programs where they are the importers.

Under a concept known as Mutual Recognition, (*see* "WCO International Security Framework and Mutual Recognition", §22.5.2 at 232), various countries will accept the other country's supply security certification. Consequently the U.S. C-TPAT program has been expanded to include U.S. exporters. (*See* "Customs Trade Partnership Against Terrorism", §22.5.1 at 22.5.1.)

---

[12] https://aesdirect.census.gov/

[13] 15 C.F.R. 30.1

[14] Safety of Life at Sea (SOLAS) – International Convention for the Safety of Life at Sea, 1 November 1974, 1184 UNTS 3 (entered into force May 25, 1980)

The United States has been a signatory to the Safety of Life at Sea Convention since September 7, 1978 (46 U.S.C § 8106.)

In 2010, the World Shipping Council (WSC) and the International Chamber of Shipping (ICS) identified the miss-declared container weights as being a significant problem.

In 2012 the United States along with several other countries and a group of five maritime industry associations lead by WSC, co-sponsored a formal proposal to the IMO to amend the SOLAS convention which would require the weight of all packed containers to be verified prior to loading on board a vessel for export,

In 2014 the Maritime Safety Commission (MSC) officially adopted the new SOLAS requirement that as a condition for vessel loading, the weight of a packed export container be verified by the shipper using one of two permissible methods with an expected entry into force date of July 1, 2016.

4. IMPORTER'S RESPONSIBILITIES & LIABILITIES

Executive Briefing

The majority of laws relating to imports hold the importer responsible.

While problems may have resulted from exporter conduct, it is the importer over whom a government has jurisdiction. Too often, importers rely upon the seller's, manufacturer's or exporter's knowledge and ability to comply with the import requirements of the importing country.

While the exporters can contractually be held responsible for any damages, their liability is only by means of indemnification. **It is the importer who will be the direct target in any domestic problems.**

Historically, there has been a very clear delineation between the obligation of the government and the importer. The importer's obligation was to make a complete disclosure of the facts relating to a transaction and to submit complete and accurate supporting documentation. The government's obligation was to make the legal determination as to the consequences of the importer's facts.

4.1. INFORMED COMPLIANCE

Under a new notion of shared responsibility, the government is still obligated to make the final legal determinations, but the preliminary burden for both factual and legal determinations has been shifted to the importer under the idea of "Informed Compliance."[15] This concept of Informed Compliance requires importers, at minimum, to exercise "Reasonable Care" in their efforts to comply with the law.

The balance between government and importer compliance responsibility has changed.

From a practical standpoint the obligation to comply rests entirely with the importer.

In meeting the "Reasonable Care" standard, the [House Ways and Means] Committee believes that

> an importer should consider utilization of one or more of the following aides to establish evidence of proper compliance; seeking guidance from the Customs Service through the pre-importation or formal ruling programs; consulting with a Customs broker, customs consultant, or a public accountant or an attorney; using in-house employees such as counsel, a Customs administrator, or if valuation is an issue, a corporate controller, who has experience and knowledge of customs laws, regulations, and procedures; or when appropriate, obtaining analyses from accredited labs and gougers for determining technical qualities of an imported product.
>
> For example, in seeking advice for a classification issue, the Committee expects an importer to consult with an attorney or an in-house employee having technical expertise about the particular

> merchandise in question. In seeking advice for a valuation question, the Committee expects an importer to consult with an attorney or a public accountant, and, as appropriate, personnel within the company knowledgeable regarding the importer's accounting system and how costs elements are booked.[16]

Based upon past practices where the law imposed a comparable standard of "responsible supervision and control," this new standard of care is likely to have the effect of imposing on the importer the obligation not just of honesty, but of correct judgment. In cases involving "responsible supervision," Customs has consistently held that, since errors would not occur if there had been responsible supervision, the existence of the error is, by definition, proof of a failure to exercise responsible supervision. So, under the newly imposed obligation of Informed Compliance, the existence of an error or the failure to discover the error may well constitute prima face evidence of a failure to exercise reasonable care.

Trade Trivia

What do these men have in common?

Chester A. Arthur, the 21st President of the United States

and

Pat Garret, the lawman who shot "Billy the Kidd"

They were all Collectors of Customs which, prior to 1913, was a prized political appointment.

Informed Compliance does not change basic obligations, but establishes a new standard of reasonable care, by which compliance is measured and imposes a greater burden on the importer at the outset.

An importer's responsibilities can be summarized as the obligation to:

- Declare goods,
- Provide complete and accurate documentation,
- Comply with legal requirements,
- Pay Duties, Taxes, and Charges, and
- Maintain Records

These obligations arise at the time that goods are exported or imported but, like a warranty, they remain continuing obligations of the importer.

4.2. DECLARED GOODS

Everything imported into the United States, unless specifically excluded, must be declared.[17] Although everything must be declared, it does not mean that everything will be subject to duty or import restrictions.

The failure to declare can result in a civil penalty or civil seizure and forfeiture,[18] and, though less likely to arise in general commercial transactions, criminal prosecution.

Non-declaration need not be intentional. It can occur inadvertently as a result of practical and normal business practice.

For example:

Take the correction of an under-shipment.

One thousand (1000) articles are ordered at $25.00 each for a total of $25,000.00 which is declared. However, it turns out only 900 were shipped. When the next order of 2000 is shipped, an additional 100 pieces are added to the shipment, to make up for the earlier short shipment. Since the 100 pieces were part of an earlier invoice, they are not invoiced in the second shipment. Consequently, there is an under declaration of 100 pieces on the second shipment. Customs considers each shipment on its own, and therefore there is an under declaration of $2,500, even though the 100 pieces had been declared in the first shipment.

If the under declaration is discovered during an inspection of the second shipment, the entire shipment could be seized and subjected to a monetary penalty. The innocent nature of the failure to declare will serve only to mitigate the extent of penalty.[19] Full and proper declaration starts with complete and accurate documentation.

4.2.1. PROVIDE COMPLETE AND ACCURATE DOCUMENTATION

The starting point for the government's determination of the admissibility of a product into the United States, and the assessment of duties and taxes, is the documentation of the international sales transaction and its shipment, e.g., invoices, transport documents, and special documentation. Importers are held responsible for the accuracy of documentation presented to the government, even though it was prepared by someone else, over whom the importer has no direct control, usually the exporter. The importer may never have seen the documentation before it was submitted to Customs. If the documentation is incomplete, inaccurate, misleading or false, the government's evaluation of the transaction is affected. Depending upon the nature of the problem with the documentation, the importer can be hampered with assessment of higher duties, penalties, exclusion of the goods from importation, seizure, or even criminal liability. (*See* "Recordkeeping" §22.3 at 222.)

4.2.2. COMPLY WITH LEGAL REQUIREMENTS

An importer's responsibility to over 40 government agencies, including Customs and Border Protection, ***does not end with the release of a shipment and payment of duties.*** Each importation carries with it a continuing obligation to comply with the law. Compliance with the law is assured through the threat of penalties, both civil and criminal, as well as liquidated damages, the payment of which is guaranteed through the posting of a bond by the importer.

4.2.3. PAY DUTIES, TAXES AND CHARGES

While Customs duties no longer represent a significant part of the revenue of the U.S., collecting them is still part of their mandate and when those revenues fall, Congress notices.

Duties are a form of tax. Inherent in every importation is the obligation to pay the taxes that are due. The liability for duties, taxes and processing fees "constitute a personal debt due from the importer to the United States which can be discharged only by payment in full."[20] The failure to pay duties (taxes) can result in an audit, penalties and various legal actions that include loss of the right to utilize certain procedures which expedite Customs clearance.

A deposit of estimated duty is due at or near the time of entry. Any additional duty found due begins to accrue interest 30 days after liquidation, reliquidation, reconciliation, or the issuance of a bill. Duty remains owing and accruing interest even if there is a dispute as to its propriety or correctness. Conversely, interest is also paid by the government on excess payments or refunds.[21]

> Customs Brokers are not agents of Customs and Border Protection therefore payment of duties to a Customs Broker does not relieve an importer of its liability to pay the duties effectively a second time should their broker fail to make the payment.

Customs duties are very often paid by the importer to the Customs Broker who is clearing the shipment, ultimately to be forwarded by the broker when due to U.S. Customs. An importer has several payment options, only two of which are discussed here.

In theory, importers still have the option of making checks payable directly to U.S. Customs which your Customs Broker will deliver to Customs when the Entry Summary (tax return) is filed.

However, in practice, payments are no longer made by check. Rather, they are made by electronic funds transfers through Customs Automated Clearing House (ACH). If you want the security of direct payment, you can set up your own ACH account rather than making payment to the Customs Broker who will then in turn make payment through its ACH account.

4.2.3.1. AUTOMATED CLEARING HOUSE (ACH)

Almost all payments today are made electronically through an Automated Clearing House (ACH) which permits Customs to withdraw the duty payments declared on a Customs Entry from the importer's or Customs Broker's bank account.[22] Unless the importer's goal is to have the Customs Broker finance their Customs duties, the use of a "zero balance" ACH account, where the duty on an entry is deposited into the account when due can provide effective financial controls. The use of ACH in conjunction with the payment under a Periodic Monthly Statement can be an effective means of managing cash flow.

4.2.3.2. PERIODIC MONTHLY STATEMENTS

The Automatic Commercial Environment (ACE) has a feature known as the Periodic Monthly Statement (PMS). This feature allows for the delay of the duty payments from the original 10th working day after date of Cargo Release to the 15th working day of the month, <u>following</u> the release of the cargo.

The entry summary (CF 7501) still has to be presented on the 10th working day, however.

4.2.4. MAINTAIN RECORDS

The entire import system is predicated on the validity and accuracy of the documents and declarations made, and the ability of the government to verify this. While questions do arise with respect to individual importations, more and more often an importer's entire operation is reviewed through a periodic audit. (Customs' sister agency had, for decades, been the IRS so a similarity of methods is to be expected).

An importer is required to maintain supporting records for five (5) years after importation[23] or starting in 2018, three (3) years after liquidation of the drawback[24] previously from payment of a drawback claim[25], in order to permit Customs or other agencies to review all the determinations as to the classification, appraisement, compliance with other laws, and the importer's right to import or export merchandise.[26] The failure to maintain or provide records can result not only in a change in position as to classification, value or admissibility; it can also result in penalties of up to $100,000 or the value of the goods at issue.[27] (*See* "Recordkeeping" §22.3 at 222.)

The fact that records must be maintained does not, however, mean that the importer itself must maintain them. The law provides for the alternative of certifying others to act as record keepers.

The law, as amended in 1993, expands the scope of record keepers beyond the importer or importer of record to include the owner, consignee, entry filer (usually the Customs Broker) or any of their agents who directly or indirectly cause the importation, transportation, or storage under bond of merchandise.[28] Nevertheless, while Customs may generally require an agent to provide documents relating to a transaction, it is ultimately the importer who will bear the consequences of the failure to maintain the required records.

> Customs Brokers are permitted to act as Third-Party Recordkeepers of your Customs related records, *however*, most Customs Brokers specifically exclude this responsibility in their Terms and Conditions unless you make specific arrangements with them to do so.

In line with Informed Compliance is an obligation to maintain the records to support your entry declarations.

– Balance of page intentionally left blank –

---

[15] 19 U.S.C. 1484 as amended by Public Law 103-182, 107 Stat 2200 Section 637(a).

[16] House Ways and Means Committee Report, H.R. Rep. No. 3450, 103d Cong., First Sess. 120. (1993)

[17] 19 C.F.R. 148.11

[18] 19 C.F.R. 148.18(a)

[19] 19 C.F.R. 148.18(b)

[20] 19 C.F.R. 141.1(b)(1) .

[21] 19 U.S.C. 1505 as amended by Public Law103-182, 107 Stat 2205, Section 642(a).

[22] 19 C.F.R. 24.25

[23] 19 C.F.R. 162.1c

[24] Changed from date of payment to date of liquidation. Trade Facilitation and Enforcement Act of 2015, Public Law No: 114-125, 130 Stat. 122 §906(c) (2016).

[25] 19 C.F.R. 191.5

[26] 19 C.F.R. 162.1a(a)

[27] House Ways and Means Committee Report, H.R. Rep. No. 103-361 to H.R. 3450, 103d Cong., First Sess. 321. (1993)

[28] 19 U.S.C. 1508 as amended by Public Law No. 103-182, 107 Stat 2057, Section 614, 19 USC 1508(a)

5. PLANNING THE TRANSACTION

Executive Briefing

Failing to take the time to address the financial and practical aspects of import and export transactions can create financial risks.

These risks range from lost opportunities to reduced costs, to the possibilities of increased costs, delays, increased duties, complications resulting from embargoes, seizure, penalties, loss, damages or non-delivery of shipments. Last, but not least, is the possibility that someone won't get paid.

Risk management must begin with the first stages of planning the transaction because the risk of importing non-conforming goods, of necessity, must start with product design and costing.

Whether you are the buyer or seller, export or importer, planning still involves essentially the same issues:

- ✓ Planning the Merchandise, §6 at page 27
- ✓ Planning the Financial Transaction, §7 at page 29
- ✓ Planning Payments – Financing the Transaction, §8 at page 35
- ✓ Planning the Procedural Operations, §9 at page 49
- ✓ Planning the Documentation, §10 at page 67

- Balance of page intentionally left blank –

– Page intentionally left blank –

6. PLANNING THE MERCHANDISE

Some importers are under the mistaken belief that they must pay the maximum amount of duty, or that the amount of duty they pay is totally beyond their control. This is not the case. The laws governing importation into the United States create a framework. Within that framework, manufacturers, importers, and exporters are free to design a product, their relationships, and all other details of a transaction to obtain the best treatment the law affords: lowest rates of duty, lowest dutiable values, and fewest restrictions.

To effect a change requires advanced planning. Once the purchase has been consummated and the shipment is on its way or has arrived, the ability to affect either classification or value is limited to the interpretation of the applicable law.

These decisions need to be made prior to consummating a transaction and should at least be considered at the planning level, and as early as product design and contracting. Often a change that may have little or no effect on marketability can reduce the duty on the article or minimize other import restrictions, both of which can affect the bottom line.

Planning needs to also take into account how parts and materials will be used subsequent to purchase and/or importation.

The origin of the parts and materials can have a serious impact on how a finished product might be marked both in terms of both domestic and international sales.

This becomes an even greater problem when materials and parts are purchased from different suppliers during the course of a year and are co-mingled in inventory, even though they are of different origins.

- Balance of page intentionally left blank –

– Page intentionally left blank –

7. PLANNING THE FINANCIAL TRANSACTION

When acquiring goods most planners focus on the product, its cost of production (the price paid for the goods) and the cost of landing it in the importing country. That view is generally product specific and often too narrow. It often ignores broader financial issues affecting transactions in general. This commonly occurs when product and financial executives act in isolation, and each is unaware of the implications of their action on the other. The way in which the financial transaction is structured can often have as great an impact as product design and price.

7.1. AGENTS & COMMISSIONS

It is not uncommon for an importer to use an agent to assist in acquiring goods or providing other services such as inspecting goods prior to shipment or arranging for shipment.

All commissions paid by the importer to an agent, in conjunction with its imported goods, must be declared to U.S. Customs. But that does not mean that the commission will necessarily be dutiable. Whether fees paid to an agent are dutiable is primarily dependent upon the type of agent and how the transaction is structured. Generally, two types of agents and commissions are encountered: buying and selling.

> Just because someone says they are a Buying Agent does not mean that Customs will agree.
>
> There is no legal requirement to have a written agency agreement, but it is better practice to have the terms in writing for several reasons:
>
> 1. It clarifies your agent's obligations to you, ensuring that they perform up to the level you are expecting.
> 2. It helps to establish to Customs that the fees you pay to the agent are non-dutiable as a buying as opposed to a selling commission.

BUYING AGENTS perform services for the buyer that the buyer could otherwise have performed for itself. The services that these agents provide and their expense are part of the "cost of goods sold" but are not part of the price paid for the goods. Commissions paid to a buying agent are usually not dutiable. The most common reasons that Customs sometimes treats buying commissions as dutiable are either that they are in excess of what would normally be expected for the services, typically 10% of the F.O.B. port of export value or less or that they are believed to actually be selling commissions.

What Every Member of the Trade Community Should Know About:

Buying & Selling Commissions

AN INFORMED COMPLIANCE PUBLICATION

CUSTOMS and BORDER PROTECTION

Buying Agents can be independent companies or, as is often the case with large importers, a wholly owned company (which adds other tax planning benefits).

SELLING AGENTS work either directly or indirectly for the seller. If

the only way to purchase articles from a manufacturer is through a particular agent, that agent is probably a selling agent, regardless of how it describes itself. Commissions paid by the buyer to the seller's agent are dutiable.

If an agent provides services other than those of a selling agent, it is possible that those services are not dutiable; however, they would need to be individually examined - a task which should be undertaken at the time the transaction is being planned.

7.2. INTEREST CHARGES

If goods are purchased in a manner that does not require immediate payment, there is generally a cost associated with the privilege of delayed payment. Whether that added cost will be dutiable depends primarily upon how the transaction is structured. The distinction is, to a large extent, based upon whether the financing cost is included as part of the cost of goods, or is broken out by being invoiced as a financing charge.

When the cost of credit is built into the price of the goods, it is dutiable.

For example:

Take an invoice for $100.00 with the terms 2/10 net 30.

If the invoice is paid within 10 days, the price paid and the dutiable value is $98.00. If paid after 10 days the price paid and the dutiable value is $100.00.

If, instead, the price was negotiated at $98.00, net 10 days, accompanied by a separate agreement to pay interest if not paid timely, then the dutiable value remains $98.00. The price for the goods was $98.00 even though the total cost of acquiring the goods including the separate interest payment may have been $100.00 or more.

7.3. QUOTA

Voluntary Restraints, more commonly known as quotas, to the extent that they limited the quantity of a textile or textile products which could be imported into the United States, have essentially been eliminated as of 2005.

This should not be confused with Tariff Rate Quotas.

7.4. TARIFF RATE QUOTAS

Tariff Rate Quotas do not limit import quantities of goods that can be imported. Instead they provide for duty-free importation for a limited quantity of imports. Once that import volume is met, the duty rates revert to their normal rate. Tariff Rate Quotas are most commonly applied to imported agricultural and dairy products.

7.5. FOREIGN CHARGES

Goods imported into the United States are valued based upon their F.O.B. Port of Export price which, by definition, includes all the costs incurred up to, and including loading the shipment onto the exporting carrier. Foreign inland freight charges are the portion of the F.O.B. price incurred in bringing a shipment from the place of purchase, (usually the factory or a warehouse) to the port, and loading it on the carrier that will bring it to the U.S. However, there are ways by which these foreign inland freight charges can be made non-dutiable, depending upon how a transaction is structured.

If goods are purchased on an F.O.B. Port of Export basis or C.I.F. (Cost of Goods, Insurance, and International Freight) basis, then foreign inland freight charges are included in the price, and are therefore dutiable. [29]

If, however, goods are purchased on an Ex-Works or Ex-Factory basis, then by definition, the price does not include a charge for foreign inland freight. Inland freight charges that are separately invoiced and paid by the purchaser to someone other than the seller will be viewed as part of the cost of acquiring the goods, but not part of the price, and are therefore not dutiable. [30]

The total cost of acquiring the goods may remain the same, but the dutiable status of the foreign inland freight charges is dependent upon the way that the transaction was structured.

7.6. TRANSACTIONS BETWEEN RELATED COMPANIES - TRANSFER PRICING

Under the World Trade Organization (WTO), as well as U.S. Customs law, the preferred basis for valuing an import transaction is "Transaction Value". It is essentially the price paid or payable for goods when they are sold for export to the United States at a price freely negotiated between an unrelated buyer and seller - an arm's length transaction.

The term 'Related' has different meanings, depending upon the laws involved. These relationships may already exist, or they can be established specifically as a duty or tax planning device.

The invoice price between unrelated parties reflects what is thought of as the major component of *cost of goods*. The key to a lower dutiable value in transactions between related parties is most easily summed up in the distinction between *cost of goods* and the *cost of doing business*. The cost of the goods is dutiable; the cost of doing business may not be.

When a company formulates a price for an arm's length sale of its goods to an unrelated party, it wants to assure itself that all costs of doing business, including its profit, are covered. Consequently, the price includes many expenses of doing business which are not actually part of the cost of the article produced.

For example:

Take a costing analysis for a shirt with 9 buttons. Since it is anticipated that a certain number of buttons will be lost or broken during manufacture, the cost of these lost or damaged buttons is covered by including 9-1/2 buttons in the costing of each 9 button shirt. The 1/2 button is a cost of doing business and a factor going into the price, but it is not part of the direct cost of the garment.

> Almost by definition, the existence of a legal relationship between a buyer and seller/manufacturer raises the question as to whether the relationship affects the price. Every buyer and seller/manufacturer hopes that there will be some monetary advantages associated with that relationship, including lower cost for goods. There is nothing wrong with that.
>
> Customs recognizes that prices between related parties may be lower than those between unrelated parties and, therefore, the resulting reductions in duty may be totally legitimate.

> Related Party pricing under Customs laws is not the same thing as Transfer Pricing under revenue and tax authority rules. In fact, the interests of the two agencies may be exactly the opposite, as an increase in revenue to one agency might result in a reduction to the other.
>
> Just because you have a Transfer Pricing Agreement that is acceptable for tax purposes does not mean that it will be acceptable for Customs' purpose.
>
> Depreciation and amortization illustrate this difference. For tax purposes, any number of accelerated write-off plans which front load deductions are acceptable. Customs, generally only accepts straight line depreciation which distributes the expense more equally over the imports.

> The cost of the 1/2 button will undoubtedly be included in the arm's length price negotiated between unrelated parties and thus be subject to duty. Between related parties it need not be. In a properly structured transaction between related parties, the price need not include many of the costs of doing business that are not directly associated with the cost of producing the article.

Moreover, an arm's length price between unrelated parties also includes business expenses that do not necessarily exist in transactions between related parties, e.g., bad debt expense. When these costs are removed from the transaction, dutiable value is reduced, which usually translates directly into lower duty.

The reduction in duty liability can be used to realize additional profit or

to reduce domestic pricing. Realizing duty savings, however, is only half of the picture. Keeping those savings safe from other taxes is the other half of the picture. Having reduced duties under Customs laws, it becomes essential not to create a corresponding increase in taxes under Internal Revenue laws.

One of the most obvious methods of reducing tax liability is by increasing tax-deductible expenses. In transactions between related parties, it is often possible to shift certain operations off shore, or to break out certain services that are costs of doing business but are not part of the cost of production. These are the business costs that would normally be included in the price when goods are sold to unrelated parties.

The key to converting customs duties and taxes into a source of profit is planning and documentation. Properly structured and documented, these services can be an important element in the overall management of the U.S. and international operations. Undertaken without proper planning, they can lead to penalties.

> Transactions between related parties are always subject to increased scrutiny by both U.S. Customs looking for under-valuations and by the Internal Revenue Service looking for overvaluations.
>
> Related Party or Transfer Pricing Transactions should only be undertaken after careful planning, with the advice of both Customs Counsel and Tax Advisers.

Not every transaction or relationship qualifies for any or all of the benefits of a related party transaction, and it may not be the best or only way to proceed. But, due to the substantial benefits that may be available to a foreign supplier or domestic importer, it is well worth the time and effort to find out just what being a related party could mean.

- Balance of page intentionally left blank -

7.7. FIRST SALE VALUATION

Executive Briefing

Imports are valued on the price paid or payable to the seller "when sold for export to the United States." However, when there are intermediaries, there is more than one "sale." Specifically, there is one sale from the factory to the middleman and another sale from the middleman to the U.S. customer.

If properly structured, duty can be paid on the lower price from the factory to the middleman as opposed to the higher marked-up price from the middleman to you.

The key to paying duty on the lower First Sale transaction price is found in the words "sold for export to the United States."

In "Nissho-Iwai" (1992)[31], it was determined that the sale destined to the U.S., even if passing through a middleman, may be used for the basis of valuation. Thus, in a sale from a foreign factory to a middleman, who then sells to the U.S. customer, it is possible to use the "First Sale" or the sale of the factory to the middleman, *if the goods were clearly destined to the U.S. and other specific required conditions* are met (e.g., back to back sale of goods).

Since the government does not like the lower duty implications, there must be a very clear trail of documentation to substantiate that the sale from the factory to the middleman was "sale for export to the United Sates." Customs may not request the documentation until well after the transaction. If you do not have the proper documentation, this may lead not only to the denial of the "first sale" valuation of this specific transaction, but a denial of all prior transactions as well. Therefore, this is one of those transactions that you do not want to undertake without advice or assistance of experts.

The following are examples of documents that may generally be requested:

- ✓ A purchase order from the U.S. customer, indicating style number or product reference.
- ✓ A purchase order from the middleman to the factory indicating that the goods are being sold from the factory to the middleman with the intent that the goods are ultimately for sale to the United States.
- ✓ Invoice from the factory to the middleman showing the style number and indicating that goods are clearly destined to the U.S.
- ✓ An invoice from the middleman to the U.S. customer showing the style number.
- ✓ Proof of payment by each party.
- ✓ Shipping documents (e.g., Bill of Lading).

– Page intentionally left blank –

---

[29] 19 C.F.R. 152.103(a)(5); Ruling 542368, dated 3-2-81

[30] 19 C.F.R. 152.103 (a)(5)(i)

[31] Nissho Iwai American Corp. v. United States, 16 Ct. Int'l Trade 86 (1992), 786 F. Supp. 1002 (1992), 982 F.2d 505 (1992).

8. PLANNING PAYMENTS - FINANCING THE TRANSACTION

There are a variety of standard methods of financing and paying for goods and a virtually unlimited number of possible variations which can be tailored to a particular transaction. The preference of one system over another generally depends upon your position as either a buyer or seller, and the laws affecting the exportation or importation. These preferences are usually based upon the premise that everything will go as planned. It is, of course, just as important to take into consideration what can go wrong.

Importers and Exporters often fail to consider the differences in culture, business practices and ethics in other countries which can affect how a transaction actually proceeds and what local remedies are available.

For example:

> Goods are sold on a C.O.D. basis. The seller believes that he will retain useful title to the goods until paid. But upon arrival, the buyer informs the seller that he has no money with which to pay for the goods. The seller may still have title, but with no practical way to dispose of the goods in the foreign country, he is at the mercy of the buyer. After the seller has had time to fully appreciate his dilemma, the buyer suddenly finds some resources with which to buy the goods at a renegotiated and substantially lower price.

The basic methods of financing a sale or purchase of goods:

- Open Account
- Cash-In-Advance
- Collection-On-Delivery (C.O.D.)
- Drafts
- Collection Against Documents (C.A.D.)
- Documents Against Payment
- Documents Against Acceptance
- Letter of Credit
- Factoring
- Consignment Sales
- Counter Trade (Barter)

> Rarely considered, but could be of great importance, is on whose books the transaction appears at the close of an accounting period, especially in terms of the Year End.

Each of these methods has its own implication to the transaction beyond the general financial issues.

8.1. OPEN ACCOUNT

In open account transactions, credit is extended by the seller to the buyer. Goods are forwarded under a contractual obligation to pay at a due date set forth in the invoice. In open account transactions, the entire cash management advantage rests with the buyer who will have goods in his possession without having advanced funds for them. The seller, however, is without merchandise or funds until the buyer pays the invoice. Clearly, purchase on open account is the buyer's most attractive choice if the option is available.

As a seller offering sales on open account to an international buyer, it is essential to measure not only the buyer's credit worthiness, but also the credit reliability of the country in which the buyer is located.

Open account terms, when not clearly documented, can vary from net thirty days in some countries, to 360 days in others, depending on the local business practice. Knowing how open account terms are construed in the country of your trading partner is important. Being clear and precise as to the terms is even more important.

There is also a risk of currency instability, making it imperative to understand and agree as to who assumes that risk.

Rarely considered at the time a deal is being consummated, but at least as important, is the availability, in the buyer's country, of an effective means of collecting payment in the event that it is not forthcoming.

It is not uncommon to see Open Account transactions secured by a "Standby Letters of Credit". (*See* §8.7.2 at 46.)

8.2. CASH-IN-ADVANCE

Cash-in-advance is usually demanded only when goods are manufactured to specification, and, as such, are not readily resalable.

In a cash-in-advance transaction, the seller will have the buyer's funds in hand and the buyer is entirely dependent upon the seller's *willingness* to fulfill the stated conditions. Cash-in-advance is as dangerous for the buyer as open account is for a seller. A buyer can, however, secure its cash advance by having the seller post a standby letter of credit payable to the buyer if the seller fails to perform.

8.3. COLLECTION ON DELIVERY (C.O.D.)

Although C.O.D. is commonly referred to as Cash-On-Delivery, it is a misnomer, as cash is only one of the forms of payment which can be used. Other forms of payment more commonly used are:

Checks: Personal, bank or certified

Drafts: Bank drafts, sight drafts, and time drafts

C.O.D. shipments are most often used when the shipper has some concern that he will not be paid for his goods. Under C.O.D., the shipper appoints an agent, typically the carrier, freight forwarder, or Customs broker, to collect payment from the consignee before completing delivery. Many carriers will not, however, act as collecting agents.

When shipping C.O.D., the shipper must clearly specify what forms of payment are acceptable; otherwise the collection agent may accept any of the forms of payment listed above.

If the shipper accepts a form of payment other than the one it specified, then the shipper assumes the risk of non-payment.

> Even in cases where there are clearly suspicious circumstances the carrier, acting as a collecting agent, is only obligated to exercise reasonable care to collect a facially valid instrument. In one case the suspicious circumstances included:
>
> *the buyer's unlisted suite number and contact person for delivery, the buyer taking possession of the computer equipment outside the office building, and presenting a cashier's check from a Fijian bank.*
>
> The court, nonetheless, found that collecting what appeared to be a facially valid instrument, despite the suspicious circumstances surrounding its collection, did not breach the collecting agent's obligation. *McCall-Thomas Eng'g Co. v. Federal Express Corp.*, 81 F.3d 28 (4th Cir. 1996) at 29, 30, 31.

C.O.D. sounds like a perfect balance between risk and costs, but in reality is anything but.

Unless given specific instructions, the collecting agent is obligated only to use reasonable care in accepting payment and may not be responsible if it accepts a payment instrument which turns out to be bad.

It is important to appreciate that, unless special arrangements are made, your collecting agent is only obligated to collect an instrument which, on its face, has the indicia of being a valid instrument.[32]

So, where it would be difficult for anyone to determine that a certified check is good or not, the carrier cannot be held responsible if the check turns out to be a forgery.

Although it appears to offer a reasonable compromise to both parties, because goods will not be delivered to the buyer without payment, the appearance of security is illusory. Payment is not generally demanded until the carrier or other third party is ready to make delivery, and consequently, the seller has no assurances that the buyer will have the funds to make the payment at the time of delivery. The goods may remain the property of the seller, but may be of little value and a substantial burden when they are in the buyer's country.

Moreover, what happens if the Customer simply refuses the shipment?

Even if you sent the goods on a "freight collect" basis, the shipper remains liable for freight and related charges for demurrage (storage) and detention (per diems) for the use of any container by virtue of being "the shipper" on transportation documents. And this remains true of vessel, rail and air shipment.

Even if you or your Customer decides to abandon the goods, these costs can continue to accrue.

While C.O.D. may be viable on domestic transactions, it may be impractical in the international marketplace. Since there are other more sure means of collecting payment from buyers, such as Letters of Credit, C.O.D. may not be the best means available to today's shipper.

8.4. CASH AGAINST DOCUMENTS (C.A.D)

As in every commercial transaction payment, security is a matter of balancing risk against benefit, as between Buyer and Seller.

Cash Against Documents (C.A.D.) provides a middle ground between sales on Open Account, and those supported by a Letter of Credit.

In the same way that a bank would exchange payment for the presentation of documents evidencing title to goods under a Documentary Letter of Credit, a bank can exchange payment for documents of title in the case of a Cash Against Documents. Collections practices normally follow the International Chamber of Commerce's Uniform Rules of Collections, URC522.

The difference is that there is a risk that the Buyer may not have sufficient funds available upon your Presentation of the Documents. In this sense a

C.A.D. is more similar to an Open Account Transaction. It does offer, however, a significant increase in security as compared to a C.O.D. transaction in that title is generally transferred before the goods leave the seller's country, as opposed to after arrival in the buyer's country. A letter of credit, on the other hand, offers the security of available funds to pay for the goods, because the bank has previously secured sufficient funds from the Buyer to pay for the goods by extending them a loan (credit).

In the end, it is a balance between the risk of non-payment and the cost of using one method over another. With security comes a cost: Letters of Credit, whether Documentary or Standby, carry higher bank fees, and are counted against the Buyer's available credit.

8.5. DRAFTS

Drafts are the most common banking documents used to effect payment. A draft is a demand for payment (bill of exchange) issued by the seller against the buyer.

Checks are forms of drafts, and both serve to request that the drawer make payment to the Payee from a specific account, according to its terms. Permissible terms between the two are very different.

On drafts, we usually refer to Drawer and Drawee. For ease of comprehension we will instead use the more familiar terms associated with checks: Payer and Payee.

A draft is a negotiable instrument when it contains the words "to order of" and can be paid "on sight" to anyone who presents a properly endorsed instrument. Payment is made from funds in a specific account at a Bank.

A draft is payable only to a named party and can be payable upon presentation ("at sight") or after a certain number of days ("time draft"). While it is like a check request for payment of funds from a specific source, that source does not have to be with a bank and can, in fact, reflect money owed by another company. It can be thought of as an assignment of debt.

A draft may be written with virtually any terms or conditions agreeable to the parties:

- Immediately payable on presentation, or
- At a fixed number of days after presentation, or
- At a specified date.

A draft can be used as a collection instrument, used to exchange possession and title to goods for payment. Or, if offered without special provisions or restrictions, a draft may be the medium of payment in a routine open account transaction, in which the buyer's bank will act as the collection agent. When a draft is accepted by the bank, the bank is substituted as the party responsible for the payment. The bank will not add its acceptance endorsement until it has secured the funds from the Payer with which to make the payment.

The difficulty with a draft is that, unless it has been accepted by a bank, like C.O.D., there is no assurance that the drawee of the draft (usually the buyer or consignee) will have the funds when the draft is presented for payment. As with C.O.D., if the draft is not paid, the seller will have title to the goods, which may be of little value when the goods are sitting in a foreign country.

8.6. ACCEPTANCE FINANCING USING TIME DRAFTS

A time draft provides for payment at a future date specified in the draft. The seller-exporter will send the time draft together with the shipping documents to the buyer-importer for the buyer's acceptance. All of this is done through banking channels and has been agreed to by both parties in the Contract of Sale described as "documents against acceptance."

The bank is instructed that the documents should be transferred to the buyer-importer *only upon acceptance*. Acceptance by the buyer-importer would be indicated by stamping or writing the date and the word "accepted" across the face of the draft.

By accepting the draft the buyer-importer buyer creates a "Trade Acceptance" which is returned to the seller-exporter through banking channels. By accepting the time draft, the buyer-importer becomes liable for payment at maturity.

The Payee (seller) then has two options as to how and when it negotiates a Time Draft. It can:

- Hold the Time Draft until the due date, say 90 days, and collect the face value of the draft, or
- Sell the Time Draft at a discount to improve its cash flow

After the addition of the Trade Acceptance, a time draft essentially functions similar to a post-dated check in that it provides payment at some later date.

Unfortunately, it also has the same limitations as a postdated check in that it represents an obligation to pay, but there is no assurance that funds will actually be available to make the payment.

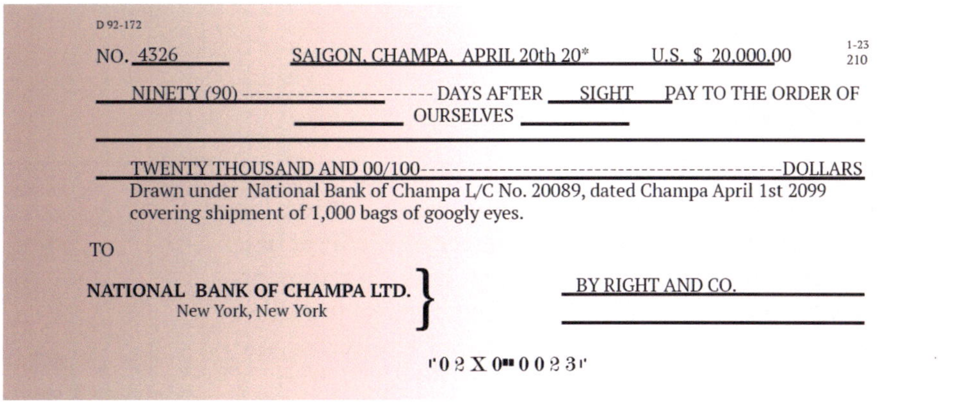
D 92-172
NO. 4326 SAIGON, CHAMPA, APRIL 20th 20* U.S. $ 20,000.00 1-23 210
NINETY (90) ------------------------- DAYS AFTER SIGHT PAY TO THE ORDER OF OURSELVES
TWENTY THOUSAND AND 00/100--DOLLARS
Drawn under National Bank of Champa L/C No. 20089, dated Champa April 1st 2099 covering shipment of 1,000 bags of googly eyes.
TO
NATIONAL BANK OF CHAMPA LTD.
New York, New York
BY RIGHT AND CO.
⑈02X0⑈0023⑈

Figure 3 - Time Draft

If, however, the Acceptance is issued by a bank, (a "Banker's Acceptance"), the bank becomes responsible for the payment. In that sense it functions similarly to a bank certifying a check.

Not surprisingly, a bank will not add its Acceptance unless it has a credit agreement with the Payer or the funds are assured through the payment of a Letter of Credit.

In the context of a Documentary Letter of Credit, a Draft is used to draw down on funds payable under the letter of credit.

The draft will be payable at the time and place that the letter of credit is payable.

A Time Draft used in conjunction with a documentary letter of credit strikes a balance between:

- A **buyer's interest** in delayed payment terms, and
- A **seller's interest** in ensuring that having given up possession and control over their goods they will get paid.

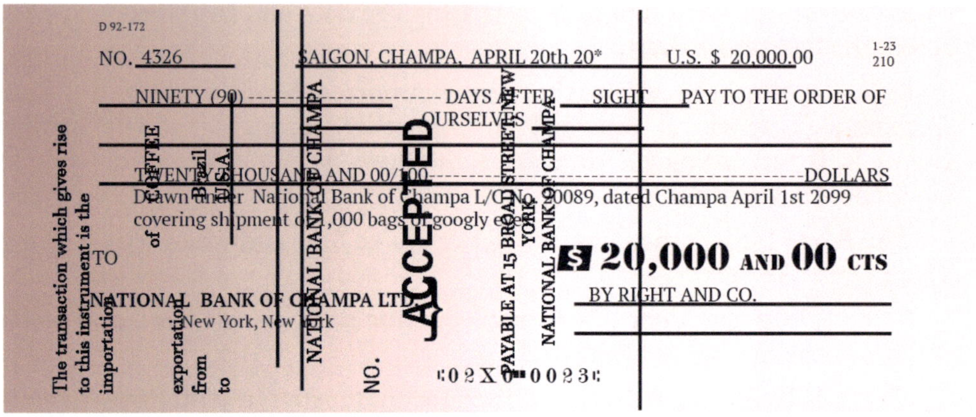

Figure 4 - Time Draft with Banker's Acceptance

Once the Time Draft has been accepted, the Payee (buyer) has the option of discounting the draft to improve its cash flow. However, without a Banker's Acceptance it is unlikely you will find someone interested in buying the Time Draft, even at a steep discount.

Once a bank stands behind the draft through the Banker's Acceptance, the risk of non-payment drops and so does the discount at which it can be sold.

8.7. LETTERS OF CREDIT

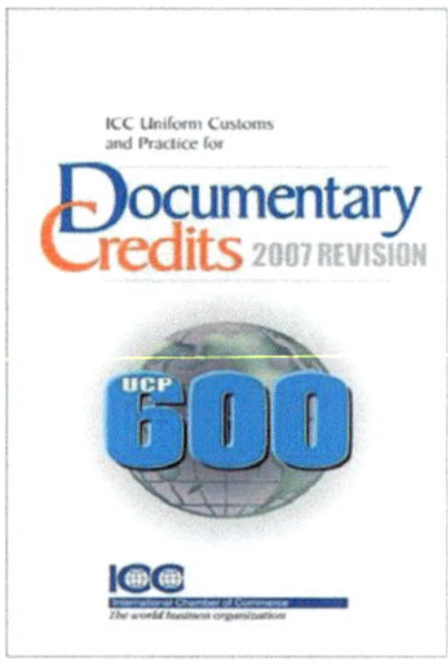

Letters of credit offer the advantage of an independent middleman, most often a bank, through which to exchange documents for money. A letter of credit is best viewed as an undertaking by a bank to make a payment, or make a payment available, to the beneficiary, provided that the beneficiary has conformed to all the terms and conditions stated within the letter of credit. Letter of Credit practices normally follow the International Chamber of Commerce's Uniform Customs and Practices for Documentary Credit, UCP600.

The terms and conditions are specified by the applicant in opening the letter of credit. Those terms reflect the basis upon which the bank will decide whether or not the beneficiary is in compliance. Letters of credit are documentary in nature, and deal with documents, not with goods. The terms and conditions must be evidenced through various documents. The bank will look only at the surface of the documents and not at the facts behind them, or even at their validity.

For example:

If the letter of credit states that payment will be against shipment of beads, and the invoice and shipping document say "beads", the bank will accept them as correct although sand was actually shipped. Conversely, most banks will refuse to pay against the documents if they say "beeds" or "bead", (instead of "beads" in the plural) even though beads were actually shipped.

- Balance of page intentionally left blank –

Case Summary

Non-Conforming Description: In disputes concerning letters of credit, the paperwork must match the letter of credit.

Courtaulds North America, Inc. v. North Carolina Nat'l Bank
528 F.2d 802 (1975)

In negotiating a Letter of Credit, the general rule is that banks will look strictly at the documents only, with no room for interpretation of the contract between the parties.

The invoice presented described the content as "Imported Acrylic Yarn." The packing list described the merchandise as "100% Acrylic Yarn." The letter of credit required that the invoice state that it covered, among other things, 100% Acrylic Yarn Package Dyed (without quotes). The bank refused to accept the drafts because of the discrepancy.

The U.S. District Court of North Carolina held that the bank was liable for the amount of the draft because "the draft complied with the letter of credit when each invoice is read together with the packing list stapled to it."

The U.S. Court of Appeals stated, however, that "after considering the insistent rigidity of the law and usage of bank credits and acceptances," they must reverse the lower court. In explaining, the Court of Appeals reasoned that:

> In utilizing the rules of construction embodied in the letter of credit -- the Uniform Customs and State statute -- one must constantly recall that the drawee bank is not to be embroiled in disputes between the buyer and seller, the beneficiary of the credit. The drawee is involved only with the documents, not the merchandise. Its involvement is altogether separate and apart from the transaction between buyer and seller; its duties and liability are governed exclusively by the terms of the letter, not the terms of the parties' contract with each other.

8.7.1. CONFIRMATION AND IRREVOCABILITY OF LETTERS OF CREDIT

There are advantages, especially to the beneficiary, in having a letter of credit that is irrevocable and confirmed by a bank in the beneficiary's country. The beneficiary obviously wants a letter of credit whose terms and conditions will remain constant. "Irrevocable" means that during the life of the letter of credit, its terms cannot be changed nor can it be revoked without the consent of the beneficiary. "Confirmation" means that a bank, other than the opening bank, accepts the responsibility of paying.

The irrevocable status of a letter of credit prevents the issuer from changing the terms of a letter of credit without consent of the beneficiary. This prevents the time for performance under the letter of credit from being shortened, or the letter of credit from being prematurely canceled.

Confirmation makes the confirming banks responsible for evaluating compliance with the terms of the letter of credit, and for payment, as though they had issued the letter of credit without deferring to the issuing bank. When a letter of credit is confirmed, the beneficiary will be paid as soon as conforming documents are presented, reviewed and approved, without having to send them overseas to obtain payment. While there is a charge for confirmation, it is well worth the cost.

Case Summary

You do not get rights under a letter of credit that you did not provide for.

Maurice O'Meara Co., v. National Park Bank of New York
146 N.E. 636 (1925)

This is another case that held that letters of credit are to be strictly construed without reference to external circumstances.

Here, there was no issue as to paperwork presented conforming to the letter of credit. The question related to the commercial aspects of the transaction and whether the goods shipped conformed to the details provided in the documents presented.

The letter of credit called for a certain size paper. It appeared that the paper was not of the tensile or bursting strength that was ordered. The Court refused to allow the plaintiff to test the paper. The letter of credit stated:

> In accordance with instructions received from the Sun-Herald Corporation of this city, we open a confirmed or irrevocable credit in your favor for account of themselves, in amount of $224,853.30, covering the shipment of 1,322 2/3 tons of newsprint paper in 72 1/2" and 36 1/2" rolls to test 11-12, 32 lbs. at 8 1/2 cents per pound net weight-delivery to be made in December, 1920, and January 1921.
>
> Drafts under this credit are to be drawn at sight on this bank, and are to be accompanied by the following documents of a character which must meet with our approval:
>
> Commercial invoice in triplicate.
>
> Weight returns.
>
> Negotiable dock delivery order actually carrying with it control of the goods.

> This is a confirmed or irrevocable credit, and will remain in force to and including February 15, 1921, subject to the conditions mentioned herein.
>
> When drawing drafts under this credit, or referring to it, please quote our number as above.

The Court refused to allow the plaintiff to test the paper before honoring the letter of credit. The Court held tight to the principle of strict adherence to the letter of credit stating:

> The bank issued to plaintiff's assignor an irrevocable letter of credit, a contract solely between the bank and the plaintiff's assignor, in and by which the bank agreed to pay sight drafts to a certain amount on presentation to it of the documents specified in the letter of credit. This contract is in no way involved in or connected with, other than the presentation of the documents, the contract for the purchase and sale of the paper mentioned. That was a contract between buyer and seller, which in no way concerned the bank. The bank's obligation was to pay sight drafts when presented if accompanied by genuine documents specified in the letter of credit.

The Court further reasoned that the defendant had no right to test the paper or even to inspect the paper because the letter of credit did not provide for that. It stated that:

> The defendant had no right to insist that a test of the tensile strength of paper be made before paying the drafts; nor did it even have a right to inspect the paper before payment, to determine whether it in fact corresponded to the description contained in the documents. The letter of credit did not so provide. All that letter of credit provided was that documents be presented which described the paper shipped as of a certain size, weight and tensile strength. To hold otherwise is to read into the letter of credit something which is not there, and this court ought not to do, since it would impose upon a bank a duty which in many cases would defeat the primary purpose of such letters of credit. This primary purpose is an assurance to the seller of the merchandise of prompt payment against the documents.

Furthermore, the Court added that:

> It has never been held… that a bank has the right or is under an obligation to see that the description of the merchandise contained in the documents presented is correct. A provision giving it such right, or imposing such obligation, might, of course, be provided for in the letter of credit. The letter under consideration contains no such provision.

Thus, the Court left open the possibility that testing may have been permitted had the letter of credit specifically provided for that, but absent that, it would read the documents strictly.

Case Summary

The principle of the independence of the letter of credit will NOT be applied where there is clear evidence of fraud and the bank received notice of the active fraud before it accepted or paid the draft.

Sztejn v. Henry Schroder Banking Corporation et. al
31 N.Y.S. 2d 631 (1941).

In this case, there was fraud in that the merchandise shipped was not what was described on the letter of credit. Indeed, instead of the contracted bristles, the merchandise was comprised of boxes filled with cowhair and worthless material with the intent to simulate genuine merchandise and defraud the buyer.

The Supreme Court of New York County first restated the traditional principle of the independence of the letter of credit:

> It is well established that a letter of credit is independent of the primary contract of sale between the buyer and the seller. The issuing bank agrees to pay upon presentation of documents, not goods. This rule is necessary to preserve the efficiency of the letter of credit as an instrument for the financing of trade. One of the chief purposes of the letter of credit is to furnish the seller with a ready means of obtaining prompt payment for his merchandise. It would be most unfortunate interference with business transactions if a bank before honoring drafts drawn upon it was obliged or even allowed to go behind the documents, at the request of the buyer and enter into controversies between the buyer and the seller regarding the quality of the merchandise shipped.

The Court, however, distinguished the current situation.

> [A] different situation is presented in the instant action. This is not a controversy between the buyer and seller concerning a mere breach of warranty regarding the quality of the merchandise; on the present motion, it must be assumed that the seller has intentionally failed to ship any goods ordered by the buyer. In such a situation, where the seller's fraud has been called to the bank's attention before the drafts and documents have been presented for payment, the principle of the independence of the bank's obligation under the letter of credit should not be extended to protect the unscrupulous seller.

The Court did state that "it is true that even though the documents are forged or fraudulent, if the issuing bank has already paid the draft before receiving notice of the seller's fraud, it will be protected if it exercised reasonable diligence before making such payment."

8.7.2. STANDBY LETTERS OF CREDIT

Standby letters are issued to guarantee an obligation or performance.

They are commonly used in conjunction with:

- ✓ Bid bonds
- ✓ Open account transactions
- ✓ Performance bonds
- ✓ Lines of credit

The obligation of the bank, in negotiating a standby letter of credit, is to examine the documents presented to ascertain that they conform to the conditions set forth in the standby credit. Issuing banks do not determine whether the actual conditions have occurred, only whether the documents evidence it. Great care must be taken in crafting the terms of a standby letter of credit. Practices relating to Standby Letters of Credit normally follow the International Chamber of Commerce's *International Standby Practices*, ISP98.

The standby letter of credit should require some form of documentation or certification issued by an independent third party as a condition of payment. If only the unverified certification of the beneficiary is required to draw down on the credit, a patently false statement conforming to the letter of credit requirements will permit the bank to pay.

For Example:

A buyer advances money to a seller against an order. In order to protect its advance, the buyer requires the seller to issue a standby letter of credit in favor of the buyer to guarantee repayment of its advance if the seller does not deliver the goods by X date. The letter of credit only requires a letter from the buyer stating that the goods have not been delivered.

The bank will pay against the standby letter of credit if it receives a letter from the buyer stating that the goods were not delivered even if the goods have been delivered. The only recourse is a civil suit against the beneficiary of the standby letters of credit, in this case the buyer.

> If a seller requests a transferable letter of credit, a buyer needs to be concerned that they might not have any contact with or control over the actual supplier of their goods. This could lead to an inability to control quality or to ensure complete and accurate documentation.
>
> Better practice would be to detail the names of eligible transferees.

8.7.3. TRANSFERABLE LETTERS OF CREDIT

A transferable credit is one which specifically provides that it can be transferred by the original (first) beneficiary to one or more other beneficiaries.

It is normally used when the first beneficiary subcontracts for some or all of the merchandise and wishes to transfer all or part of his rights and obligations under the letter of credit to the subcontractor(s) as secondary beneficiary(ies).

If a buying agent is the beneficiary of a transferable letter of credit, care should be taken to make sure that the buying agent is not, in reality, acting as a seller, making a mark-up as opposed to a commission, which could impact on the duty due Customs. (*See* "Agents & Commissions" §7.1 at 29 and "Selling Commissions" §11.2 at 75.)

8.7.4. ASSIGNMENT OF PROCEEDS OF A LETTER OF CREDIT

Any beneficiary of a letter of credit may choose to assign some or all of the rights (proceeds) of the letter of credit to a third party without the knowledge or consent of the applicant. In order to assign these rights, a document of assignment must be executed, naming the party to whom the assignment has been made. The paying bank will then pay proceeds to the assigned in accordance with the executed document. In this way, a seller who is the beneficiary of a letter of credit from a buyer could pay or guarantee payment to his supplier, and/or commission to an agent or broker.

Assignments of proceeds are tied to specific letters of credit, not orders or transactions. It is not a guarantee of payment, only a guarantee of payment of funds received from a particular letter of credit. Thus, an assignment becomes void if the letter of credit expires or is not complied with by the beneficiary. This sometimes occurs accidentally, but assignments can also be circumvented by an unscrupulous beneficiary.

For example.

> A seller obtains a letter of credit against which it issues an assignment of proceeds to its supplier. The seller requests modifications of the letter of credit, but has the buyer issue a new letter of credit rather than amending or extending the existing one. This is easy to do when the letter of credit has or is about to expire.
>
> The original letter of credit against which the assignment was made no longer exists and neither does the assignment. The seller will obtain the full value of the new letter of credit. The supplier receives nothing.

8.8. FACTORING

Factoring is a form of third party financing secured by both title to goods, and the expected proceeds from the resale of those goods.

One major difference between factoring a transaction and obtaining bank financing, is whose credit will be evaluated. The only credit evaluated by a bank is that of the buyer. A factor will take into consideration not just the importer's credit, but also the credit worthiness of the resale purchaser, since it is the resale purchaser which is the first source of its repayment.

A second advantage of factoring is that the factor may be willing to advance the funds necessary to produce the goods.

Factoring does not alter the relative interests of buyer and seller; however, there may be less flexibility as to acceptable terms because of security concerns of the factor.

Factoring to provide funds for production is usually predicated upon the existence of a confirmed order. The prior existence of resale orders, in conjunction with the structure of a transaction required by the factor's security interests, can conflict with what may be the most efficacious form of a transaction from a duty or tax standpoint. Importers contemplating using a factor for financing should carefully evaluate its effects on the import transaction. This is especially true if it will result in a change in the way both the import and resale transactions have been structured.

8.9. CONSIGNMENT SALES

In consignment sales, goods are delivered to a buyer and payment to the seller is usually contingent upon future resale by the buyer. If the goods are not resold, the buyer can either pay for the goods or return them to the seller. Similar to the sale of goods on terms, when goods are sold on consignment, the entire cash advantage rests with the buyer who will have possession of goods without paying for them.

Clearly, every buyer would prefer to buy on a consignment, but most sellers will not sell on these terms. International sales on consignment are usually limited to specific industries where it has become the custom in the trade.

Consignment sales raise practical and legal questions as to the dutiable value of the merchandise both as to what should be declared at the time of entry and what may have to be restated after a sale.

8.10. COUNTER TRADE (BARTER)

Counter Trade addresses more precisely the currency of the transaction rather than the means of financing. The valuation of goods being exchanged should be given serious consideration as to its effect on the transaction. Different values might be more desirable depending upon the purpose for which they will be used.

From the standpoint of liability for Customs duties, a lower value would be preferable.

If the goods are being pledged as security in consideration of credit, or are being insured against loss, then a higher value may be preferred.

Finally, both Customs and Internal Revenue laws look to the cost of acquiring the goods which are used as the medium of payment.

---

[32] *Milam Audio Co. v. Federal Express Corp.*, 1994 U.S. Dist. LEXIS 15585 (C.D. Ill. 1994) at 9, 10,

9. PLANNING THE PROCEDURAL OPERATIONS

The viability of a transaction is dependent upon, not just its economics, but also upon its smooth and timely execution. All too often the procedural aspects of a transaction are handled as an afterthought to the acquisition of the product, when it should have been part of the planning.

9.1. TRANSPORTATION

There are a number of different modes of transportation which are very often used in combination: air, water, truck, and rail.

These services can either be contracted for individually, or as part of a combined service called "intermodal."

Services may be provided either directly by the carrier operating the transportation vehicle, e.g., airline or shipping line, or by non-carrier operating third parties who contract for space with carriers and then resell the transportation service often in combination with other services.

Different documents are issued, depending upon the mode of transportation.

A Bill of Lading is a contract for carriage of goods entered into by a shipper with a carrier. It is a receipt, and can serve as a Document of Title[33] for the goods evidencing the type, condition and quantity. It usually has terms and conditions on its back which, among other things, imposes limitations on their liability. Terms and Conditions are also made publically available through the carrier's tariff.

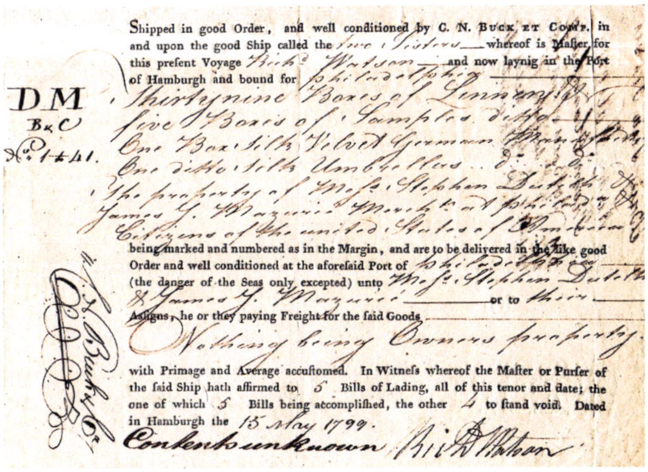
Shipped in good Order, and well conditioned by C. N. Buck et Comp. in and upon the good Ship called the ... whereof is Master for this present Voyage ... and now laying in the Port of Hamburgh and bound for ...

DM

being marked and numbered as in the Margin, and are to be delivered in the like good Order and well conditioned at the aforesaid Port of ... (the danger of the Seas only excepted) unto ... or to ... Assigns, he or they paying Freight for the said Goods ...

with Primage and Average accustomed. In Witness whereof the Master or Purser of the said Ship hath affirmed to 5 Bills of Lading, all of this tenor and date; the one of which 5 Bills being accomplished, the other 4 to stand void. Dated in Hamburgh the 15 May 1799.

Contents unknown

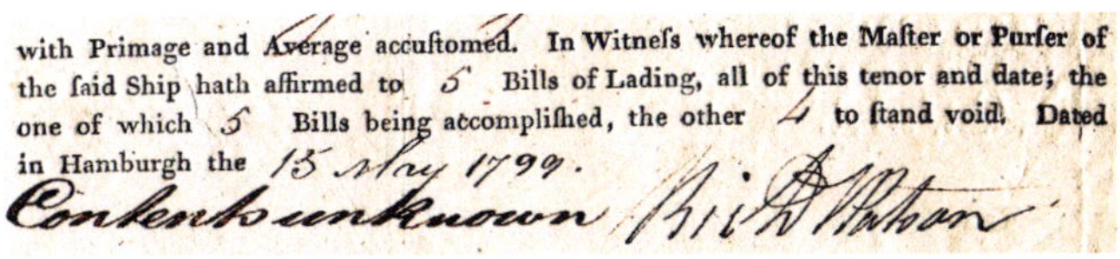
with Primage and Average accustomed. In Witness whereof the Master or Purser of the said Ship hath affirmed to 5 Bills of Lading, all of this tenor and date; the one of which 5 Bills being accomplished, the other 4 to stand void. Dated in Hamburgh the 15 May 1799.

Contents unknown

In witness whereof the carrier by its agent has signed 3 Bills of Lading all of the same tenor and date, one of which being accomplished, the others stand void.

2016

Trade Trivia

Many of the terms used on Bills of Lading today have remained essentially unchanged for hundreds of years.

In witness whereof the carrier by its agent has signed 3 Bills of Lading, all of the same tenor and date, one of which being accomplished, the others stand void.

It is the same in 2016 as it was in 1799.

A Waybill is a document often used by NVO's and freight forwarders. It looks very much like a Bill of Lading and provides shipping details and instructions relating to a shipment, however, it cannot serve as a Document of Title of goods.

An Air Waybill is a document of transportation for shipments by air. It is, however, not a document of title and cannot be issued as negotiable.

> Bills of Lading can be both instruments of title and transportation. Waybills, however, are only instruments of transportation.
>
> Only Bills of Ladings (and Warehouse Receipts) can be made Negotiable by use of the term "To Order Of".
>
> While for transport purposes both may be acceptable, when financing and security interest is concerned, generally Bills of Lading will be required.
>
> Air Waybills are never negotiable.

Consolidators for air shipments and Non Vessel Operating Common Carriers (NVOCC) for water borne shipments provide a practical and economical way for companies who ship less than a full shipping unit (igloo for air, container for sea, and trailer for truck) to still gain an advantageous rate. In many instances, consolidators can even provide competitive rates for full loads.

The basic rate available in all modes of transportation is a commodity specific rate. Generally, a reduced rate is available when a large volume of cargo is shipped over a period of time. In addition, depending upon the mode of transportation, a special service contract may be available which tailors both rates and services to an individual shipper's needs.

In addition, there may be an association of shippers of a particular commodity that has negotiated a time/volume discount based upon the aggregate freight of its members.

Air freight carriers are not regulated. The rates that they charge can differ from shipper to shipper, and from time to time. Airlines tend to maintain a tariff, and, therefore, their rates tend to be less flexible. Consolidators are often more flexible as to freight rates. In general, air freight rates are a matter of contract and negotiation.

Vessel, interstate or international truck and rail freight carriers are regulated. In general, the rates charged by the regulated common carriers are required by law to be published in their tariff. In order to be fair to all shippers, only the rates published in their tariffs may be charged. Rates differing from those in a carrier's tariff may be negotiated, but the negotiated rates must be filed with the regulatory government agency to be effective. It is sanctionable if other than the tariffed rate is charged, and carrier may be subjected to a fine by its regulating agency. The shipper and carrier may be subjected to a fine if the lower rate was obtained through collusion.

A shipper will be liable for payment of whatever rate is filed or published in the tariff for vessel, interstate or international truck and rail freight, even if an undercharge was the result of a unilateral act of the carrier misquoting or misrepresenting its tariff, or negotiating a rate and then failing to file the rate.

> If enough money is involved, you might consider suing the carrier for their failure to file the rate. This does not cancel the liability for the freight but it can be the source of damages in an amount sufficient to offset the liability.

If the carrier has breached its contract with the shipper, the shipper may have a legal action against the carrier for damages in an amount equal to the benefit of the rate that it should have gotten. But the two issues of payment of freight and damages are independent: the freight is regulatory and the damages are a civil action.

Two carriers, one an NVOCC, the second a major interstate trucking company now in bankruptcy, were found to have failed to file the rates that they negotiated with shippers, and consequently failed to charge the tariffed rate. Both carriers commenced several hundred lawsuits to collect the undercharges. The shippers were not responsible for the carriers' failure to file the negotiated rate, but under prevailing law, they are nevertheless responsible for payment.[34]

Almost any rate negotiated with a carrier can be made lawful if it is published and made available to all similarly situated shippers. If any substantial cargo is to be shipped under a particular rate, it is probably worth the shipper's effort to make sure that the rate to be used is a published rate. A few rates, such as Special Contracts with Freight Forwarders and Truck Contract Carrier rates do not generally need to be published.

Each mode of transportation and individual carrier imposes certain limits on its liability. In most instances, these limits are noted on the shipping documents. While the precise limitations will vary according to the law governing the mode of transportation, liability is usually, at most, only several hundred dollars per package or per kilo lost or damaged.

Unless a decision is made to self-insure, consideration should be given either to obtain insurance on your own or to declare a higher value with the carrier, if possible, in order to increase the carrier's limits of liability. (*See* also "Declaration of Higher Value" §9.4.1 at 61.)

9.2. LIABILITY FOR FREIGHT, CHARGES AND SERVICES.

There are three basic questions relative to liability for shipment related expenses.

1. Who is supposed to pay them?
2. Who in the end will have to pay them?
3. How much might you have to pay?

The legal issue of who has to pay in the first instance is a contractual matter between the buyer and seller and, secondarily, between the shipper who is most often the seller, and the carrier.

The practical issue, however, deals with what happens when the contractually obligated party doesn't pay.

The commercial term 'freight charges' actually covers two types of charges; freight which is the actual cost of the physical transportation and other related services provided by the carrier, such as consolidation charges. No distinction needs to be made between them unless there is a dispute as to liability, in which case liability might depend, in part, on the type of charge.

As a practical matter, when looking at liability, it is better to consider all vendor services involved with the shipment, including freight forwarders, warehouses, truckers, and Customs Brokers.

9.2.1. WHO PAYS

Carriers, forwarders, and Customs Brokers are entitled to get paid. The contractual arrangements between the buyer and seller are of no concern to them.

Their terms and conditions, whether found in a carrier's Waybill, tariff, or documents, or online, generally seeks to draw in almost anyone who has contact with the shipment, not just the Shipper, Consignee, Importer or Exporter.

By way of illustration, one carrier's Waybill provides that:

> "Merchant" means the shipper, consignee, receiver, holder of this Bill of Lading, owner of the cargo or person entitled to the possession of the cargo and the servants and agents of any of these, all of whom shall be jointly and severally liable to the Carrier for the payment of all Charges, and for the performance of the obligations of any of them under this Bill of Lading.

Because the seller is normally the one who arranges for shipping and acts as shipper they will generally be liable for payment of freight charges. However, regardless of what terms appear on the Bill of Lading or Waybill, by law, the consignee becomes equally liable for freight charges when it accepts the benefit of the services by accepting delivery of the shipment.[35] Even a disclosed agent named as the consignee may become liable to the carrier if it accepts actual delivery, despite the disclosure of the principal beneficiary.

There are limited situations where a consignee will not be liable for certain freights. For that to happen advanced planning is required.

9.2.2. THE SHIPMENT AS SECURITY FOR PAYMENT

Regardless of who you think should pay for these services, in the end it usually comes down to the simple fact that carriers, NVOs, forwarders, warehouseman, truckers, and customs brokers, all have at least Specific Liens against either cargo and/or documents for the work they perform, or the moneys they advance with respect to that cargo. The shipment serves as collateral securing that debt. Maritime and Mechanic's Liens are nothing new. They have been around for hundreds of years.

If you want the goods or documents, you will have to satisfy that lien. Today, it is not uncommon to find that they have a General Lien which essentially means that if they release one shipment to you, they will substitute the next shipment as security for the money due against both the released shipment as well as the current shipment. This is particularly the case where you have been extended credit.[36]

9.2.3. HOW MUCH ARE YOU LIABLE FOR

It is important to keep in mind that certain charges such as demurrage, storage, and detention continue to accrue until the goods are released and delivery is taken.

When it comes to liability for freight, the most important rule and the one that overrides all other rules is that where a carrier is required by law to post a tariff it has a duty to collect the full tariffed amount. Collecting less than the rate tariffed and charged against one shipment is tantamount to permitting one shipper to obtain transportation at a lower rate than other comparably situated shippers. What follows is merely sorting out from whom the carrier must collect and under what circumstances.

Clearly, the primacy of the rule that the carrier must be paid, or the presence of various liens securing payment sometimes creates the possibility that a person, most likely the consignee, will have to pay freight, charges and service fees twice.

This occurs most often when the selling price was inclusive of freight and/or services, but the seller or freight forwarder did not pay the carrier, forwarder or broker and payment is demanded from the consignee/buyer before delivery is made.

The risk of double liability, from a practical standpoint can only be prevented through advance planning. Consider buying on an FOB foreign port or Freight Collect basis rather than on a CFR, CIF, or DDP basis or paying through a Documentary Letter of Credit requiring proof of payment to the carrier or other parties as a documentary requirement.

There are a variety of rules under which incentivized rates can be negotiated. They must, however, be negotiated in advance of shipment or carriage which means that they will not help to reduce your liability after the fact.

Those programs include:

- Service Contracts with liquidated damages for failure to ship the contracted quantities.
- Time-Volume rates which provide for reduced rates as the volume shipped increases.[37]
- Negotiated Rate Agreements (NRAs).

Airfreight, forwarder, warehouse and Customs Broker rates are unregulated so, in simple terms, rates are the result of market rates and negotiations. While the carrier or service provider has more leeway to negotiate a settlement, in light of their liens, reduction in the liability should not be assumed.

Interstate Trucking has presented a special problem for shippers. Interstate trucking rates are tariffed[38] and, like other carrier rates, often discounted. Those discounts may, however, be discounted not on volume, but on condition of timely payment. If payment is not rendered timely, the rate reverts to usually very high undiscounted tariff rates. This can be a particular problem when you contract indirectly with the trucker through a

An FMCA Broker, also commonly known as a Freight Broker, can look like a trucker, and even issue transportation documents, but, having no trucks of their own, has to contract with an actual carrier, to move the goods. The problem for you as a shipper is that they act as a principal when it comes to collecting from you, but as your agent when it comes to paying the underlying trucker.

Here is what you need to know:

1. If you pay the freight broker and they don't pay the trucker, the risk is that the trucker will try to collect from you.

2. You will not necessarily know the broker's terms with that trucker. So you will not know if you are dealing with a rate conditioned upon timely payment.

3. You also may not know the carrier's limitations of liability in the case of loss or damage.

freight broker or forwarder, or online services which do not make timely payments to the trucker.

9.2.4. UNDELIVERABLE CARGO – LIABILITIES AT THE FOREIGN PORT

A growing problem today is the issue of abandoned freight. While the seller may have been paid for the goods, and under the terms of the sales agreement, the buyer is responsible for all foreign charges; the shipper remains liable to the carrier for all charges related to the abandoned cargo. That includes, foreign charges, demurrage, detention, and the cost of abandoning or destroying the goods.

Abandonment seems to be a more common occurrence today with respect to goods of marginal value such as used, recycled, or inexpensive items or materials, and goods exported on speculation.

9.3. INCOTERMS

Executive Briefing

Importers, exporters, carriers and others are free to establish whatever terms they deem desirable or appropriate to their business. However, the possibility that those terms might be interpreted differently by each of the parties, as well as the possibility that laws may differ between countries, make it preferable to use standard commercial terms with established meanings. Moreover, because the interpretation of even standard commercial terms can be affected by local law, a reference to the source of the definitions and, where possible, the law to be applied should also be included in any agreement.

INCOTERMS do not cover all issues, but they still provide a common ground with respect to basic terms.

Case Summary

Where the contracting parties' countries are signatories to United Nations Convention on Contracts for the International Sale of Goods (CISG) its terms will apply unless the parties have expressly Opted Out of its application.

The mere designation of a Choice of Law in an agreement does not constitute an express Opting Out, of the application of CISG.

BP Oil International v. Empresa Estratal Petroleos de Ecuador
332 F.3d 333 (US CA 5th Cir. 2003)

There are a number of sources of standard commercial terms. The most commonly used terms are INCOTERMS, published by the International Chamber of Commerce, and those incorporated into the Uniform Commercial Code, as adopted by each state of the United States.

If no reference is made in the sales/purchase agreements as to which definitions or law the parties want to apply, by default, the law of the state or country in which the contract was executed, or is to be performed, will generally govern.

Case Summary

Where the law to be applied in interpreting the definition of the term CIF was not supplied by the parties, Incoterms meanings would apply.

The Court concluded that since United Nations Convention on Contracts for the International Sale of Goods (CISG) applied to the underlying contract because each of their respective countries were a "Contracting Party" to the treaty, "[i]ncoterms are incorporated into the CISG through Article 9(2) which provides that,

The parties are considered, unless otherwise agreed, to have impliedly made applicable to their contract or its formation a usage of which the parties knew or ought to have known and which in international trade is widely known to, and regularly observed by, parties to contracts of the type involved in the particular trade concerned".

St. Paul Guardian Insurance Co. v. Neuromed Medical System & Support GmbH
53F. App'x 173, 173 (USCA 2d Cir. 2002)

– Continued on next page –

The basic INCOTERMS® as of 2010[39] are:

DEPARTURE		GOODS ARE DELIVERED FREE OF RISK AT THE NAMED FACILITY.
	EXW	Ex Works (named place of delivery)
MAIN CARRIAGE UNPAID		BUYER BEARS MOST COSTS AFTER THE TRANSFER OF RISK OF LOSS OR DAMAGE
	FCA	Free Carrier (named place of delivery)
	FAS	Free Alongside Ship (named port of shipment)
	FOB	Free On Board (named port of shipment)
MAIN CARRIAGE PAID		SELLER MUST BEAR CERTAIN COSTS EVEN AFTER THE TRANSFER OF RISK OF LOSS OR DAMAGE
	CFR	Cost and Freight (named port of destination)
	CIF	Cost, Insurance and Freight (named port of destination)
	CPT	Carriage Paid to (named place of destination)
	CIP	Carriage and Insurance Paid to (named place of destination)
ARRIVAL		THE GOODS MUST ARRIVE AT THE NAMED DESTINATION
	DAT	Delivered at Terminal (named terminal at port or place of destination)
	DAP	Delivered at Place (named place of destination)
	DDP	Delivered Duty Paid (named place of destination)

Figure 5 - INCOTERMS® 2010

The following illustrates the differences between what is covered in terms of cost as compared to when risk of loss normally transfers:

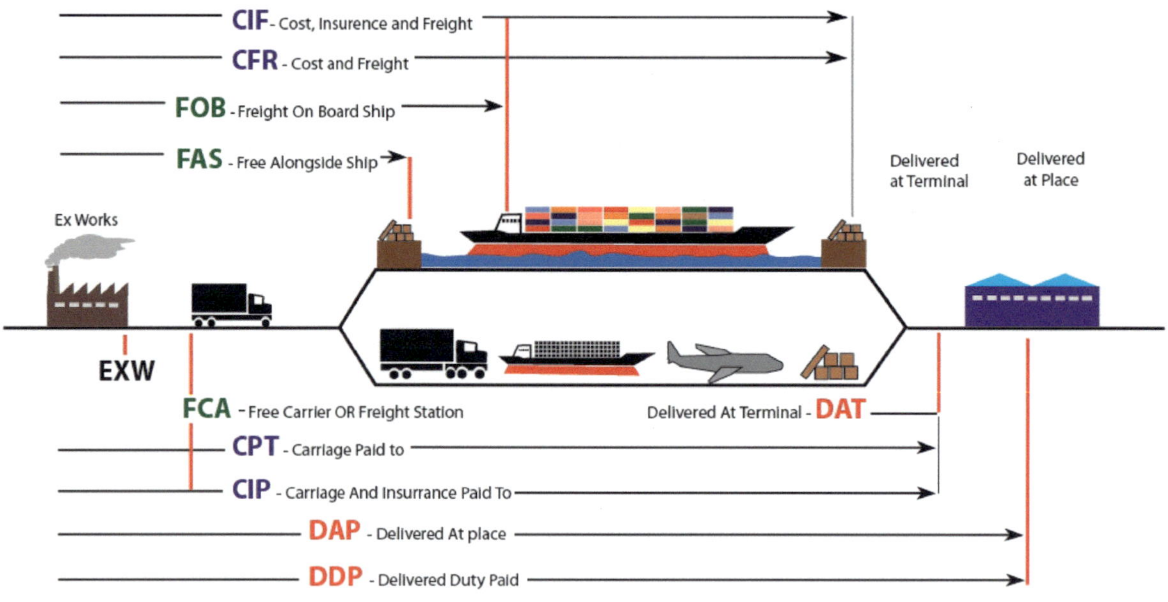

Figure 6 - Transfer of Risk of Loss

While, for diagramming purposes, an Incoterm may appear to have a ridged application they can be, and are often adapted to the needs of the parties.

By way of example, Frank Reynolds, author of *Incoterms® for Americans®*, has observed that:

FCA can be used with any agreed place on the seller's side (most often either the seller's premises or buyer's-appointed carrier terminal / forwarder's consolidation point.)

CPT/CIP can be used to terminate costs at any point, not just at the arrival terminal, but also can be, and often are used with door-to-door transportation.

The choice of terms is not just a matter of price, because terms which may yield the same end result when a transaction proceeds as planned, can yield substantially different results when something goes wrong.

Take for example:

Two orders for identical goods are placed.

The first is purchased CIF New York.

The other is purchased DAT New York.

The price of the goods is the same and the total cost, including transit and insurance to New York, are the same.

If the shipment arrives in good order, there is effectively no difference.

However, if there is loss or damage while in transit, from both a practical and legal standpoint, these two terms yield very different results.

On the DAT New York shipment the problem belongs to the Shipper, who is generally the seller.

On the CIF shipment it is the problem of the Consignee, which is usually the buyer.

Trade terms mean different things to different people and in different countries.

It is important to make it clear that your definition is under Incoterms, e.g.,

DAP New York, INCOTERMS.

INCOTERMS change over time.

For example, the term for Cost & Freight has changed over time from C&F to CNF and now to CFR.

Certain terms have been eliminated, e.g., Delivered Duty Unpaid (DDU).

And still other terms have had their commercial meaning changed, as in the case of FOB, which has shifted the transfer of risk from "over the rails" of the ship to "when placed aboard the vessel at the point of shipment

It is therefore better to include a reference to the publication year:

DAP New York, INCOTERMS 2010

In terms of a timely delivery, when a date is specified in conjunction with "DAT New York" it means the date by which the cargo must be delivered at New York. However, under the term "CIF New York" it only requires delivery to the carrier in the foreign port by that date.

For the DAT New York shipment, risk of loss remained with the shipper until the goods arrived at New York, so an in-transit loss is the problem of the shipper. With CIF New York, risk of loss passed to the purchaser when the goods were delivered to the carrier in the foreign port, and thus, the problem rests with the purchaser. Insurance may cover the loss, but the cost and burden of dealing with the claim has shifted from the Seller to the Buyer.

Even though the CIF price includes the cost of insurance and freight, these are obtained by the seller for the account and risk of the purchaser. Unless otherwise specified, the insurance and transportation obtained by the seller will usually be the minimum that meets the terms of the sale. This may not be adequate to protect the purchaser and is certainly not the same as allowing the risk of loss to remain with the seller until the goods arrive at the destination, as in FOB New York or, today, more appropriately DAT or DAP New York. (*See* "Insurance" §9.4 at 60.)

Any term can be modified, but modifications always raise the possibility of unforeseen issues, including misinterpretation or differing interpretations. Therefore, great care should be taken to make them as clear as possible.

We have included what is considered common practice with respect to when risk passes. While Title to the Goods is assumed to pass simultaneously along with Risk of Loss, Incoterms do not expressly address the passage of Title to Goods. In addition, Customs may, depending upon the valuation method you use, demand proof of when title passed. (*See* "Title to Goods" §9.3.1 at 59.)

Case Summary

The default meaning of any particular trade term can be modified by the express agreement of the contracting parties.

While under the term CIF, risk passes from Seller to Buyer when the cargo is delivered to a carrier. The appellate court held that additional terms which the parties added to their contract of sale, relating to title and payment, could modify the terms of delivery to such an extent as to nullify the passing of risk pursuant to the default rules of CIF.

Kumar Corp. v. Nopal Line
462 So. 2nd 1178 (CA Florida, 3rd Dist. 1985)

While Incoterms address a number of important contractual issues between the buyer and seller, with respect to their respective responsibilities regarding purchase and delivery of goods, they do not address all purchase and delivery issues. And many of those not addressed are significant.

Those issues raise questions of a balance between security of payment and the risks associated with non-payment.

- ✓ When does title to the goods transfer?
- ✓ When is payment due?
- ✓ In what form is the payment to be made?

- versus -

- ✘ What happens if the buyer doesn't pay?
- ✘ What happens if the goods are never picked up?
- ✘ Who is responsible for charges related to the goods that are not collected, including return or abandonment?

One factor rarely considered is who will be the Shipper on your transportation document.

Sellers assume that the buyer is responsible for all charges after delivery of goods to the exporting carrier. The buyer may be contractually obligated to make these payments, however, if things go wrong, being the Shipper on the transport document can render you primarily liable for domestic and foreign charges as well as freight.

> On exports, if you can get paid prior or contemporaneous to delivery of goods to the buyer's control, then perhaps you might consider having the buyer act as the shipper on the transport documents so that you can avoid being held responsible for future expenses.

If you need to use various INCOTERMS, *Incoterms® for Americans®* should be part of your reference library. A good companion to it is the *Incoterms® 2010* source book, issued by the International Chamber of Commerce.

store.iccwbo.org/incoterms-2010

www.incoterms-4-americans.com/
www.amazon.com

Figure 7 - Incoterms Publications

9.3.1. TITLE TO GOODS

While it is commercially common for title to pass simultaneously with the risk of loss, there are many circumstances where the seller does not want title to pass until payment is made.

> Title has business and tax implications beyond risk of loss. It can affect which transaction governs value for Customs purposes and on whose books and in what physical year the transaction appears.

When title passes is a matter of contract. INCOTERMS do not control the transfer of title.

Care should be taken when crafting title transfer language against unanticipated results. Separating the transfer of title and risk of loss may give the appearance of having the security of title, as might be required by a letter of credit, while leaving the risk of loss and the attendant responsibility with the Seller. While this might be practical with an established domestic seller, the cost of enforcing a foreign seller's performance after having been paid could be very high. In practice, it might be the equivalent of self-insuring.

9.3.2. RISK OF LOSS OR DAMAGE

Inherent in transportation is the risk of loss from damage or theft.

Traditionally, by obtaining insurance, a business protects itself from risks it cannot afford.

Insurance, as a practical matter, often refers to more than just liability protection offered by a third party. For a shipper, the bottom line is how to balance the risk of loss with the cost of protection.

Protection from loss is available as:

- Third party insurance obtained from an insurance underwriter or its agent
- Declaration of Higher Value to the carrier
- Insurance

9.4. INSURANCE

The most common form of protection is insurance underwritten by an independent insurance company. Coverage is available either for single shipments or on an open policy covering all shipments.

> A Seller's failure to place the insurance required under the sales agreement has, in various cases, resulted in the seller being liable as though it were the insurer.

There are various types of insurance to cover loss or damage to a shipment.

> Insurance will not cover you for your own deficiencies. It remains your obligation to ensure that the goods are properly packed for shipment, to provide proof as to what you actually shipped, and, if required, have the cargo inspected prior to shipment.

Ocean policies are generally referred to as Open Marine, although today open coverage can be arranged for ocean, air, rail and trucking transit risks, as well as warehousing, deconsolidation, and the like. Open policies terminate only by cancellation; generally, they do not have an expiration date. The main advantage of open coverage is that it automatically covers all shipments that are contractually required to be insured and, therefore, coverage is not subject to the risk of a traffic department's failure to apply for coverage on an individual shipment.

If you do not have enough shipments to warrant an open policy, a freight forwarder or customs broker can generally obtain insurance for individual shipments. A shipper would find that trying to place a "stray" risk itself is very expensive and, in fact, many insurance companies will not accept a stray risk. Alternatively, a freight forwarder or Customs Broker may be able to cover the shipment under its own open marine policy, but it is up to the shipper or consignee to clearly specify the coverage that is required.

The broadest standard coverage is against "All Risks," which protects the shipment against physical loss or damage from external causes, except those resulting from the natural tendencies of the goods, (e.g., deterioration due to expiration of shelf life), or delay.

As a general rule, a purchaser is better off obtaining its own insurance or at least specifying the coverage it wants. While, for example a C.I.F. contract requires the seller to obtain insurance on the shipment, the seller's interest is in obtaining the least expensive insurance that meets the contract, not in providing the best protection for the purchaser.

A seller also has an interest in obtaining insurance, even if it sells goods on terms that do not require it to obtain insurance. When goods are sold on open account or sight draft terms, the purchaser should be the party to arrange for insurance. But, if the purchaser forgets or purchases inadequate coverage, and the shipment then suffers a loss or damage, the purchaser often times simply says that he can't pay for the goods. The seller could be legally entitled to payment, but unable to collect in a foreign country. To protect against these types of situations, "Unpaid Vendor's Insurance" may be available, which would pay the seller provided that the loss falls within the terms and conditions of the coverage.

The key is that under a marine policy, nothing is written in stone. Anything an importer or exporter may need can be discussed with underwriters and, in many instances, special coverage can be arranged.

There are many customs variations in coverage that should be considered because what appears to be "All Risk" coverage has limitations. Given issues of worldwide political and labor instability, depending upon the countries and ports with which you are doing business, additional coverage should be considered for strikes, riots, civil commotion (SRCC) and war.

There are specialized insurance brokers, commonly known as Ocean Marine Insurance Brokers, who can assist both the seller and purchaser, not only in obtaining the correct coverage, but also in arranging for required surveys and submitting claims.

9.4.1. DECLARATION OF HIGHER VALUE

All carriers limit their liability for loss or damage for shipments they carry. Exact limitations may vary based on package count or weight and depending upon the type of carrier: air, water, land or rail. Limitations generally range from fifty ($50) to five hundred ($500) dollars per shipping unit, depending upon terms and conditions of carriage, and local and international law.[40] A forty foot container can, under certain circumstances, be treated as a single shipping unit limited to a five hundred dollar recovery. Limitations for air shipments are based upon weight, and are generally about $0.15 per lb.

Carriers can permit a shipper to declare a higher value to increase the carriers' liability limits.[41] The carrier will, of course, charge a higher rate for this increase in liability. This is not insurance, and it may be very limited as to the types of losses covered.

Declaring higher value to a carrier should not be confused with third party insurance provided by a freight forwarder or Customs Broker under its open policy, which is true insurance. (*See* "Insurance" §9.4 at 60.)

9.4.2. SELF-INSURANCE

There are times when a shipper may want to consider a limited form of self-insurance. When shipping by water, you need to take into consideration the risk of "General Average" in addition to the value of your goods. Under General Average a shipper is responsible for its proportional share of the total value of other shippers' cargo lost at sea in an attempt to save the vessel or other cargo.

If a shipper is reasonably assured that the risk of damage, breakage, or pilferage is low, a shipper can purchase a special type of limited insurance known as F.P.A. or "Free of Particular Average" which gives the shipper coverage. Simply stated, this limited form of insurance will not pay for losses unless there is a sinking, stranding, burning, etc., as well as collision and upset of overland conveyance. In this way a shipper can self-insure for the manageable risks while protecting itself from a disaster.

> The likelihood of being subject to General Average is relatively low, but the loss could be substantial.
>
> The likelihood of being at risk due to a Carrier bankruptcy is even more remote, but bankruptcies such as Hanjin in 2016 are not unknown.

9.5. PRE-SHIPMENT INSPECTION

One daunting question facing every purchaser, assuming that their order is shipped: does the shipment conform to the order as to quantity, design, quality specifications, and timeliness? While many payment terms make payment conditional on submission of proof that something purporting to be the goods ordered were shipped on time, the purchaser has no assurance that the goods actually conform to the order.

A buyer can assure itself that conforming goods are shipped only through physical examination of the goods before they are shipped. Inspection can be performed by an employee of the buyer, a buying agent, or an independent inspection company. Payment can then be conditioned, not just upon proof of shipment, but upon presentation of documentation establishing that the shipment has been inspected and that the inspector finds that the goods conform. (*See* "Drafts" §8.5 at 38 and "Letters of Credit" §8.7 at 40.)

Non-conforming international orders spawn issues beyond those which would result in domestic transactions and beyond the obvious issue of price adjustment. The condition of the goods, their return, correction of defects, and/or price reductions, can all affect the amount of customs duty due on the shipment.

If goods do not conform:

- The product provided may be prohibited entry, e.g., shoes ordered with a non-endangered species of snake skin as trim arrives with a different species requiring a CITES certificate of origin, or the goods may be a prohibited endangered species.
- A different classification carrying a higher rate of duty might apply, e.g., a jacket with sufficient plastic coating to make it water resistant is dutiable at 7.6%[42], but if the coating is insufficient it would be dutiable at 29.5 % [43].
- If the shipment does not conform to the order because it was

shipped late, there can be other consequences, including a plan for change in duty rates.

- The rate of duty might have changed because:
  - The article no longer qualifies for a duty free benefit,
  - A temporary duty suspension has expired, or
  - A supplemental duty has been imposed.
- The way in which either the defect is corrected or the price is adjusted may bring into play factors independent of the defect itself.
- If a lower price is negotiated for the goods, it may be possible to use the reduced price as the dutiable value, which would reduce the customs duty proportionally. (*See* "Transaction Value for the Goods Being Imported" §11.1 at 75.)
- If the goods are returned, a refund of 99% of the duty paid may be available under drawback. (*See* "Duty Refund" §0 at 117.)
- If goods are exported for repair and then re-imported, duty may be due only on the value of the repairs. (*See* "Articles Not Advanced or Improved In Condition" §0 at 117.)
- If some or all goods are replaced rather than repaired, the replacements will be assessed duty on their full value even if nothing additional had to be paid for them. Consider exporting the defective goods under drawback. (*See* "Duty Refund" §13.5 at 122.)

9.6. CUSTOMS CLEARANCE, FORWARDING AND OTHER SERVICES

Most importers use a professional known as a Customs Broker to clear their shipments through U.S. Customs and other agencies, and to coordinate related activities including forwarding or trucking.

Customs Brokers are generally individuals or corporations licensed by Customs to transact Custom Business on behalf of others[44]. An importer is not required to use a Customs Broker to clear its shipments, but even large experienced companies should give serious thought to the consequences of not doing so. As one former career Customs Officer once said: "*Of course you can make entry yourself. You can also amputate your right arm by yourself. I don't recommend either.*"

> Perhaps of greatest importance to an importer is a good Customs Broker since they are generally one of the best, first sources of information, advice and aid in spotting import problems before they become insurmountable.

Customs clearance is often viewed by importers as a procedural inconvenience, clerical in nature, and the costs associated with it unwarranted; consequently, the service is often purchased on price alone. Nothing could be further from the truth or a bigger mistake.

A Customs Broker does more than just clear goods through Customs. They are *jacks of all trades* related to clearance and movement of a shipment. They are the procedural grease for the importation. A Customs Broker can normally arrange for any other related services that an importer or exporter may need, from warehousing to repacking to forwarding to final delivery to ultimate consignees and even the collection of payment.

Few importers realize that what a good Customs Broker can save an importer in handling expenses, problems, and penalties, usually exceeds the difference in cost between the least and most expensive brokerage services, and are probably less than the legal fees necessary for resolving problems. Unfortunately, these types of savings are unquantifiable.

All too often, costs become the sole criteria in acquiring Customs Brokerage services. This can be penny wise and pound foolish. Given the importance of the services performed by a Customs Broker, it is important to shop for quality services first and last.

Customs Brokers differ in size, scope of practice, and number of offices. There is not necessarily any correlation between those factors and the quality of service. Individual offices can vary significantly even within one company. If you can, select the best broker at each port. Period! Most brokers have correspondent brokers at other ports if they don't have their own offices, and are accustomed to working with and coordinating with, other brokers. Further, most entries only require action at a single port.

Freight forwarders arrange for the physical movement of goods. For vessel export shipments from the U.S., they are licensed by the Federal Maritime Commission (FMC). No license is required for domestic or air shipment. Many Customs Brokers also do forwarding and many are also FMC licensed.

9.7. POWER OF ATTORNEY

In international trade, a Power of Attorney is commonly required to authorize a logistics provider to file documents with government agencies. This is as true for filing Electronic Export Information[45] (EEI, formerly SED) on exports as it is for filing Customs Entries[46] on imports.

What many importers do not appreciate is that when a Customs Broker or Logistics Provider, e.g., Forwarder or NVO, signs documents, they are signing them in YOUR name, as your agent, which makes you directly responsible for their statements or misstatements.

Think about the signature line on your tax return. You are swearing that the information you have provided is true and accurate. It is the same on your import and export filings with the government, except that you will likely not see the documents until after they are filed.

This is one of the reasons why buying these services by price alone, or letting another person make the choice of who will be signing your name as either Importer of Record or U.S. Principal Party in Interest, can be risky. So, make sure you know who you are giving your authorizations to.

CAUTION

Who would you just let anyone sign YOUR name to YOUR tax return?

When you grant a power of attorney to a Customs Broker, Freight Forwarder, NVO, or other logistics provider, that is essentially what you are authorizing.

Since it is not practical to operate without giving out these authorizations unless you want to sign each entry document yourself...

Make sure you know to whom you are granting that authority.

Just as you will want to know the bona fides of those you authorize to act as your agent, the government, as well as Customs Brokers, NVOs, and Forwarders, are each equally concerned about YOUR bona fides.

[33] U.C.C.- Article-7 (amended 2003)

[34] Maislin Indus. v. Primary Steel., 497 U.S. 116, 110 S. Ct. 2759 (1990)

[35] 49 USC 10744

[36] In re World Imports Ltd. v. OEC Grp. N.Y., 820 F. 3d 575 (2016)

[37] 49 U.S. Code §13702 (b) (4); 49 U.S. Code 1101 (rail)

[38] 49 U.S. Code 13501i; 49 U.S. Code 13702 (truck)

[39] INCOTERMS® 2010

[40] Carriage of Goods by Sea Act (C.O.G.S.A.) 46 USC 1304(5)

[41] Carriage of Goods by Sea Act (C.O.G.S.A.) 46 USC 1304(5)

[42] Item 6201.93.30 HTSUS (1994)

[43] Item 6201.93.35 HTSUS (1994)

[44] 19 USC 1641, 19 C.F.R. Part 111

[45] 15 C.F.R. Part 30 subpart A

[46] 19 C.F.R. part 141 subpart C

– Page intentionally left blank –

10. PLANNING THE DOCUMENTATION

Executive Briefing

Documentation is the primary basis for all decisions made by the government and those handling the practical aspects of an international transaction. The absence of complete and accurate documentation can result in erroneous decisions, as well as delays and expense(s).

10.1. INVOICING

An invoice fulfills more functions than just documenting the commercial transaction. Various government agencies, other than Customs, use the information found in the commercial invoice to determine compliance with import and export laws. Beyond documenting a sale, the regulatory need for information dictates what must appear on an invoice, such as the species name for the Federal Trade Commission Fur Product Labeling Act and the Fish & Wildlife Service.

A separate invoice is required for each shipment. Normally, only one distinct shipment, from one manufacturer/seller/shipper, to one consignee, carried by one commercial carrier, should be included on a single invoice.

Required information that does not appear on the invoice as originally prepared should be provided on attachment(s) to the invoice.

Invoices and all other attachments covering shipments to the U.S.A. must be in English or must be accompanied by an accurate English translation.

The precise contents of an invoice will vary depending upon the nature of the transaction. In certain situations, such as in the case of footwear, special invoices may be required in addition to the commercial invoice.[47]

Each of the elements of information required in the invoice has a consequence for the value, classification or admissibility of a shipment. Custom has been endeavoring to set forth product specific invoice guidelines. Until such guidelines are published, it is up to the importer to make sure that the description and information necessary to properly classify, appraise and admit the shipment are presented in the invoice and accompanying documents.

The Customs Modernization Act of 1993 updates invoicing requirements to take into consideration current business practices, enforcement needs, and the electronic nature of business and customs transactions. Of significance to importers will be the ability to transmit invoice and other information electronically to U.S. Customs.[48] Moreover it may be possible for Customs to act on incomplete information subject to a subsequent "Reconciliation."[49] In combination, electronic filing and post entry reconciliation can be of tremendous advantage to fast moving transactions where information often lags behind, and may not be available until year's end.[50]

10.2. DOCUMENTS OF TRANSPORTATION

Bills of Lading and Air Waybills are the usual documents under which goods are transported. Bills of Lading (for water or ground transportation) and Air Waybills (for air transportation) fulfill a variety of functions beyond evidencing the contract of carriage.

Bills of Lading and Air Waybills:

- Are contracts of carriage,
- Evidence a right to delivery or possession of a shipment and may, in certain cases, be the instruments of title,
- Evidence the right to make a Customs entry, and
- Establish the carrier's responsibility or limitations of liability for loss or damage to goods while in transit.

Carrier certificates are an alternate form of evidence of the right of a consignee to make entry with U.S. Customs. While no longer required by U.S. Customs, they are still commonly issued by carriers, most often airlines or deconsolidators, as a substitute for Air Waybills. The carrier certificate can cover an entire shipment or only a portion of a shipment.

Trade Trivia

Ever wonder what Marks and Numbers are?

Marks were your secret code for identifying your shipment.

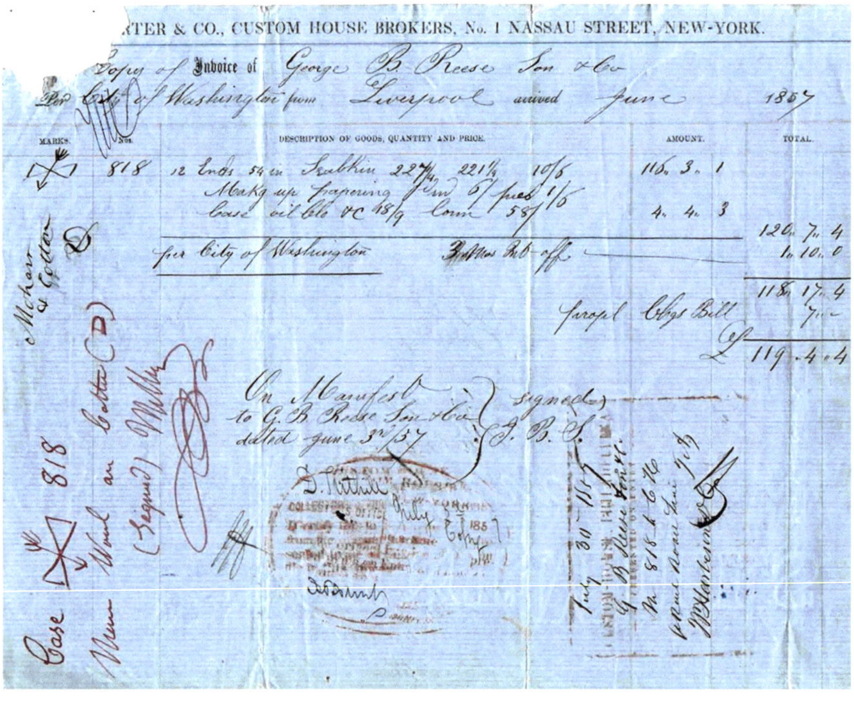
...RTER & CO., CUSTOM HOUSE BROKERS, No. 1 NASSAU STREET, NEW-YORK.

Copy of Invoice of George B. Reese Son & Co

Per City of Washington from Liverpool arrived June 1857

MARKS.	Nos.	DESCRIPTION OF GOODS, QUANTITY AND PRICE.	AMOUNT.	TOTAL.
	818			

When cargo was shipped loose (and at this time ALL cargo was shipped loose) you did not want to put your name on your packages because it would allow thieves to easily identify which goods to steal.

Marks were a substitute for the Consignee's name.

Figure 8 - Customs Broker Cargo Receipt – 1857

10.3. CERTIFICATES OF ORIGIN

Certificates of Origin are simply documentary declarations as to the identification and Country of Origin of imported goods.

> Generally, if the program is concerned with enforcement, the lack of a proper certificate of origin will preclude admission of the shipment. Under certain programs such as the Endangered Species Act, shipments not accompanied by a valid Certificate of Origin are not only refused admission, but are subject to seizure and forfeiture.

A number of special programs relating to enforcement of import controls or restrictions, as well as those granting preferential treatment as to rates of duty, are dependent upon the identity of the goods and the Country of Origin. Each program has its own requirements as to the form of the information or document. This can range from as little as a statement in a commercial invoice, to an export license or visa, or an independent document entitled Certificate of Origin.

Depending upon the program, Certificates of Origin may be prepared and executed by the exporter, may require certification or endorsement by a Consulate or Chamber of Commerce, or may require validation by a government agency in the exporting country and, in that sense, they constitute a Foreign Export License.

The significance of the certificate is based upon the type of program to which it relates.

Most U.S. programs that grant preferential duty treatment require the certificate at the time the benefit is claimed.

Some programs such as Generalized System of Preferences (GSP), Caribbean Basin Initiative (CBI), U.S.- Israeli Free Trade Agreement, or North American Free Trade Agreement specifically provide a means for claiming the benefit after importation. (*See* "520 (a, b, d) Claim" §20.2.2.2 at 200.) Many other programs do not specifically provide this option, requiring the importer to have to resort to alternate means of making the claim. (*See* "Post Entry Amendment" §20.2.3 at 200 and "Protest" §20.2.1 at 198.)

Not all declarations of identity and origin are called Certificates of Origin or require specific form. It is important to determine in advance which one is required.

10.4. U.S. EXPORT LICENSES

Export licenses are government authorizations to export a restricted or controlled product to a specified country or person. It is a unilateral control imposed by the exporting country, sometimes as a result of an international trade agreement. Each country has its own laws and regulations governing which products require export authorization, the type of license required and the requirements of that license.

> While the name has changed, the Electronic Export Information or E.E.I, still performs essentially the same function as what was previously known as a Shipper's Export Declaration or S.E.D.

All goods exported from the United States are subject to licensing requirements of the U.S. Department of Commerce, but not all shipments will require a formal license. Most shipments will be NLR (No License Required) and as a practical matter satisfied by the filing of the Electronic Export Information.

Most U.S. exports will not require an export license. Every shipment, however, needs to be reviewed to confirm it.

Export licenses are government authorizations to export a restricted or controlled product to a specified country. It is a unilateral control imposed by the exporting country, sometimes as a result of an international trade agreement.

High-tech items and those items which potentially have a military use will be covered by export regulations of the Department of Commerce or other agencies. Obviously this means that most exports ultimately will not be subject to Export control's requirements.

Items being exported need to be classified to determine if they are high tech or military in nature and if they require a license. Even so, a majority of items will be classified as EAR 99, which indicates that a particular item is subject to Export Administration Regulations (EAR) but not specifically described by an Export Control Classification Number (ECCN) on the Commerce Control List (CCL). In other words, the product is subject to the Department of Commerce rules but does not require a license. Such items will be NLR (No License Required).

Regardless, for items that do not fall under the EAR 99 exception, or are EAR 99, if being shipped to a particular person of concern or in support of a prohibited end-use, they will generally require an export license.

The Department of Commerce does not license products for importation.

The State Department licenses both imports and exports of defense related articles, even if imported on only a temporary basis for testing and/or repairs, requires a formal license.

Failure to have the required license, or a false declaration in the documentation, can result in an inability to export the goods, their seizure, forfeiture, and/or substantial penalties, including suspension of export privileges and potential criminal liability, depending on the commodity and destination.[51]

Because of the risks associated with not having a proper export license, a prudent purchaser can make payment to the supplier, contingent upon providing the proper license.

If an export violation, or even suspicion of one is identified while your shipment is still in possession of the carrier, the U.S. can, and has, asked for its return: at your expense, of course.

10.5. U.S. IMPORT LICENSES

In the same way that certain exports are controlled by specific licensing requirements of the exporting country, so too are certain imports controlled unilaterally by the importing country.

Each country has its own rules for determining which products are affected and the qualifications for the license.

The following is a partial list of products which typically require U.S. Import Licenses:

- Milk, cream & certain cheeses - Department of Agriculture
- Biological products - Animal & Plant Health Inspection Services
- Fish, wildlife and articles made from them - Fish & Wildlife

- Petroleum & petroleum products - Department of Energy
- High Technology equipment with a potential military application - Department of State

In the United States, import licenses are controlled by the agencies having jurisdiction over the product. The import license requirement is in addition to any other requirements imposed on the product. For example, while the Fish and Wildlife Service issues import licenses for certain seafood, the import license requirement is in addition to the requirements for a CITES Certificate of Origin, and Food and Drug Administration and U.S. Customs.

Goods imported without the required license may be refused entry or may be subject to seizure or forfeiture, and the importer may be subject to a penalty.[52]

Import licenses are not automatically or rapidly available just because the product meets an agency's requirement.

10.6. VISAS

Visas were used to control or limit the total quantity of goods of a particular origin into the United States by controlling the export from that other country. There are no longer any products that require this type of visa for importation into the United States.

This should not, however, be confused with import licenses which still apply to any number of products.

10.7. INTELLECTUAL PROPERTY

U.S. Law protects Intellectual Property rights in the form of Copyrights[53], Trademarks and Trade names[54], and Patents[55].

These protections apply to goods being imported into the United States,

those being held in a Foreign Trade Zone (which, while physically in the United States are outside of the Customs territory), goods merely transiting the United States which are not intended for entry into the U.S. market, as well as those being exported.

Regardless of the Intellectual Property involved and whether the goods are being imported, exported, or domestically distributed, it remains your responsibility to ensure that the goods and marks are legitimate and that you possess the required authorization to use them.

While each of these different Intellectual Property rights are protected under differing laws and regulations, the most basic of the rules is that the goods must be genuine. Counterfeit or Piratical Copies will always be subject to seizure, forfeiture, and penalties at the corporate level, and, in some cases, the personal level.[56]

In May of 2016 the "Defend Trade Secrets Act" was signed into law. This new law provides for a federal right of action that complements the existing state laws under the Uniform Trade Secrets Act, thus creating a more uniform and expeditious avenue for pursuing violations of intellectual property rights. It provides whistleblower protections to those who disclose violations and a financial incentive for disclosure by way of *Qui Tam* actions.

10.7.1. TRADEMARKS AND TRADE NAMES

Trademarks and Trade Names are protected by U.S. Customs to the extent that they are cross-filed with Customs and Border Protection as well as the U.S. Patent and Trademark Office.

Customs will protect a registered and recorded mark from both:

- Goods which bear a counterfeit mark which is defined as a "a spurious mark that is identical with, or substantially indistinguishable from, a registered mark"[57] and
- Goods bearing marks which, although, are neither identical nor substantially indistinguishable from protected marks, are nevertheless "Confusingly Similar" to those marks.[58]

> The costs of cross filing a registered trademark with Customs and Border Protection are so miniscule compared to the protections offered that doing so should be considered a good practice.

Genuine goods which are generally foreign-manufacture bearing a valid U.S. trademark that are imported into the U.S. without the consent of the U.S. trademark owner are termed Gray Market goods, or Parallel Imports.[59] The protection of genuine Gray Market goods is much more limited generally based upon who owns and controls the mark. If the mark is owned and controlled in the United States, the trademark owner's permission is even required to import goods bearing genuine marks. [60]

> Owners of valuable marks and names sometimes find it prudent to use different marks for goods distributed in the United States as a means of controlling gray market imports.

Trademarks and Trade Names filings can be checked at:

Patent & Trademark Office: www.uspto.gov/trademark

CBP Intellectual Property: iprs.cbp.gov

10.7.2. COPYRIGHTS

Copyrights commonly protect Software Programs/Games, and Video and Audio Recordings. Copyrights must be recorded in the U.S. Copyright Office but, unlike trademarks and trade names, do not have to be cross filed with Customs and Border Protection to be entitled to protection by Customs.[61]

Goods containing Copyrighted materials which are imported without the approval of the copyright owner will be considered piratical[62] and, as an infringement, subject to seizure, forfeiture and penalties.

Copyrights can be searched at:

U.S. Copyright Office: www.copyright.gov/records

10.7.3. PATENTS

Patents are protected by Customs to the extent that the patent holder has obtained U.S. International Trade Commission section 337 Exclusion Order, which addresses Unfair Trade Practices.[63]

The pendency of Unfair Trade Practice proceedings and resulting orders are a matter of public record.

Patents and Exclusion orders can be checked at:

Patent and Trademark Office: patft.uspto.gov

International Trade Commission:

https://pubapps2.usitc.gov/337external/

10.7.4. REQUIRED DOCUMENTATION/LICENSES

It is your responsibility to make sure that you have documentation supporting your right to use the protected Intellectual Property. If you are dealing with trademarks filed with Customs and Border Protection, you will be expected to provide that proof; otherwise your shipment will be subject to seizure.

> **If you are not acquiring your right directly from the owner of the intellectual property it is good practice to obtain a copy of the original license as a backup to whatever sub-license you received.**

10.7.5. LICENSE FEES

Whether the price you pay for a license to use the Intellectual Property is dutiable dependent upon the basis on which the fee is paid. If the fee is based upon post importation sales, the license fee will not be dutiable. If, however, you are paying a license fee based either on production or the right to import, it will be subject to duty. (*See* "Royalties and License Fees" §11.2.4 at 77.)

---

[47] 19 C.F.R. 141.89(a)

[48] 19 U.S.C. 1481 as amended by Public Law 103-182, 107 Stat 2057 Section 636(c).

[49] 19 U.S.C. 1481 as amended by Public Law 103-182, 107 Stat 2057, Section 636(b).

[50] Public Law 103-182, 107 Stat 2057, Section 636

[51] United States Export Control, Section 9.3

[52] 19 USC 1595a(c)

[53] Copyright - 17 U.S.C. 101 et. seq.19 USC 1595a , 19 CFR 133

[54] Trademarks and Trade names - 15USC 1051 et. seq.__19 USC 1595a , 19 CFR 133

[55] Patent and Unfair Competition - 35 USC 101, 19 USC 1337, 19 CFR 201, 210

[56] 19 USC 1595a

[57] 15 USC 1127 19 CFR 133.21

[58] 15 USC 1114, 1125, 1127, 19 CFR 133.22.

[59] K Mart Corp. v. Cartier, 486 U.S. 281, 285 (1988)

[60] 19 U.S.C. § 1526(a), 19 CFR 133.23, Lever Bros. Co. v. United States, 981 F.2d 1330 (D.C. Cir. 1993), K Mart Corp. v. Cartier, 486 U.S. 281, 285 (1988)

[61] 19 C.F.R. 133.31 (a)

[62] 19 CFR 133.42 "piratical" is defined as copies that are unlawfully made. "Clearly Piratical" is defined as overwhelming and substantial similarity between the copyrighted elements of the protected work and the suspect item so as to clearly indicate that one work was based upon the other.

[63] 19 USC 1337

– Page intentionally left blank –

11. VALUATION

Executive Briefing

The duty, and taxes and Customs fees due on an imported article are in most instances a percentage of its dutiable value. The "dutiable value" is determined by the valuation process known as appraisement, discussed below. The dutiable value is multiplied by the duty rate as determined through classification according to the Harmonized Tariff Schedules.

Improper valuation of goods initially affects duty liability. Inflated value or the inclusion of non-dutiable charges can result in payment of excessive duty. Conversely, under valuation or the failure to declare an element of value can result in additional duty liability and, in certain cases, substantial penalties, including potential criminal liability.

While value determinations are primarily made based upon commercial documentation, Customs does have the authority to require the submission of verified statements from manufacturers or producers to establish costs,[64] or such other documentation as it deems necessary for appraisement. [65]

11.1. TRANSACTION VALUE FOR THE GOODS BEING IMPORTED

The dutiable value of most imported articles is their "transaction value" which is the "price actually paid or payable" for the articles, "when sold for export to the United States."[66]

The price "paid or payable" for an article is generally based upon its FOB price at the port of export [67], which means that it includes any costs incurred to bring the shipment to the port of export (foreign inland freight) and of lading it onto the carrier. [68] In a properly structured transaction, a lower, Ex-Factory (EXW Incoterms® 2010) price may qualify as the "price paid or payable". (*See* "Incoterms" §9.3 at 54.)

If the terms of the sale include charges for things which occur after the cargo is placed on board the carrier, then for duty purposes, the invoice price will be adjusted back to an FOB price.[69] For example, if the terms of sale were C.I.F. (Cost, Insurance & Freight), the cost of insurance and international freight could be deducted from the C.I.F. price to determine an FOB price. (*See* "Incoterms" §9.3 at 54.)

Under normal circumstances, the price "paid or payable" by the purchaser to the seller will be the "transaction value." With certain exceptions, this "transaction value" will be the "dutiable value" upon which Customs will base its duty assessment.

11.2. ADDITIONS TO TRANSACTION VALUE APPRAISEMENT

In order for the price "paid or payable" for an article to be considered its dutiable value, it must include all elements of value.

Consequently, the costs associated with missing charges must be added to the Transaction Value, to the extent that they are not already included in the transaction price. Customs may require only the following charges, incurred by the buyer, be added to transaction value:[70]

- ✓ Packing Costs
- ✓ Selling Commissions
- ✓ Assists
- ✓ Royalties
- ✓ Proceeds of a Subsequent Sale

11.2.1. PACKING COSTS

Packing costs are any costs incurred by the buyer for labor and materials of whatever kind used in packing goods to make them ready for exportation.[71] It typically includes items such as:

- Boxes, cartons & wrapping
- Hangers
- Poly bags
- Spools
- Inedible coatings on food
- Labels
- Labor costs related to all of the above

Under most Incoterms, including EXW, the seller is required to place the goods in a condition ready for transport. In certain instances such as where special packing is required, there may be an additional packing charge which is invoiced separately from the Commercial Invoice accompanying the shipment. Those additional charges need to be added to the transaction value in calculating Dutiable Value.

On the other hand, additional packaging for re-packing goods, after they have been made ready for export, e.g., changing labels on cans, might not be packing which will be added to the transaction value of imported goods.[72]

11.2.2. SELLING COMMISSIONS

A selling commission is any commission paid to the seller's agent.[73] A selling agent is anyone who is related to, controlled by, works for, or on behalf of, the manufacturer or seller.[74] For Customs Valuation purposes, payments made to a Selling Agent are treated the same as a payment to the seller itself. (*See* "Selling Commissions" §11.2.2 at 76.)

Traditionally, such undisclosed payments by an importer have led to penalties.

11.2.3. ASSISTS

An assist is anything that the buyer provides to the manufacturer and/or seller, directly or indirectly, either free of charge or for less than the arm's length price, and for which the manufacturer/seller would otherwise have to charge the buyer, if not so provided.[75]

For example:

- ✓ Materials, components, parts and similar items incorporated into a final product;
- ✓ Tools, dies, molds and similar items used in producing the goods;
- ✓ Materials consumed in the production of goods;
- ✓ Engineering, R&D, artwork, design work, and plans produced or undertaken outside the United States.

Like commissions, all assists must be declared, although not all will be dutiable. For example, the cost of foreign produced engineering, development, artwork and designs provided to the manufacturer by the buyer is dutiable. If, however, the same work is produced in the U.S., it is still an assist, but it is not dutiable.[76]

> Assists are perhaps the most frequently omitted value declarations.
>
> This error is often not one of intention but by oversight because assists are very often purchased either independently from the product itself by someone other than the person responsible for handling the importation.

An assist can be declared and duty paid for it on the first importation, or it can be amortized over the life of the production or on any other business basis which is consistent with Generally Accepted Accounting Principles (GAAP).[77]

The failure to properly report assists to Customs is one of the major sources of importer liability.

11.2.4. ROYALTIES AND LICENSE FEES

Royalty and license fees that a buyer is required to pay either directly or indirectly to the seller or manufacturer as a condition of sale of the merchandise for exportation to the United States are dutiable.[78]

> Royalties, like Assists, are often not disclosed because importers mistakenly view them as separate and distinct from the imported goods. These are dutiable on value.
>
> However, if the transaction is properly structured and based on other than imported value, e.g., domestic sales, then it will not generally be considered as dutiable.

Fees or commissions for trade names, marks and logos, paid to other than the manufacturer/seller in such a way that the sale of the goods is not conditioned on payment, are generally not dutiable.

11.2.5. PROCEEDS OF SUBSEQUENT RESALE THAT ACCRUE TO THE SELLER

If, subsequent to importation, an importer pays or is required to pay more for the imported goods than was declared at the time of entry, those additional payments constitute part of the price paid for the goods. This frequently occurs in industries where the final price for the imported goods is based upon the price at which the goods are ultimately resold.

For example:

Goods are purchased for $100.00 on the condition that if the goods are ultimately resold for more than $150.00, the profit would be split or a commission would be due.

If the article sells for $200.00 then $25.00 is owed to the manufacturer. This subsequent payment constitutes part of the price paid for the goods: $100 + $25.

Additional payments due to the seller as a result of a post entry sale are rarely disclosed.

Any subsequent payments to the seller will be presumed to be part of the price paid or payable for the goods, and are probably dutiable, and must be declared.[79]

If the additional payments are made before the entry is liquidated, then they can be declared through a Post Entry Amendment. (*See* "Post Entry Amendment" §20.2.3 at 200.) If not known until substantially later and especially if this is a common situation, consider discussing your options with a Customs Attorney. An exception might be if the payment constituted a one-time retroactive price increase, which might not be dutiable. How it will be treated can be evaluated only in the context of the entire transaction and course of prior dealings.

11.3. TRANSACTION VALUE BETWEEN RELATED PARTIES

Executive Briefing

The existence of specific interrelationships between a buyer and seller raises the question whether the price at which goods are bought and sold between them constitutes an arm's length price or whether the relationship has resulted in an artificially low price.

The validity of the price charged by a seller to a related buyer will, at some point, have to be substantiated.

The value acceptable for transactions between unrelated and related parties may be different and, in a properly structured transaction, may legitimately be lower, resulting in a reduced duty liability.

Parties are considered related[80] if they are:

- Members of the same family, including brothers, sisters, spouse, parent or child, ancestor or lineal descendants
- Officers or directors of both entities or a common entity
- Partners
- Employer and employee
- Direct or indirect ownership or the right to vote 5% or more of

stock

- Two or more persons directly or indirectly controlling, controlled by, or under common control with, any person

The fact that parties are related does not mean that the transaction value for a particular importation will be rejected, only that its legitimacy has to be verified.

The law recognizes that prices between related parties can be justifiably lower than those between unrelated parties. The price paid will be accepted as its "transaction value" provided that it closely approximates what Customs would calculate to be its "Computed Value." Thus, when properly structured, transactions between related parties can be financially advantageous. (*See* "Transactions Between Related Companies - Transfer Pricing" §7.6 at 31 and "Deductive or Computed Value" §11.5.2 at 80.)

11.4. FIRST SALE

In a "First Sale" transaction there are at least two sales transactions that bring goods to the United States. The first is a sale from the factory to the middleman. The second is from a middleman to the U.S. customer.

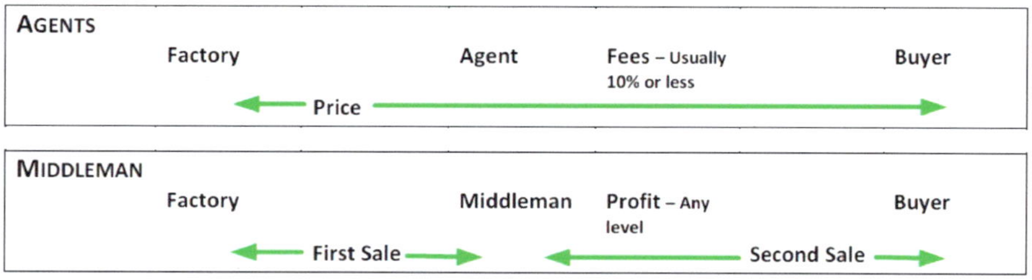

Figure 9 - Buying Agent vs Middleman Transaction

As long as the goods are "clearly destined for export to the U.S." and there was a bona fide arm's length sale, they may be entered under the lower price of the "first sale" from the factory to the middleman. There must be sufficient documentation to prove a back-to-back sale and, most importantly, that the seller knew at the time of sale that goods were destined for export to the U.S. (*See* "First Sale Valuation" §7.7 at 33.)

11.5. ALTERNATIVES WHEN THERE IS NO TRANSACTION VALUE

While the majority of transactions will be valued on the basis of transaction value, there will be times when the transaction value cannot be determined by available documents, or cannot be used for other reasons.

For Example:

> If the price paid by the buyer was contingent on other factors, such as the volume of future sales, the price paid or payable could not be determined at the time of import.
>
> If the goods were imported on a contingency basis, with part of the proceeds to be paid to the exporter when a buyer appeared, the goods were not "sold for export."

If "transaction value" cannot be used as the basis for dutiable value, the law provides for alternate means of appraising the merchandise to establish dutiable value.

For most importers, it is not important to know the details of the alternate forms of appraisement. It is generally sufficient to know of their existence.

11.5.1. TRANSACTION VALUE OF IDENTICAL OR SIMILAR MERCHANDISE

The transaction value of identical merchandise is used when the transaction value of the current shipment cannot be determined. The alternate items used for valuation must be identical in all respects, must have been imported from the same country, and preferably from the same company at about the same time.[81]

If identical merchandise cannot be found, then a transaction of similar merchandise can be used. The alternate items used for this valuation must be commercially interchangeable with those of the current shipment, and must also have been produced in the same country and preferably by the same company.[82]

11.5.2. DEDUCTIVE OR COMPUTED VALUE

When there are no transactions of identical or similar merchandise to compare with, or the transaction was between related parties, dutiable value is determined by accounting for the actual cost of the product either by accumulating all of the costs of production or deducting extraneous costs from a domestic price.[83]

In a transaction between related parties, if this computed cost closely approximates the price charged between the parties, that price will be deemed to be the transaction value and will be acceptable, even if it is lower than would exist in sales between unrelated parties.[84] (*See* "Transaction Value Between Related Parties" §11.3 at 78.)

Computed value is essentially calculated by adding up all the costs of production. Deductive value starts with a U.S. sales price and then backs out costs not related to production. Which one an importer uses is a matter of both the available evidence and which works best.

The computed value of an article is the sum of the costs of

MATERIALS	actually used in production *plus*
LABOR	directly used in the production *plus*
OVERHEAD	apportioned to this product *plus*
PROFIT	which need not be the same or as high as sales between unrelated parties, provided that it is reasonable and is consistent with profits on comparable sales *plus*
PACKING	to make the merchandise ready for export transportation.

Figure 10 - Required Additions to Transaction Value

11.5.3. FALLBACK VALUE

Occasionally, the facts of a given importation do not provide a basis for appraisement on one of the four bases discussed in §§ 11.5.1 and 11.5.2 above. Customs is then empowered to set a value on the merchandise by devising a formula based on one of the statutory methods of appraisement modified to suit the facts of the case.[85]

---

[64] 19 U.S.C. 1481 as amended Public Law 103-182, 107 Stat 2057 Section 632(g)

[65] 19 U.S.C. 1508 --- Record Keeping

[66] 19 U.S.C 1401a(b)(1), 19 C.F.R. 152.103(a)(1), 152.102(f)

[67] 19 U.S.C 1401a(b)(4)(A), 19 C.F.R. 152.102(f)

[68] 19 C.F.R. 152.102(b)

[69] 19 U.S.C 1401(a), 19 C.F.R. 152.105(d)(2)

[70] 19 USC 1401a(b)(1), 19 C.F.R. 152.103(b)

[71] 19 USC 1401a(h)(3), 19 C.F.R. 152.102(e)

[72] Customs Value Encyclopedia

[73] 19 C.F.R. 152.102(b)

[74] 19 C.F.R. 152.102(b)

[75] 19 USC 1401a(h)(1), 19 C.F.R. 152.102(a)

[76] 19 USC 1401(h)(1)(A)(iii)

[77] 19 C.F.R. 152.103(e)

[78] 19 USC 1401a(b)(1)(D), 19 C.F.R. 152.103(f)

[79] 19 USC 1401a(b)(1)(E), 19 C.F.R. 152.103(g)

[80] 19 USC 1401a(g)(1), 19 C.F.R. 152.102(g)

[81] 19 USC 1401a(c)(1), 19 C.F.R. 152.104

[82] 19 USC 1401a(c)(1), 19 C.F.R. 152.104

[83] 19 USC 1401a(d)(1), 19 C.F.R. 152.105, 152.106(a)(2)

[84] 19 USC 1401a(d)(1), 19 C.F.R. 152.103(j)(2)

[85] 19 USC 1401a(f), 19 C.F.R. 152.107

– Page intentionally left blank –

12. CLASSIFICATION

Executive Briefing

Classification is the process through which goods are categorized according to a uniform identification system for the purpose of assessing duty or taxes and/or imposing restrictions upon imports.

Incorrect classification can result, not only in improper duty liability, but also in a change in import requirements or eligibility for duty free programs. Changes in tariff rate can positively or negatively affect the financial viability of a transaction.

While often addressed only after importation, classification should more appropriately be considered during the design, costing, and sourcing of a product.

Classification of goods requires four (4) things:

- ✓ A detailed understanding of your product
- ✓ An understanding of the tariff page
- ✓ An understanding of the language of the tariff
- ✓ An understanding of how to apply the tariff rules and how they affect your classification

12.1. HARMONIZED SYSTEM OF CLASSIFICATION

The United States subscribes to the Harmonized System of Classification ("Harmonized System"), commonly referred to as the Harmonized Code. Most major trading countries also subscribe to the Harmonized System of Classification convention.

The Harmonized System functions at two levels: International and National (Country Specific). At the International level, a product should be classified the same in all countries that subscribe to the Harmonized Code. Unfortunately, it is at the National level, where each country maintains its own detailed and individualized description breakout, upon which rates of duty and import restrictions are set.

Most executives dealing with imports or exports do not need to be able to classify goods themselves because their Customs Broker, Forwarder, or in-house specialist will take care of it. But since it is both advantageous and proper to design an article so that it qualifies for the lowest rate of duty, it is important to understand how to achieve the most beneficial classification.

Classification of goods under the Harmonized System is governed by a series of General Rules of Interpretation (GRI), Legal Notes, Rulings and Legal Decisions. The General Rules of Interpretation are, just as the term implies, the general rules applicable throughout the tariff, while the Legal Notes are the specific rules applicable to particular classes of merchandise. Most of the General Rules of Interpretation and Legal Notes apply to classification at both the international and national level.

Duty rates and import restrictions are country specific and, more directly, affected by the Additional Legal Notes, Rulings and Legal Decisions.

Classifying an article within the Harmonized Tariff is relatively simple IF we know in simple terms and language what it is that we are trying to classify, meaning articles which are:

- ✓ Known by a single name,
- ✓ Complete,
- ✓ Assembled, and
- ✓ Composed of a single material, or have a single function.

There are, of course, many articles which do not fall within that limited class. While there are six (6) General Rules of Interpretation (GRIs) at the multi-national level, the primary rule that applies to the simple product is GRI 1:

> ***[C]lassification shall be determined according to the terms of the headings and any relative section or chapter notes and, provided such headings or notes do otherwise require...***

Many of the remaining General Rules of Interpretation address how to remove complicating factors that impede classification. This is done, in part, by looking at complex articles as though they were in fact simple ones. Unfortunately, many of these decisions that need to create such a fiction are highly subjective.

12.2. PRINCIPLES OF CLASSIFICATION –HOW GOODS ARE CLASSIFIED

Classification, for practical purposes, requires the resolution of two issues.

- ✓ The first is to identify the article in simple terms.
- ✓ The second is to identify the article for tariff purposes.

Two approaches to classification are presented here:

- ✓ A Conceptual Approach, which is sufficient for most business planning purposes, and
- ✓ A more Formal Approach which addresses the technicalities.

In either approach, classification starts with:

- ✓ An accurate picture and understanding of the article being classified. Written descriptions are rarely an adequate substitute for a sample of the article itself or a picture of the article, and a detailed understanding of what it is, how it was made, what it is made of, and how it is used. If a full written description is insufficient, then the shorthand designations often used in commercial invoices aren't likely sufficient either, and
- ✓ An understanding as to the structure of and how to use the tariff.

12.2.1. U.S. TARIFF LAYOUT

The pages of the Harmonized Tariff Schedules of the United States (HTSUS or HTS) are divided into various columns, the most important of which, to most Importers are: Description, Rates of Duty and Special which details the available duty reduction programs.

> The tariff schedule is packed with useful information IF you understand how to read it.

Harmonized Tariff Schedule of the United States (20)
Annotated for Statistical Purposes

XVI
84-78

Heading/ Subheading	Stat Suf-ix	Article Description	Unit of Quantity	Rates of Duty		
				1		2
				General	Special	

Figure 11 - Tariff Page Organization

- "Heading/Subheading" and "Stat, Suffix" columns contains the tariff item number that codes its classification.
- The "description" column contains the Harmonized Codes' uniform description. A description includes all of the superior (less indented and less specific) text. The tariff is hierarchically organized by indents levels.

> Tariff numbers have no direct meaning; they are merely a way of organizing the tariff into standard designations.

Heading/ Subheading	Stat. Suf-fix	Article Description	Unit of Quantity	Rates of Duty		
				1		2
				General	Special	
8472		Other office machines (for example, hectograph or stencil duplicating machines, addressing machines, automatic banknote dispensers, coin-sorting machines, coin-counting or wrapping machines, pencil-sharpening machines, perforating or stapling machines):				
8472.10.00	00	Duplicating machines	No.	Free		25%
8472.30.00	00	Machines for sorting or folding mail or for inserting mail in envelopes or bands, machines for opening, closing or sealing mail and machines for affixing or canceling postage stamps	No.	1.8%	Free (A, AU, BH, CA, CL, CO, D, E, IL, JO, KR, MA, MX, OM, P, PA, PE, SG)	35%
8472.90		Other:				
8472.90.05	00	Addressing machines and address plate embossing machines	No.	Free		25%
8472.90.10	00	Automatic teller machines	No.	Free		35%
8472.90.40	00	Pencil sharpeners	No.	Free 1/		40%
8472.90.60	00	Numbering, dating and check-writing machines	No.	Free		25%
8472.90.90		Other		Free		35%
	40	Desktop note counters and note scanners	No.			
	60	Other currency and coin handling machines	No.			
	80	Other	No.			

Figure 12 – HTS – Organization of Article Description

- The "Unit of Quantity" column indicates the type of unit, e.g., m2 kg, doz, and is used for purposes of trade statistics.
- The "Rates of Duty" column is divided into two main divisions: Column 1 (General) for articles from Most Favored Nations and Column 2 for products from all other countries, (e.g., North Korea and Cuba). The rates of duty for goods from a Column 2 country are usually many times higher than those from a Column 1 country. Column 2 rates are usually those that were in effect in the Smoot-Hawley Tariff of 1930. Column 1 rates are those which have been reduced to improve International Trade.
- Column 1 is further subdivided: The left hand column indicating the usual rate of duty, and the column labeled SPECIAL, indicating special programs which are available for this item and the rate of duty which is accorded articles qualifying for these programs.

> Just because there is a tariff rate for a product doesn't mean that you can import the product from every country.
>
> Embargoes trump tariff rates.

> Just because there is a tariff rate does not mean that it is the only amount of duty or fees due with respect to the shipment.
>
> Anti-Dumping Duties, Countervailing Duties, Trade Sanctions and similar charges are in addition to these published rates.

Tariffs are about both revenue, and business interest, both as to trade promotion as well as protectionism. The Special column provides for programs intended to promote trade. On the other side, Tariff Rate Quotas, implemented through Legal Notes rather than being detailed in the Duty Rate columns, seek to protect domestic industries by providing low rates of duties for limited annual imports only.

Duty rates are either:

AD VALOREM	A percentage of the dutiable values. *For example:* 1.8%
SPECIFIC	A specific charge per unit of quantity. *For example:* 2.5¢ each
COMPOUND	Subject to both an Ad Valorem and Specific Rate. *For example:* 5% + $0.44 each.

Figure 13 - Types of Duty Rates

12.2.2. HARMONIZED TARIFF SCHEDULE – WHERE INTERNATIONAL ENDS AND U.S. BEGINS

The harmonized system and the U.S. Tariff Schedules have their own terminology, and the rules of classification are keys to that terminology.

As a practical matter, the U.S. tariff page is divided into two distinct areas:

Multi-National Level - Tariff Numbers and descriptions which pertain to all countries using the Harmonized System.

County Specific Level (in this case the U.S.) - Portions of the tariff number, descriptions and rates of duty which are unique to each country.

U.S. Tariff Numbers are 10 digits long (0000.00.0000) of which the first 6 contain information which is applicable in all countries using the HTS.

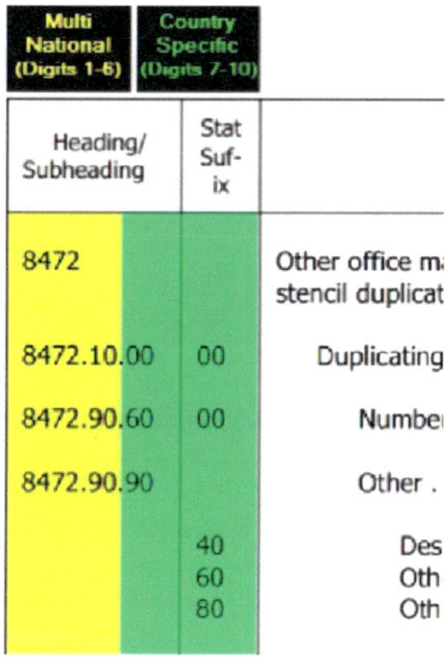

Figure 14 - The Tariff Divide Between Multi-National and Country Specifics

Classification Rules, Legal Notes, Customs Rulings and Court decisions are set forth in terms of the Harmonized Tariff Nomenclature.

– Balance of page intentionally left blank –

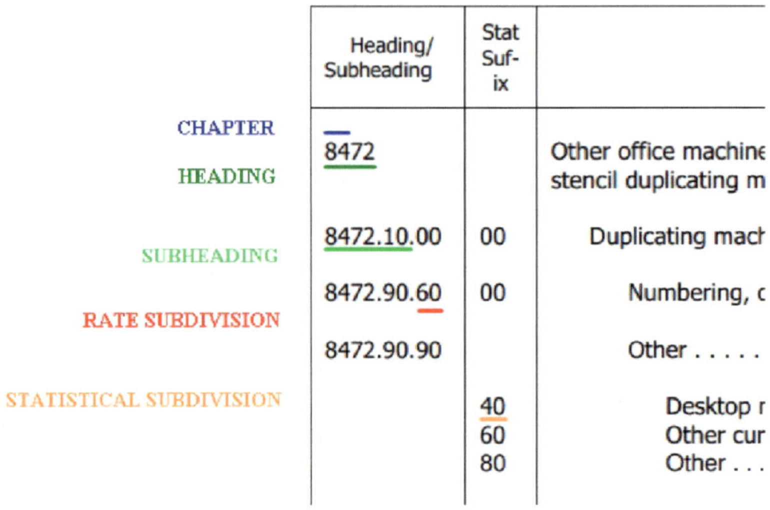

Figure 15 – HTS Terminology - Tariff Numbers Breakdown

CHAPTERs are grouped into SECTIONs, generally by industry, so that rules specific to an entire section can be more conveniently presented. There is no section identifier in the tariff number. It is found in the upper margin of the tariff page.

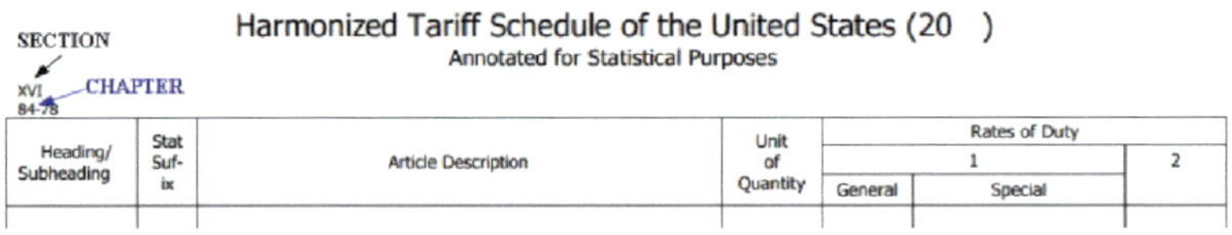

CHAPTER 0000.00.0000

HEADING

SUB-HEADING

Most of the classification rules apply to HEADINGs and SUB-HEADINGs.

Unfortunately, what business is really interested in are the Rates of Duty which are unique to each country as are the Statistics that each country maintains for trade analysis purposes. They are represented in the last 4 digits of the HTS.

RATE SUBDIVISION

0000.00.0000

STATISTICAL SUBDIVISION

RATE SUBDIVISION contains the following:

- General Rates applicable to most countries.
- Special rates are reduced rates that benefit only specific countries

Rates of Duty		
1		2
General	Special	
1.6%	Free (A,AU,BH,CA, CL,CO,E,IL,JO, KR,MA,MX,OM,P,PA, PE,SG)	25%
1.8%	Free (A,AU,BH,CA, CL,CO,E,IL,JO, KR,MA,MX,OM,P,PA, PE,SG)	35%

Figure 16 - Rate Subdivision – Where The Money Is

- Column 2 rates are applicable to those few countries which are not signatories under the WCO. (Products from embargoed countries are not eligible for importation regardless of any rate shown in the tariff.)

The Rate Subdivision numbers, which are the 7th and 8th digits of the number appearing in the Heading/Subheading column, do not indicate a rate of duty. All products classified under that Rate Subdivision number will, however, be subject to the same Rates of Duty.

Heading/ Subheading	Stat Suf-ix	Article Description	Unit of Quantity	Rates of Duty 1 General	Rates of Duty 1 Special	2
8472		Other office machines (for example, hectograph or stencil duplicating machines, addressing machines, automatic banknote dispensers, coin-sorting machines, coin-counting or wrapping machines, pencil-sharpening machines, perforating or stapling machines):				
8472.10.00	00	Duplicating machines.	No. . . .	1.6%	Free (A,AU,BH,CA, CL,CO,E,IL,JO, KR,MA,MX,OM,P,PA, PE,SG)	25%
8472.90.60	00	Numbering, dating and check-writing machines	No. . . .	Free		25%
8472.90.90		Other	. . . . . .	1.8%	Free (A,AU,BH,CA, CL,CO,E,IL,J, KR,MA,MX,OM,P,PA, PE,SG)	35%
	40	Desktop note counters and note scanners. . .	No.			
	60	Other currency and coin handling machines. .	No.			
	80	Other	No.			

STATISTICAL SUBDIVISIONs

group articles together for purposes of accumulating the trade statistics which are set forth in the Units of Quantity column. It is not related to the duty rate.

Heading/ Subheading	Stat Suf-ix	Article Description	Unit of Quantity	Rates of Duty 1 General	Rates of Duty 1 Special	2
8472.90.90		Other	. . . . . .	1.8%	Free (A,AU,BH,CA, CL,CO,E,IL,J, KR,MA,MX,OM,P,PA, PE,SG)	35%
	40	Desktop note counters and note scanners. . .	No.			
	60	Other currency and coin handling machines. .	No.			
	80	Other	No.			

12.2.3. CONCEPTUAL APPROACH TO CLASSIFICATION

Executive Briefing

Most businesses handle a limited class of goods or some variation of the same goods on a continuing basis. Documenting how you classified one type of product will make it easier to classify the next product, as well as providing good documentation for the next person doing the job, and will serve to demonstrate Informed Compliance; all of which will help to reduce risks.

The easiest way to do this is also the simplest.

1. **Copy the pages of the Tariff that apply to your product.**
2. **Copy ALL of the tariff rules and notes that go along with that section and chapter.**
3. **Outline your classification and cross out or highlight those things that are respectively applicable or not applicable to your product.**
4. **Annex any opinion letters from counsel, Customs Broker or consultant along with any customs or court decisions you have.**
5. **If you can't make heads or tails out of the tariff for your product, or the rules seem to conflict, ask your Customs Broker or Trade Counsel for help; it is cheaper to resolve issues ahead of time.**

There are 6 General Rules of Interpretation ("GRI"s) which govern classification at the multi-national level, and several more that are country specific. Each rule has its own complexities.

For most people in business, it is not necessary to be totally conversant on how to classify goods under the HTS. It is more important that you understand what issues can be encountered. So, while the full details of the rules are provided later in this book, below is a conceptual, rather than legal, approach to working with the Tariff and Classification Rules.

Under this conceptual approach we will pretend that, rather than there being 6 General Rules of Interpretation ("GRI"s) at the multi-national level and several more that are country specific, there is instead only one, General Rules of Interpretation 1.

Most business people do not need to master the entire tariff.

Most will only need to master the few sections affecting their product line.

The best way to read a tariff page is with the aid of ruler and highlighter. The ruler will ensure that you compare descriptions that are at the same level of indentation. The highlighter will allow you to annotate the tariff with your logic. Doing so will also make it easier the next time you need to reference the same sections.

Classify your product according to the language in the heading and any relevant legal notes.

The HTS, unfortunately, only provides for the classification of simple goods - those which are:

- ✓ Complete
- ✓ Assembled
- ✓ Made of One Material or Component
- ✓ Have only One Function
- ✓ Known by One Name and
- ✓ Packed

Clearly, not all goods will meet all of those criteria. The remaining rules of Classification essentially instruct us on how to pretend – yes pretend – that for classification purposes, we can treat more complex goods as simple ones in order to make classification easier.de

Maybe your goods are simple. U.S. Customs and Border Protection has stated that they believe that 80% of all goods can be classified by reference to GRI 1 alone.

The balance of the GRI's primarily tell us how to *pretend* that a complex article is actually a simple one for tariff classification purposes. We will examine how the GRI's do this in the Formal Approach. (See "Formal Approach to Classification", **§12.2.4** at 94.)

Reading the tariff is relatively straight forward if you keep in mind that it is hierarchal in design, and that hierarchy is portrayed visually through indent levels.

Heading/ Subheading	Stat. Suf- fix	Article Description	Unit of Quantity	Rates of Duty 1 General	Rates of Duty 1 Special	Rates of Duty 2
8472		Other office machines (for example, hectograph or stencil duplicating machines, addressing machines, automatic banknote dispensers, coin-sorting machines, coin-counting or wrapping machines, pencil-sharpening machines, perforating or stapling machines):				
8472.10.00	00	Duplicating machines	No.	Free		25%
8472.30.00	00	Machines for sorting or folding mail or for inserting mail in envelopes or bands, machines for opening, closing or sealing mail and machines for affixing or canceling postage stamps	No.	1.8%	Free (A, AU, BH, CA, CL, CO, D, E, IL, JO, KR, MA, MX, OM, P, PA, PE, SG)	35%
8472.90		Other:				
8472.90.05	00	Addressing machines and address plate embossing machines	No.	Free		25%
8472.90.10	00	Automatic teller machines	No.	Free		35%
8472.90.40	00	Pencil sharpeners	No.	Free 1/		40%
8472.90.60	00	Numbering, dating and check-writing machines	No.	Free		25%
8472.90.90		Other		Free		35%
	40	Desktop note counters and note scanners	No.			
	60	Other currency and coin handling machines	No.			
	80	Other	No.			

Classification is the process of comparing Article Descriptions at the same indent level and then repeating the step for each indent level in the hierarchy.

Following indent levels on chapters which covers several pages can be difficult. Try noting the indent levels on the pages you are working with.

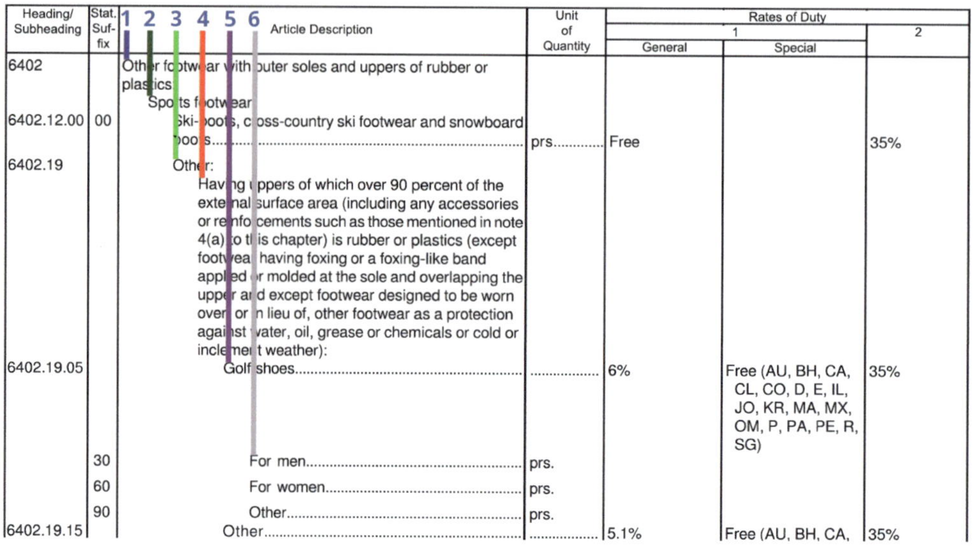

Heading/ Subheading	Stat. Suf-fix	Article Description	Unit of Quantity	Rates of Duty 1 General	Rates of Duty 1 Special	2
6402		Other footwear with outer soles and uppers of rubber or plastics				
		Sports footwear:				
6402.12.00	00	Ski-boots, cross-country ski footwear and snowboard boots	prs.	Free		35%
6402.19		Other:				
		Having uppers of which over 90 percent of the external surface area (including any accessories or reinforcements such as those mentioned in note 4(a) to this chapter) is rubber or plastics (except footwear having foxing or a foxing-like band applied or molded at the sole and overlapping the upper and except footwear designed to be worn over, or in lieu of, other footwear as a protection against water, oil, grease or chemicals or cold or inclement weather):				
6402.19.05		Golf shoes		6%	Free (AU, BH, CA, CL, CO, D, E, IL, JO, KR, MA, MX, OM, P, PA, PE, R, SG)	35%
	30	For men	prs.			
	60	For women	prs.			
	90	Other	prs.			
6402.19.15		Other		5.1%	Free (AU, BH, CA,	35%

Figure 17 - Classification - Following the Indentations

The Harmonized Tariff Numbers, or the rates of duties set out on a tariff page, are the end result of the classification process and should otherwise be ignored. The following illustrates how to work with the tariff.

- ✓ Have a photograph and other detailed specification of your product, along with marketing materials available to you for reference.
- ✓ Print out a copy of the relevant sections of the tariff INCLUDING the Section and Chapter Notes.
- ✓ Use a ruler to ensure that you are comparing indents at the same level.
- ✓ Use a highlighter to trace out your logic.
- ✓ Highlight any Section or Chapter Notes which apply to your product.

Most companies find that their products are classified under a limited number of tariff numbers. Outlining your classification process will make it easier to maintain consistency.

– Continued on next page –

By way of example, let's classify this old bank coin counter and sorter.

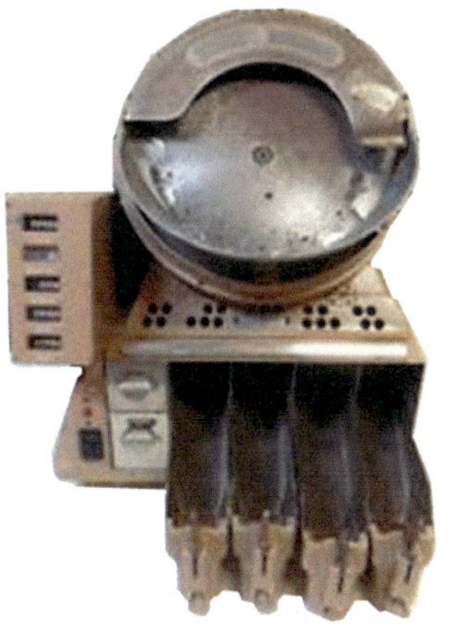

Figure 18 - Desktop Coin Counter

Where to start? Start with the Tariff Index. Look up ALL words that you think describes any feature of your article.

The index will not provide you with a classification, but it may point you to chapters or headings to look at and to compare.

It looks like something used in a bank

BANDSAW BLADES	
of base metals	8202.20
BANJOS	9202.90
BANKNOTE DISPENSERS	
automatic	8472.90
BANKNOTES	4907.00
BARBECUES	
of iron or steel	7321

A bank note dispenser sounds similar in function to a coin dispenser, so 8472.90 looks like a possibility.

It dispenses coins

COIL-WINDERS	
for electric wire	8479.81
COIN	71-US2, 7118.10-90
COIN-COUNTING OR WRAPPING MACHINES	8472.90
COIN-OPERATED RECORD-PLAYERS	8519.10
COIN-SORTING MACHINES	8472.90
COIR	5305.11-19

Coin-Sorting Machine and Coin-Counting Machines both looks like possibilities and both refer to 8472.90.

Figure 19 - HTS Index

Even when you think you know the correct subheading (6 digits) it is best to always start by comparing all of the Headings (4 digit numbers) that you think might apply to your goods.

- Continued on next page –

Heading/ Subheading	Stat. Suf-fix	Article Description	Unit of Quantity	Rates of Duty 1 General	Rates of Duty 1 Special	Rates of Duty 2
8472	(1)	Other office machines (for example, hectograph or stencil duplicating machines, addressing machines, automatic banknote dispensers, coin-sorting machines, coin-counting or wrapping machines, pencil-sharpening machines, perforating or stapling machines):				
8472.10.00	00	Duplicating machines	No.	Free		25%
8472.30.00	00	Machines for sorting or folding mail or for inserting mail in envelopes or bands, machines for opening, closing or sealing mail and machines for affixing or canceling postage stamps	No.	1.8%	Free (A, AU, BH, CA, CL, CO, D, E, IL, JO, KR, MA, MX, OM, P, PA, PE, SG)	35%
8472.90		(2) Other:				
8472.90.05	00	Addressing machines and address plate embossing machines	No.	Free		25%
8472.90.10	00	Automatic teller machines	No.	Free		35%
8472.90.40	00	(3) Pencil sharpeners	No.	Free 1/		40%
8472.90.60	00	Numbering, dating and check-writing machines	No.	Free		25%
8472.90.90		Other		Free (FINISHED)		35%
	40	Desktop note counters and note scanners	No.			
	60	(4) Other currency and coin handling machines	No.			
	80	Other	No.			

12.2.4. FORMAL APPROACH TO CLASSIFICATION

Classification under The Harmonized Code is determined by application of a series of GENERAL RULES OF INTERPRET-ATION, referred to as GRIs.

While the Conceptual approach to tariff classification is sufficient for most executives, the Formal Approach is provided both for contrast as well as for those who prefer a more hands on approach.

There are six (6) GENERAL RULES OF INTERPRETATION in the International System and one (1) U.S. Rule with four (4) subparts. These rules are intended to be applied sequentially, starting with GRI 1, until a classification is determined. In order to better illustrate the concepts and issues involved in classification, a different approach is employed here.

- Continued on next page –

GENERAL RULES OF INTERPRETATION

Classification of goods in the tariff schedule shall be governed by the following principles:

1. The table of contents, alphabetical index, and titles of sections, chapters and sub-chapters are provided for ease of reference only; for legal purposes, classification shall be determined according to the terms of the headings and any relative section or chapter notes and, provided such headings or notes do not otherwise require, according to the following provisions:

2.

(a) Any reference in a heading to an article shall be taken to include a reference to that article incomplete or unfinished, provided that, as entered, the incomplete or unfinished article has the essential character of the complete or finished article. It shall also include a reference to that article complete or finished (or falling to be classified as complete or finished by virtue of this rule), entered unassembled or disassembled.

(b) Any reference in a heading to a material or substance shall be taken to include a reference to mixtures or combinations of that material or substance with other materials or substances. Any reference to goods of a given material or substance shall be taken to include a reference to goods consisting wholly or partly of such material or substance. The classification of goods consisting of more than one material or substance shall be according to the principles of rule 3.

3. When, by application of rule 2(b) or for any other reason, goods are, prima facie, classifiable under two or more headings, classification shall be effected as follows:

(a) The heading which provides the most specific description shall be preferred to headings providing a more general description. However, when two or more headings each refer to part only of the materials or substances contained in mixed or composite goods or to part only of the items in a set put up for retail sale, those headings are to be regarded as equally specific in relation to those goods, even if one of them gives a more complete or precise description of the goods.

(b) Mixtures, composite goods consisting of different materials or made up of different components, and goods put up in sets for retail sale, which cannot be classified by reference to 3(a), shall be classified as if they consisted of the material or component which gives them their essential character, insofar as this criterion is applicable.

(c) When goods cannot be classified by reference to 3(a) or 3(b), they shall be classified under the heading which occurs last in numerical order among those which equally merit consideration.

4. Goods which cannot be classified in accordance with the above rules shall be classified under the heading appropriate to the goods to which they are most akin.

5. In addition to the foregoing provisions, the following rules shall apply in respect of the goods referred to therein:

(a) Camera cases, musical instrument cases, gun cases, drawing instrument cases, necklace cases and similar containers, specially shaped or fitted to contain a specific article or set of articles, suitable for long-term use and entered with the articles for which they are intended, shall be classified with such articles when of a kind normally sold therewith. This rule does not, however, apply to containers which give the whole its essential character;

(b) Subject to the provisions of rule 5(a) above, packing materials and packing containers entered with the goods therein shall be classified with the goods if they are of a kind normally used for packing such goods. However, this provision is not binding when such packing materials or packing containers are clearly suitable for repetitive use.

6. For legal purposes, the classification of goods in the subheadings of a heading shall be determined according to the terms of those subheadings and any related subheading notes and, mutatis mutandis, to the above rules, on the understanding that only subheadings at the same level are comparable. For the purposes of this rule, the relative section, chapter and subchapter notes also apply, unless the context otherwise requires

Figure 20 - HTS General Rules of Interpretation

ADDITIONAL U.S. RULES OF INTERPRETATION

1. In the absence of special language or context which otherwise requires—

(a) a tariff classification controlled by use (other than actual use) is to be determined in accordance with the use in the United States at, or immediately prior to, the date of importation, of goods of that class or kind to which the imported goods belong, and the controlling use is the principal use;

(b) a tariff classification controlled by the actual use to which the imported goods are put in the United States is satisfied only if such use is intended at the time of importation, the goods are so used and proof thereof is furnished within 3 years after the date the goods are entered;

(c) a provision for parts of an article covers products solely or principally used as a part of such articles but a provision for "parts" or "parts and accessories"; shall not prevail over a specific provision for such part or accessory; and

(d) the principles of section XI regarding mixtures of two or more textile materials shall apply to the classification of goods in any provision in which a textile material is named.

Figure 21 - HTS GRIs Additional U.S. Rules of Interpretation

✓ A number of the General Rules of Interpretations set forth some basic and often common sense rules to observe when reading The Harmonized Tariff.

Heading/ Subheading	Stat Suf-ix	Article Description	Unit of Quantity	Rates of Duty 1 General	Rates of Duty 1 Special	2
8472		Other office machines (for example, hectograph or stencil duplicating machines, addressing machines, automatic banknote dispensers, coin-sorting machines, coin-counting or wrapping machines, pencil-sharpening machines, perforating or stapling machines):				
8472.10.00	00	Duplicating machines.	No. . . .	1.6%	Free (A,AU,BH,CA, CL,CO,E,IL,JO, KR,MA,MX,OM,P,PA, PE,SG)	25%
8472.90		Other				
8472.90.05	00	Addressing machines and address plate embossing machines.	No. . . .	2.1%	Free (A,AU,BH,CA, CL,CO,E,IL,JO, KR,MA,MX,OM,P,PA, PE,SG)	25%
8472.90.10	10	Automatic teller machines.	No. . . .	Free		35%
8472.90.40		Pencil sharpeners.	No. . . .	2.6% 1/ See Notes	Free (A,AU,BH,CA, CL,CO,E,IL,JO, KR,MA,MX,OM,P,PA, PE,SG)	40%
8472.90.90		Other . . .		1.8%	Free (A,AU,BH,CA, CL,CO,E,IL,J, KR,MA,MX,OM,P,PA, PE,SG)	35%
	40	Desktop note counters and note scanners. . .	No.			
	60	Other currency and coin handling machines. .	No.			
	80	Other	No.			

✓ Titles and Indexes are for reference only and have no effect on classification.

✓ Do not read in language that is not in a Heading or Subheading.

✓ Only compare language at comparable levels: Headings (4 digits) to Headings, Subheadings (6 digits) to Subheadings, etc.

Tariffs are read based upon the hierarchical organization of text as set forth in the Article Description.

Make sure that you compare descriptions at the same indentation level and ignore the tariff numbers. Try drawing lines with a ruler to keep you on track.

The same rules that apply to a classification at Heading level apply in spiral fashion to each indentation level sequentially.

The GENERAL RULES OF INTERPRETATION are, as their name implies, the general rules. LEGAL NOTES are the specific rules that detail the twists and turns of classification, especially those that relate to classification of goods imported into the United States. While the LEGAL NOTES are often voluminous, several pages per CHAPTER, they must be read in order to find a valid classification under the HTSUS.

In addition to setting out particular rules, the LEGAL NOTES also act as sign posts to other classifications. The first section of each LEGAL NOTE applies either to the Section or to only a single Chapter.

Both specify what

> "[t]his chapter does not cover"

Both will very often point to alternate provisions.

GRI 1 is the first rule in the traditional approach. For instructional purposes, it is the only rule of classification. GRI 1 provides that:

> ***[C]lassification shall be determined according to the terms of the headings and any relative section or chapter notes and, provided such headings or notes do otherwise require...***

In other words, if an article is identified in a HEADING, that is where it is to be classified.

The only exception will be if the language of the HEADING or a LEGAL NOTE specifically excludes it from that classification.

SECTION XVI
MACHINERY AND MECHANICAL APPLIANCES;
ELECTRICAL EQUIPMENT; PARTS THEREOF; SOUND
RECORDERS AND REPRODUCERS, TELEVISION IMAGE
AND SOUND RECORDERS AND REPRODUCERS, AND PARTS
AND ACCESSORIES OF SUCH ARTICLES

Notes

1. This section does not cover:
    (a) Transmission, conveyor or elevator belts or belting, of plastics of chapter 39, or of vulcanized rubber (heading 4010), or other articles of a kind used in machinery or mechanical or electrical appliances or for other technical uses, of vulcanized rubber other than hard rubber (heading 4016);

.....

Additional U.S. Note

1. For the purposes of this section, the term "printed circuit assembly" means goods consisting of one or more printed circuits of heading 8534 with one or more active elements assembled thereon, with or without passive elements. For the purposes of this note, "active elements" means diodes, transistors and similar semiconductor devices, whether or not photosensitive, of heading 8541, and integrated circuits of heading 8542.

Statistical Note

1. Provisions for semiconductor manufacturing and testing machines and apparatus cover products for the growth and processing of semiconductor materials, such as silicon and gallium arsenide, the processing of such materials into semiconductor devices and the testing of such devices (in general the testing equipment, as well as some of the processing equipment, is classified in chapter 90). More specifically the goods include the following:
    (a) Wafer manufacturing equipment:

.....

Figure 22 – HTS Section Notes

CHAPTER 84
NUCLEAR REACTORS, BOILERS, MACHINERY AND
MECHANICAL APPLIANCES; PARTS THEREOF

Notes

1. This chapter does not cover:

(a) Millstones, grindstones or other articles of chapter 68;

(b) Machinery or appliances (for example, pumps) of ceramic material and ceramic parts of machinery or appliances of any material (chapter 69);

. . . . .

2. Subject to the operation of Note 3 to Section XVI and subject to Note 9 to this chapter, a machine or appliance which answers to a description in one or more of the headings 8401 to 8424, or heading 8486 and at the same time to a description in one or more of the headings 8425 to 8480 is to be classified under the appropriate heading of the former group or under heading 8486, as the case may be, and not the latter group.

. . . . .

Heading 8422 does not cover:

(a) Sewing machines for closing bags or similar containers (heading 8452); or

(b) Office machinery of heading 8472.

. . . . .

7. A machine which is used for more than one purpose is, for the purposes of classification, to be treated as if its principal purpose were its sole purpose.

8. For the purposes of heading 8470, the term "pocket-size" applies only to machines the dimensions of which do not exceed 170 mm x 100 mm x 45 mm.

. . . . .

Subheading Notes

1. For the purposes of subheading 8471.49, the term "systems" means automatic data processing machines whose units satisfy the conditions laid down in note 5(C) to chapter 84 and which comprise at least a central processing unit, one input unit (for example, a keyboard or a scanner), and one output unit (for example, a visual display unit or a printer).

. . . . .

Additional U.S. Notes

. . . . .

2. Subheading 8443.99.20 covers the following parts of printer units of subheading 8443.32.10:

(a) Control or command assemblies, incorporating more than one of the following: printed circuit assembly, hard or flexible (floppy) disk drive, keyboard, user interface;

. . . . .

Statistical Note

1. For the purposes of statistical reporting number 8472.90.9040, the term "note counters and note scanners" means document handling machines that count currency bills, bank notes, coupons, script or other value-based paper documents and to stack them in an organized fashion. Note counters and note scanners can both incorporate a sensor for detecting suspect (i.e., counterfeit) documents. Note scanners have additional sensors that enable the machines to distinguish documents by denomination.

Figure 23 – HTS Chapter Notes

– Continued on next page –

Case Summary

Classification is a very subjective process, especially when it is a question of legal interpretation of the Court.

Camel Manufacturing Co., v. U.S.
686 F.Supp.912 (1988)

Relatively heavy tents holding between 5 and 9 persons were held to be other textile products dutiable at 25 cents per pound plus 15% ad valorem instead of sports equipment dutiable at 10% ad valorem.

The Court rejected a prior case where tents were classified as sports equipment by distinguishing it from the current merchandise based on weight. The Court said that the subject tents were too heavy to be used as a backpacking activity.

The Court also heavily weighed the testimony of a National Import Specialist regarding the definition of the term "sport" within the meaning of the Tariff Schedule. "Sport" was defined as "an activity in which a progressive level of skill is recognized and for which a certain recognized methodology of practice exists." Simply setting up quarters outdoors was determined not to be a sport and therefore the tents were not classified as sports equipment but rather other textile articles.

12.2.4.1. UNASSEMBLED OR INCOMPLETE GOODS

Many articles are unassembled or incomplete when imported. The U.S. Harmonized Tariff is almost 1,000 pages, and primarily addresses single function, complete, assembled products composed of a single material. Classification would be virtually impossible if a tariff had to provide for every combination of article, function, material and whether it was complete, incomplete and assembled, unassembled or disassembled. GRI 2(a) simplifies classification by allowing us to classify certain articles as though they were complete and assembled, even though they are not.

The rule focuses on the essential character of the article. "Essential Character" is not only not defined in the law; it is acknowledged that what constitutes "essential character" will vary depending upon the article. The best way to identify "essential character" for purposes of GRI 2 is to answer the question "Can you recognize the thing for what it was intended to be?" If you can, then the article has the "essential character" of an assembled and complete article and, for the purpose of simplifying classification, we can pretend that it is assembled and complete.

Take a bicycle, for example.

Most bicycles come unassembled. Since, we can normally recognize the parts for the assembled bicycle they will become we can say that the parts have the essential character of an assembled bicycle. Then, for classification purposes we can pretend that we have an assembled bicycle. If not, the parts do not have the essential character of a complete and assembled bicycle, but are separate parts, each of which is separately classifiable.

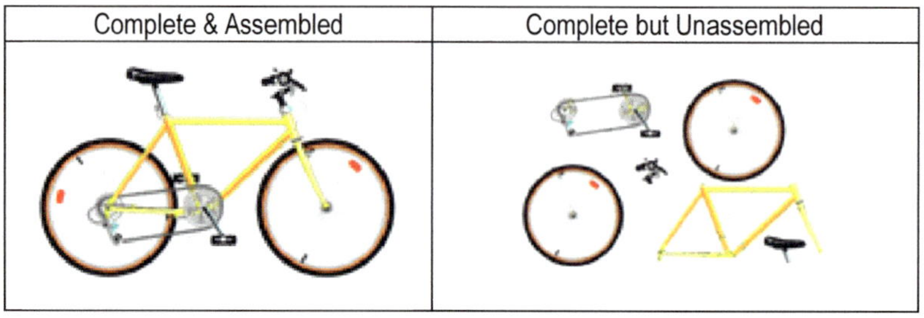

Figure 24 – GRI - Complete and Assembled

Suppose that a bicycle is incomplete or unassembled when imported. Which of the following incomplete or unassembled bicycles on the exhibit page can be said to still have the essential character of a complete bicycle?

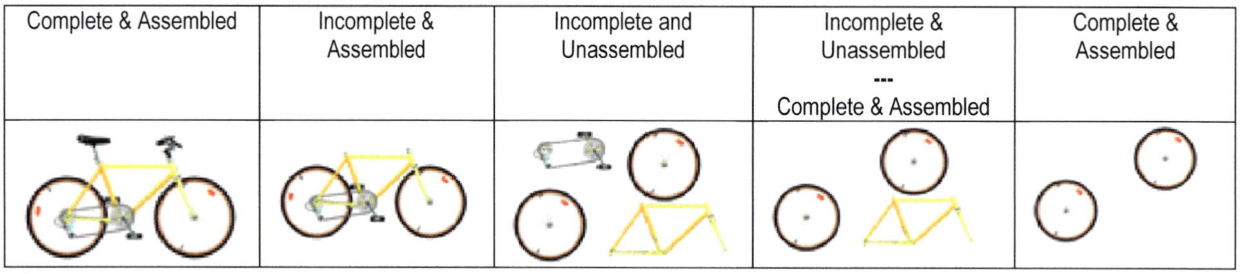

Figure 25 – GRI - Complete and Incomplete

12.2.4.2. MULTIPLE DESCRIPTION OR NAMES

Sometimes there is more than one word or way the tariff describes an article. For example, a carburetor is also a part of an engine. GRI 2(b) is a sign post which requires us to give consideration to each heading which identifies by name, language or description any part of an article. Obviously, this can lead to a problem since we cannot classify in one heading an article that cannot be described in only one way.

	Handbag Purse Satchel Pocketbook Shoulder bag

Figure 26 - Not Known by a Single Name

GENERAL RULES OF INTERPRETATION 3, which is divided into three subsections again deals with simplifying the identification of the article.

12.2.4.3. RELATIVE SPECIFICITY

Under the Harmonized Code, more specific language is always preferred to general language. Therefore, GRI 3(a) prescribes that the term which more precisely describes an article is preferred, and any others will be ignored. The concept is simple, as are all of the GRI concepts; applying them is not necessarily as simple, especially since the Harmonized System confirms that "[i]t is not practicable to lay down hard and fast rules by which to determine whether one heading more specifically describes the goods than another..."[86]

In general "a description by name is more specific than a description by class" and a description that more completely describes an article is preferable to a less complete description.

For example:

> According to the Explanatory Notes, a tufted textile carpet for use in an automobile is more specifically described as "tufted carpet" than "accessories for motor cars" [87]

GRI 3(a) MOST SPECIFIC

THE HEADING WHICH PROVIDES THE MOST SPECIFIC DESCRIPTION SHALL BE PREFERRED TO THE HEADINGS PROVIDING A MORE GENERAL DESCRIPTION.

A description by name is more specific than a description by class.	HEADING
Shaver and hair clippers with self-contained electric motor	85.10
Electro-mechanical tool for working in the hand	85.08
Electro-mechanical domestic appliances with self-contained electric motor	85.09
A description which more clearly identifies them is more specific than one where identification is less complete.	
Tufted textile carpets, identifiable for use in motor cars	57.03
Accessories of motor cars	67.08

"It is not practicable to lay down hard and fast rules by which to determine whether one heading more specifically describes the goods than another...".
Explanatory Notes Rule 3(a)(IV)

Figure 27 – GRI - Most Specific

12.2.4.4. Composite Goods, and Goods Put Up in Sets for Retail Sale

> "The factor which determines essential character will vary as between different kinds of goods."
>
> Although somewhat oversimplified, the question can be framed as: ***What is the primary element that is causing the purchaser to buy the article?***

Relative Specificity as between different components is not the determining factor when dealing with composite goods or mixtures, where the language in competing headings each name only part of the article.

COMPOSITE GOODS - When an article is a mixture or a composite, consisting of different materials, or made up of different components, or goods put up in sets for retail sale, we have the type of complex article that cannot be easily classified under the Harmonized System. In order to classify the article, we again need to fictionalize how to simplify it. Like unassembled or incomplete articles, this is done by looking to the essential character of the article. In this case, however, essential character is best thought of as that characteristic which imparts the essence of the article. "For classification purposes we need to pretend that articles consist of only that one item which imparts the essential character to the whole."

- Continued on next page –

For example :

The essential character of a fax machine incorporating a telephone and answering machine is the fax machine. Thus, this article would be classified as if it were only a fax machine.

Figure 28 – GRI - Essential Character of items with multiple functions

SETS FOR RETAIL SALE - Goods imported in sets for retail sale are treated like composite goods and duty is assessed on the single article which imparts the essential character to the set. Not all commercial sets are, however, "sets for retail sale" for tariff purposes. If it does not qualify as a "sets for retail sale", duty is then assessed on each article in the set separately. In order for a set to qualify as a "set for retail sale" it must:

- ✓ Have two or more articles with different classifications,
- ✓ Have a single commercial purpose, and
- ✓ Be packaged ready for sale.

If you have a "set for retail sale," we can again pretend we have a simple article made entirely of the element which imparts the essential character. If we do not have something which qualifies as a "Set for Retail Sale," then we have several separately classifiable items.

- Continued on next page –

For purposes of this Rule, the term "goods put up in sets for retail sale" shall be taken to mean goods which:

(a) Consist of at least two different articles which are prima facie, classifiable in different Headings. Therefore for example, six fondue forks cannot be regarded as a set within the meaning of this Rule.

(b) Consist of products or articles put up together to meet a particular need or to carry out a specific activity; and

(c) Are put up in a manner suitable for sale directly to users without repackaging (e.g. in boxes or cases or on boards).

Hair grooming kit consists of	
Electric Hair Clippers	Heading 8510
Combs	Heading 9615
Scissors	Heading 8213
Fitted Leather Case	Heading 4202

Figure 29 – GRI - Sets for Retail Sale

Case Summary

In dealing with classifying an article under the HTSUS, one must understand that the Tariff is designed to accommodate products made of a singular material or of one component. When there are multiple materials and/or components, or the articles are part of a set, a "fiction" is created to deal with the article as if it was in fact made of only the one material or component which imparts its "essential character."

Thus the process becomes a highly subjective one in determining the classification.

The Shower Curtain Case exemplifies how difficult it can be to determine the essential character of a particular product when it contains several elements or a set.

Better Home Plastics Corp. v. U.S.
("Shower Curtain Case")
916 F. Supp. 1265 (1996)

The product in this case was a shower curtain set consisting of:

1. An outer textile curtain
2. An inner plastic liner
3. Plastic hooks

Customs had classified the product based upon its outer textile curtain under

Heading 6303 for curtains. The importer insisted that the "essential character" test must be applied and that the product should be classified based upon the inner plastic liner under Heading 3924.

Customs' position was that the items should be classified in accordance with GRI 3(a), which is also known as the rule of relative specificity. This rule states that when "goods are *prima facie*, classifiable under two or more headings," the court must classify the merchandise pursuant to the heading which provides the most specific description.

There is, however, an exception to this rule in that when two or more headings each refer...to *part only of the items* in a set put up for retail sale, those headings are to be regarded as equally specific...even if one [heading provides] a more complete or precise description of the goods.

Thus, the Court stated that the rule that applies in that situation is GRI 3(b) which directs that goods be classified by the "component which gives them their essential character."

Specifically, GRI 3(b) provides that:

> Mixtures, composite goods consisting of different materials or made up of different components, and goods put up in sets for retail sale, which cannot be classified by reference to 3(a), shall be classified as if they consisted of the material or component which gives them their essential character...

The Explanatory Notes (EN (VIII)) to GRI 3(b) states that:

> The factor which determines essential character will vary as between different kinds of goods. It may, for example, be determined by the nature of the material or component, its bulk, quantity, weight or value, or by the role of the constituent material in relation to the use of the goods.

With these rules in mind, the Court looked at the following factors:

1) The use of each of the component parts;

2) The nature of the material of each of the component parts;

3) The relative value of each of the component parts;

4) The invoice description of the product.

Customs' argument focused on the following factors to prove that the textile curtain imparted the "essential character" of the product:

1) The plastic liner is replaceable at 1/3 to 1/4 the price of the set;

2) The consumer purchases the set because of the decorative function of the outer curtain, and not for the protection afforded by the liner;

3) The liner is used for a limited period that someone is utilizing the shower, whereas the decorative outer curtain is used, at a minimum when the bathroom is used, and as much as 24 hours a day; and

4) The invoice describes the product as "Fabric Shower Curtain and Liner."

The Court held the following:

1) While stating that the relative cost of the component parts is a factor, this point alone "is not dispositive, nor very persuasive against the competing arguments."
2) The consumer purchases the set to serve the function of protecting water from leaking out which is performed by the plastic liner.
3) The plastic liner protects the outer decorative curtain from mildew and soap scum.
4) The invoice description "does not definitively determine which component provides the essential character of the set ...the invoice description is intended to characterize the shipped item; it is not a declaration of the relative importance of its component parts."

Essentially, the Court reasoned that "it is the plastic liner that provides the *indispensable* property of preventing water from escaping the shower enclosure" in that it:

(1) Prevents water from escaping when the shower is in use;

(2) Protects the Nonmember bank curtain from mildew and soap scum; and

(3) Conceals the shower and provides privacy when the shower is in use.

Based on the above, the Court stated that the "essential character" is imparted by the plastic liner.

The determination of "essential character" is very fact specific. Just because two items may appear the same does not mean that they will be classified or analyzed in the same manner. In this regard, the Court stated that its ruling is limited to the low-end market of shower curtain sets and may not necessarily apply to similar items in a different market price range.

12.2.4.5. MORE THAN ONE ESSENTIAL CHARACTER

Finally, if the article has more than one essential character, or we cannot tell what the essential character is, the Harmonized System provides a solution of last resort. Although we have more than one way to describe an article, each of these terms or possible essential characters was presumably found under a different heading (different tariff number). If we cannot logically determine which one represents the article, the Harmonized System will determine it arbitrarily under GRI 3 (c) by looking to the feature or element that appears in the tariff heading that appears last numerically. Thus, we again have a simple article; one which for classification purposes, we will pretend is made solely of that feature or element that was identified in the last heading.

As between those headings which merit equal consideration,
Classify under the heading which occurs last in numerical order.

Hair grooming kit consists of	
Electric Hair Clippers	Heading 8510
Combs	Heading 9615
Scissors	Heading 8213
Fitted Leather Case	Heading 4202

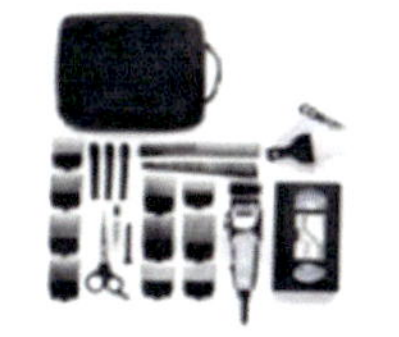

Figure 30 – GRI - Heading which occurs last

Under GR 3(b) mixtures are classified based upon their essential character. While relative weight is a consideration; focus more often is on "the role of the consistent materials or components in relation to the use of the goods..."[88] However, when dealing with mixtures of textile fibers, under US. Additional Note (1)(d), it is the weight of the fibers that predominates by weight over all other fibers, that controls. (*See* Figure 31 – GRI - Principal Weight at 109.)

12.2.4.6. NOWHERE IDENTIFIED

At the outset, it was stated as a cardinal rule that nothing should be read into the language of the tariff. If we simply take the language as we find it, a situation can develop in which we cannot find any language that identifies the product we are trying to classify. No matter how well a system is designed, it is inevitable that something will have been excluded or that the natural changes which occur over time could not be foretold. This is resolved in GRI 4, by pretending that the article has changed to one named in the tariff, to which it is most akin or similar.

12.2.4.7. PACKING AND PACKAGING

The preceding rules dealt with the character of an article. GRI 5 doesn't address how to classify an article. It addresses whether certain types of packing are to be treated as part of an article, or must be classified separately as independent articles.

FITTED CASES such as camera cases, musical cases, gun cases, drawing instruments cases, necklace cases and similar containers, specifically shaped or fitted to contain a specific article or set of articles, suitable for long-term use, and entered with the articles for which they are intended, are to be classified with such articles when of a kind normally sold with them. The same fitted cases imported separately would be classified under their own classification as containers, e.g. packing tea in a silver chalice, the chalice would be classified under its own number; so must we classify reusable packing and containers of all kinds.

USUAL AND ORDINARY PACKING MATERIALS are classified with imported articles, but reusable packing and containers are separately classifiable.

12.2.4.8. U.S. ONLY RULES

The U.S. GENERAL RULES OF INTERPRETATION provide definitions and interpretations of the HTSUS specifically applicable to imports to the U.S.

Many items are classified based upon their composition or general characteristics. There are also many others which are classified by reference to their "use" or suitability for a use, e.g., glassware of a kind used for table, kitchen, etc., 7013. What constitutes "use" can be highly subjective and can vary from location to location and change over time. U.S. Rule 1(a) simply provides a reference point for the determination of what "use" means.

Under U.S. GRI 1(a), when a tariff classification is controlled by use (other than actual use), use refers to the principal use in the United States, at, or immediately prior to, the date of importation, of goods of that class or kind to which the imported goods belong.

Certain articles are given preferential treatment in the tariff based upon their use. This infers more than mere suitability for a use, it is actual and documented use in a particular application, e.g. tractors are dutiable at 2.2% under 6701.90.50 HTSUS. However, when actually used for agricultural purposes they are duty free under 6701.90.10.

Under U.S. GRI 1(b), when a tariff classification is controlled by the actual use to which the imported goods are put in the United States, that use must be intended at the time of importation and proof of the actual use must be furnished within 3 years after the date the goods are entered.

U.S. GRI 1(c) amplifies the rule of relative specificity as it relates to parts. It provides that a provision for parts of an article covers products solely or principally used as parts of such articles, but a provision for "parts" or "parts and accessories" shall not prevail over a specific provision for such part or accessory.

U.S. GRI 1(d) extends certain principles in the International Harmonized System relating to the articles classified in the textile sections. The textiles and wearing apparel section of the International Harmonized System provides that for classification purposes, we should pretend that a textile article is made entirely of the one fiber that predominates by weight over each other fiber. U.S. GRI 1(d) extends this principle to all textile articles wherever found in the U.S. HTSUS.

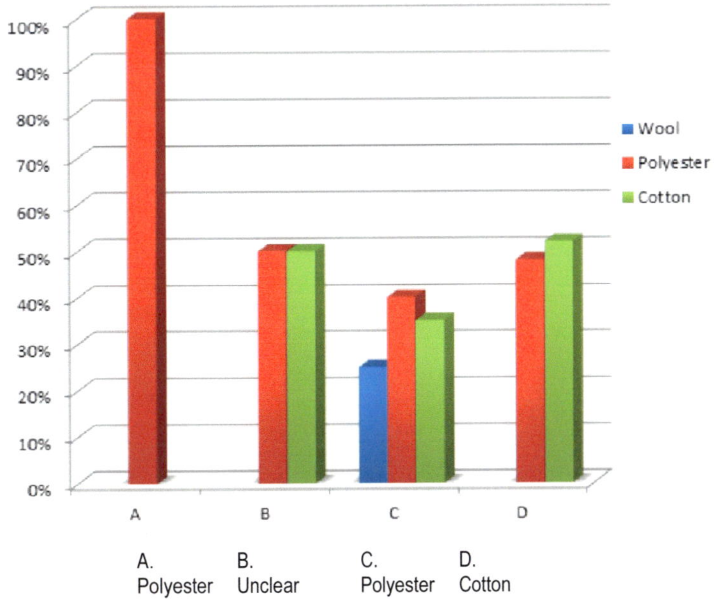

Figure 31 – GRI - Principal Weight

12.3. INTERPRETATIVE AIDS

Interpretive aids fall into two categories: authoritative and persuasive. Only decisions issued to the importer by Customs on the same merchandise are absolutely authoritative, all other decisions, even those of the courts, are generally viewed by Customs as persuasive, not binding.

In addition to the decisions of the Court of International Trade (CIT) and the Court of Appeals for the Federal Circuit (CAFC), there are administrative decisions issued by Customs and Border Protection (CBP) and the Department of the Treasury. These decisions are public, but they are not always available or easy to locate. Specialized publications listing them exist, including those in the form of electronic data bases.

There are now several on-line resources such as the Customs Ruling Online Search System (CROSS) http://rulings.cbp.gov.

The Explanatory Notes are a series of volumes setting forth an international consensus as to classification under the HTS, but only at the international level.

Although merely informational, trade publications and trade association newsletters often provide notice of changes in interpretation.

---

86 Harmonized System Explanatory Notes, Rule 3 EN IV

87 Harmonized System Explanatory Notes, Rule 3 EN IV(b)(1)

88 Headquarters Ruling Letter 964851 dated April 18, 2001

– Page intentionally left blank –

13. CONDITIONAL VARIATIONS IN DUTY

Executive Briefing

There are numerous special programs which can benefit a transaction by reducing duty liabilities (sometimes to zero), improving cash flow or even refunding duties.

It is the responsibility of the importer or exporter to seek out these benefits and take the steps necessary to qualify for them, since the government has little or no incentive to inform you of an opportunity to improve your financial position at the expense of the government.

And yes, there are circumstances where a product might be subject to additional duties beyond those that are set out in the tariff, but you are clearly better off knowing about them in advance.

In addition to the duty provisions found in Chapters 1 - 97 of the Tariff, there are a number of special programs which can have significant benefits to business, including reduction in duty rates or delaying when and if duty has to be paid.

13.1. DELAYED DUTY PAYMENT

While it may be inevitable that duty will have to be paid, there are circumstances and programs that will delay those payments and at the same time, permit the goods to be available so that they may be subject to certain pre-distribution processing.

13.1.1. BONDED WAREHOUSE

Customs bonded warehouses are specially licensed warehouses within the Customs' territory of the United States, in which merchandise, which has not yet finally cleared Customs, may be stored. Merchandise held within a Customs bonded warehouse is still in Customs custody. It has not been released and duty has not been paid.

Customs Bonded Warehouses and Foreign Trade Zones both provide a means of delaying the payment of duty until the goods are consumed in the United States or to avoid payment altogether if all or some of the goods will be exported.

Each has their advantages and disadvantages.

The primary advantage of a Customs Bonded Warehouse is that Customs duties do not have to be deposited until the goods are withdrawn from the warehouse.[89] The duty applicable will be in effect at the time the goods are withdrawn from the warehouse for consumption, not when deposited into the warehouse.[90] If the goods are withdrawn for export, no duty is ever paid[91], improving cash flow and eliminating the need to seek a refund of duty through a drawback claim. (*See* "Drawback" §13.5.1 at 122.)

One major advantage of a Bonded Warehouse is that you can have one in your own facility.

Unless you are a major manufacturer it is unlikely that you could gain authorization for a private sub-FTZ.

Merchandise can be retained in a bonded warehouse for up to five (5) years before it must be entered for consumption, exported or abandoned.[92] In addition, it can be withdrawn as needed in less than full shipment quantities.

Bonded warehouses are either public facilities, where space and services are provided for a fee, or they can be private facilities maintained for one company. A private bonded warehouse can be located at a company's own facility and be as large as a full building or as small as a safe or closet, depending upon particular needs.

Storage at a public bonded warehouse costs more than at a general warehouse, but generally less than at a carrier's facility or at a Customs general order warehouse.

What can be done to merchandise while in a Customs bonded warehouse is fairly limited unless a special manufacturing warehouse is established. Manipulation of warehoused goods is generally limited to cleaning, sorting, packing or repacking or other processing which, although it might change its condition, is not considered manufacturing.[93] Prior approval from Customs is required.

Customs' control over goods held in a bonded warehouse is through documentation and periodic inspection and audit. Merchandise cannot be deposited into the warehouse or withdrawn from it without prior Customs approval obtained through the filing of an entry or warehouse withdrawal.

13.1.2. FOREIGN TRADE ZONE

A U.S. foreign trade zone (FTZ) is a designated area located within the United States, but is considered to be outside of the Customs Territory (a Bonded Warehouse is inside Customs Territory). It is generally operated as a public utility, very often as an "Authority" and is supervised by U.S. Customs. A U.S. foreign trade zone is similar to Europe's free ports. Sub-zones are special purpose facilities for companies that are unable to operate effectively at an existing zone site, e.g., an automobile factory.

Like a bonded warehouse, many other prerequisites to entry for consumption do not need to be addressed until and unless the goods are withdrawn for consumption. Both foreign and domestic goods may be stored in a Foreign Trade Zone for an unlimited period, unlike a bonded warehouse, which permits storage of only dutiable imported goods and then limits storage to five (5) years.

> One particular advantage of a FTZ is that goods may be transferred to a foreign trade zone with less formality than if deposited in a bonded warehouse and goods can be more freely handled.

Unique to a foreign trade zone is that it provides an area within which both domestic and imported materials and goods can be stored, manipulated, processed or manufactured in a domestic location prior to entry into domestic commerce or prior to exportation to a foreign country.

Foreign Trade Zones are often used as a domestic location within which to combine, assemble or manufacture both imported and domestic materials and components prior to importation. Domestic merchandise may be withdrawn from the zone, duty-free, regardless of whether it was segregated or combined with imported goods. Customs duties are due only upon the foreign goods and only at the time they are withdrawn from the FTZ and entered for domestic consumption. Neither the final product nor its domestic or foreign content will be subject to U.S. Customs duties if the final product is exported.

One of the most important features of a Foreign Trade Zone is the ability to elect a "privileged" status for foreign goods entered into the zone.[94]

PRIVILEGED status merchandise is dutiable based upon the condition of the goods and the rate of duty in effect when goods were deposited into the zone, even though their conditions may have changed or the rate of duty may have changed by the time of withdrawal.[95] This can be of substantial advantage if goods withdrawn from the zone have been processed into articles that are subject to a higher rate of duty than the components or materials deposited in the zone.

NON-PRIVILEGED status goods are dutiable based upon the condition of goods and the rate of duty in effect when withdrawn from the Zone, and are entered for consumption.[96] The big advantage of the FTZ is to combine a process or manufacture foreign goods in the FTZ into articles that may be withdrawn at lower rates of duty. If foreign goods are not changed in condition and classified in FTZ, the rules are much the same as when goods are withdrawn from a bonded warehouse and entered for consumption.

13.2. DUTY REDUCTION OR ELIMINATION

The United States has a number of special programs that grant preferential treatment in the form of duty reduction or elimination. There are four basic categories for such treatment:

- ✓ **Temporary Legislation** – This is private legislation that usually lasts for up to 2 years.
- ✓ **Less Developed Country Programs** – Generally, these countries are either economically or industrially less developed and the duty eliminations last until the countries reach a certain level of development.
- ✓ **Product Specific Programs** - This is in the form of U.S. legislation.
- ✓ **Bi-lateral or multilateral agreements for countries** which afford essentially reciprocal treatment to products of the United States. These programs are not likely to change as readily.

> If you are going to make use of a program that is going to exempt you from duty, you will, at some point, be asked to prove that you are actually qualified.
>
> Prudence dictates that you make this evaluation before you start using the program rather than after Customs asks.

13.2.1. SECURITY OF CONCESSION

Each type of program is subject to its own rules:

Temporary duty reductions under Chapter 99 of the tariff generally afford a benefit for two (2) years only. Renewals seem to be at the whim of the economic policies of the party in power at the time, so renewal should not be assumed.

Programs intended to assist Less Developed Countries are intended to terminate, either with respect to the country as a whole, or as to specific products as the country's economy becomes competitive. It is impossible to predict when that will occur but examination of their trade statistics can provide insight.

Product Specific Programs are a legislative prerogative but seem to be very stable.

Bi-lateral and multi-lateral programs, being treaties, are unlikely to be subject to change except in the case where there is a break in relations.

- Trumping all of the security built into the duty concession programs is that disputes between countries or related to specific products can, and have, led to temporary duty increases or embargoes.
- Presidential Proclamations tends to provide little advanced warning but are also generally of short duration.

Trade cases, including Anti-dumping, Countervailing, and Unfair Competition cases normally provide substantial advance warning, but also tend to be of multi-year duration.

13.2.2. QUALIFICATIONS

Each of the programs requires that the article that will be entitled to benefits under the program must have originated in a beneficiary country. If the article is produced of material that was imported into the beneficiary country, the material must be transformed by some process or manufacture into a product of that country.

For GSP, CBI, and IFTA programs, the determination of origin is based upon Customs' general rules of origin. Under these rules, a subjective evaluation is made as to whether the materials or products have undergone a substantial transformation. (*See* "Country of Origin" §14 at 131.)

In addition to the origin requirements, a specified minimum value of direct labor and local origin material must be added in the beneficiary country.

For NAFTA and most other U.S. free trade agreements the determination of origin is based upon a schedule of tests which set forth specific changes in classifications, and in some cases, a specified amount of direct labor and local origin material which must be added.

Simple operations such as the following are, alone, generally insufficient to affect a change in the origin of an article or to otherwise make it eligible for duty-free treatment:

- ✓ Combining or packaging operations, *or*
- ✓ Mere dilution with water or another substance that does not materially alter the characteristics of the article.

Value Requirements - The amount of value to be added generally consists of:

- ✓ Materials produced in the beneficiary country, *plus*
- ✓ Direct costs of processing operations performed in the beneficiary country.

This added value is measured against the appraised value of the article at the time of its entry into the Customs' territory of the United States, and must equal or exceed the amount required under the program. Under GSP, CBI and IFTA, 35% of the appraised value must have been added. Under NAFTA and other free trade agreements the amount generally varies depending upon the commodity and test.

If non-beneficiary country material is to be counted, it must first undergo a substantial transformation itself into a product of the beneficiary country before it is used in the manufacture of the finished product. This is, in effect, a "double substantial transformation" requirement.

If non-beneficiary materials are used, but were not first transformed into a product of the beneficiary country so that they can be counted toward the value added requirement, their cost is, nonetheless, counted in the appraised value of the article against which the percentage is measured. Consequently, the effect of non-beneficiary labor and material is effectively multiplied.

13.2.3. DOCUMENTATION

A Certificate of Origin which sets forth the origin and basis for qualification is required. Under most programs, a Certificate of Origin must be filed for each entry in which special treatment under the program is claimed. (*See* "Certificates of Origin" §10.3 at 69.)

13.2.4. DIRECT SHIPMENT

Some programs require the article to be imported into the Customs territory of the United States directly from the beneficiary country. Those that do not require direct shipment prohibit further processing after exportation from the beneficiary country.

13.3. TEMPORARY DUTY REDUCTION OR REMISSION PROGRAMS

These are both product specific and of limited duration. There is no assurance of renewal and, even if renewed, no guarantee that the same rate reductions will apply. Being solely the product of U.S. legislation, current and expired provisions are generally listed in Chapter 99. Proposed future reductions or remissions are generally made part of an Omnibus Trade Bill.

Harmonized Tariff Schedule of the United States (2013) (Rev. 1)
Annotated for Statistical Reporting Purposes

XXII
99-II-7

Heading/ Subheading	Stat. Suf-fix	Article Description	Unit of Quantity	Rates of Duty 1 General	Rates of Duty 1 Special	Rates of Duty 2	Effective Period
9902.24.67	1/	Unicycles (provided for in subheading 8712.00.50).	1/	Free	No change	No change	On or before 12/31/2012

Figure 32 - Temporary Duty Reduction

13.3.1. PROGRAMS BENEFITTING LESS DEVELOPED COUNTRIES

TITLE	COUNTRIES OR FULL TITLE	TARIFF CODE	APPLICABLE RULES
CAFTA	Central America Free Trade Agreement	"P" or "P+"	GN 29 - 19 C.F.R. 10.581-625 (Subpart J)
CBERA	Caribbean Basin Economic Recovery Act	"E"	GN 7 - 19 C.F.R. 10.191-10.199
CBPTA	Caribbean Basin Trade Partnership Act	"R"	GN 17 - 19 C.F.R. 10.221-10.237
GSP	Generalized System of Preferences *(lapsed 7/31/2013 renewed retroactively almost two years later on 6/20/015 effective 7/29/2015* [97]	"A"	GN 4 - 19 C.F.R. 10.171-10.178
AGOA	African Growth and Opportunity Act	"D"	GN 16 - 19 C.F.R. 10.178a

Figure 33 - Trade Programs for Less Developed Countries

13.3.2. PRODUCT SPECIFIC PROGRAMS

Product specific rather than country specific programs. This is in the form of U.S. legislation.

PROGRAM	TARIFF CODE	APPLICABLE RULES
Automotive Products Trade Act	"B"	GN 5
Agreement on Trade in Civil Aircraft	"C"	GN 6
Agreement on Trade in Pharmaceutical Products	"K"	GN 13
Uruguay Round Concessions on Intermediate Chemical for Dyes	"L"	GN 14

Figure 34 - Product Specific Programs

– Balance of page intentionally left blank –

13.3.3. BI-LATERAL OR MULTI-LATERAL AGREEMENTS

Bi-lateral or multi-lateral agreements afford essentially reciprocal treatment to products of the United States. These programs are not as likely to change.

The number of bi-lateral trade agreements has increased dramatically over the last decade so careful attention should be paid to the status of new agreements with the country you are looking to as a either a purchase source or a sales target.

TITLE	COUNTRIES	TARIFF CODE	APPLICABLE RULES
NAFTA	Canada	"CA"	GN 12 - 19 C.F.R. 181, 19 C.F.R. 102
NAFTA	Mexico	"MX"	GN 12 - 19 C.F.R. 181, 19 C.F.R. 102
USIFTA	Israel	"IL"	GN 8
US-Australia FTA	Australia	"AU"	GN 28
US-Bahrain FTA	Bahrain	"BH"	GN 30 - 19 C.F.R. 10.801-827 (Subpart N)
US-Chile FTA	Chile	"CL"	GN 26 - 19 C.F.R. 10.401-490
U.S.- Colombia Trade Promotion Agreement	Colombia	"CO"	GN 34 - 77 FR 29519
US-Jordan FTA	Jordan	"JO"	GN 18 - 19 C.F.R. 10.701-712 (Subpart K)
US-Korea FTA	Korea	"KR"	GN 33
US-Morocco FTA	Morocco	"MA"	GN 27 - 19 C.F.R. 10.761-787 (Subpart M)
US-Oman FTA	Oman	"OM"	GN 31 - 19 C.F.R. 10.861-890 (Subpart P)
US – Panama Trade Promotion Agreement	Panama	"PA"	GN 35
US-Peru Trade Promotion Agreement	Peru	"PE"	GN 32
US-Singapore FTA	Singapore	"SG"	GN 25 - 19 C.F.R. 10.501-570 (Subpart 1)

Figure 35 - Free Trade Agreements

In January 2017 the United States initiated procedures to renegotiate NAFTA. Focus and impact is still uncertain.

In 2015, the United States concluded negotiations of a Trans Pacific Partnership (TPP) to create multi-national free trade areas much like the North American Free Trade Agreement (NAFTA) did as between the U.S., Canada, and Mexico, providing for duty free trade between all of the signatories and just the United States.

CAUTION

As of 2017, the United States has withdrawn from Trans Pacific Partnership.

It is yet to be seen if the U.S. will pursue individual bi-lateral agreements with Japan, Malaysia, New Zealand and/or Vietnam in lieu of the multi-lateral TPP.

If you are merely importing into or exporting from the United States to a country which already has a free trade agreement with the U.S., there is no clear advantage to the TPP.

Existing Trans Pacific Partnership County	Existing Free Trade Coverage
Australia	Australia FTA
Brunei Darussalam	
Canada	NAFTA
Chile	Chile FTA
Japan	
Malaysia	
Mexico	NAFTA
New Zealand	
Peru	Peru FTA
Singapore	Singapore FTA
Vietnam	

Figure 36 - Trans Pacific Partnership Countries

13.4. OTHER DUTY REDUCTIONS

A general rule of the U.S. tariff is that articles imported into the United States are subject to duty, unless specifically exempted. Chapter 98 of the U.S. Harmonized Tariff provides a number of special programs for the exemption, reduction or elimination of duty on specific imported goods or goods imported under certain circumstances.

Articles that have been exported from the U.S. and subsequently re-imported, may qualify for partial duty exemptions. The mere fact that an article is of U.S. origin, or that it was previously imported into the U.S. does not mean that it can automatically be exported and re-imported into the U.S. duty-free. Articles imported into the United States are dutiable every time they enter the U.S., unless specifically exempted.[98] The type and extent of the exemption depends upon the origin of the goods, whether they have been advanced or improved in condition while abroad, and the type and nature of any processing that they have undergone.

13.4.1. ARTICLES NOT ADVANCED OR IMPROVED IN CONDITION

The tariff sets forth narrow and specific rules that must be met if an article is to be exempted and admitted duty free as Goods Not Advanced or Improved in Condition While Abroad. Most require supporting documentation to exist PRIOR to export from the U.S.

Commonly used provisions are:

- American Goods Returned. (HTS 9801.00.10)
- Articles exported under lease. (HTS 9801.00.20)
- Articles re-imported because they did not conform to samples or specifications. (HTS 9801.00.25)
- Articles exported for temporary exhibition abroad at public expositions, fairs or conferences or for examination, experimental, scientific or educational purposes. (HTS 9801.00.60 and 9801.00.40)

13.4.2. ARTICLES ADVANCED OR IMPROVED IN CONDITION

Goods being imported under the following provisions are generally subject to duty only on the cost or value of foreign processing. The type and degree of processing permitted to advance or improve the condition of an article is set forth in the tariff and Customs regulations and extensive legal decisions. Fairly precise compliance with the regulations is generally required.

> There is no general duty exemption for U.S. content.
>
> Exemptions only apply under specific circumstances and are subject to special documentation requirements.

Commonly used provisions are:

- Articles assembled abroad in whole or in part of U.S. fabricated components (HTS 9802.00.80) (*Formerly known as "807"*).

Under this provision, imported goods are assessed duty on only the non-U.S. components of the final cost of the assembled product; essentially, the cost or value of the labor and non-U.S. components along with the cost of shipping the U.S. components abroad.

When components of U.S. origin are sent abroad for assembly, the U.S. portion of the new article can be exempted from duty upon return to the United States. There is no general exemption for U.S. content, only an exemption for those U.S. components that are ready for assembly when exported from the U.S.[99] Foreign material substantially transformed in the U.S. into components ready for assembly will also qualify for duty exemption.[100]

"Assembly" means that only minimal processing, incidental to assembly, may be applied to the components. Incidental processing would include: oiling, painting, cutting to length, minor trimming and adjusting, and the like.[101].

> U.S. goods processed abroad, even if eligible for duty free re-importation, lose their identity as U.S. origin good for marking purposes.
>
> They will be subject to the same marking and labeling rules as any other goods of foreign origin.

The imported article is considered to be of foreign origin, even if all of the components are of U.S. origin. As a foreign article, it remains subject to all other import restrictions[102] and subject to the same marking and labeling requirements. [103]

The key to successful use of these provisions is preparation to ensure that contemplated operations qualify, and that required documentation is maintained and available in proper form.[104]

- Articles exported for repairs or alterations (HTS 9802.00.40).

Goods sent abroad for alteration or repair, upon re-importation are dutiable only on the cost or value of the repairs or alterations.

It is advisable to determine, in advance of exportation, if the work to be performed abroad will be considered a repair or alteration. Replacing a defective component may constitute more than repair and be deemed to be a new product, subject to full duties.

Documentation indicating your intent to have the goods repaired or altered must exist PRIOR to exportation from the U.S. and, in some cases, be signed off by Customs.

13.4.3. SAMPLES FOR SOLICITING ORDERS

Samples used for taking orders may be imported duty free provided that they are samples as defined by the tariff.[105] "Samples for Soliciting Orders" has a much narrower meaning for tariff purposes than it does for commercial purposes. In general, for an article to be considered a sample eligible for importation free of duty it must be:

> **Just because you use an article commercially as a sample does not mean that it will be treated as a duty free sample.**

- ✓ Valued not over $1 each, ***or***
  - ✓ (a) marked, torn, perforated, or otherwise treated so that it is unsuitable for sale or use other than as a sample, ***and***
  - ✓ (b) be used in the United States only for soliciting orders for products of foreign countries.

The samples must be marked or mutilated prior to importation. If it is to be marked, the marking should read "SAMPLE" and "NOT FOR SALE," and must be permanent, and at least two inches in height. If it is to be mutilated, perforations should be at least 1 inch in diameter, and any tears or cuts must be sufficient to make the article unusable for its intended purpose.[106]

-Continued on next page -

Figure 37 - Mutilation is not always a viable option.

It is not always possible or practical to mutilate commercial samples so that they will qualify as samples for Customs purposes. In that case they will be viewed as any other commercial shipment and be subject to full duty and all other applicable requirements.

13.4.4. DUTY AVOIDANCE BY TEMPORARY IMPORTATION

While the object of most importations is to enter goods permanently for consumption, there are times when goods are needed in the United States only for a temporary period, after which they can be exported or destroyed.

If it is intended from the outset that importation is only to be temporary, then it may be possible to avoid paying or advancing any customs duties at all by making Temporary Importation under Bond or making use of an ATA Carnet.

If the determination to re-export the imported article is not made until after importation, a refund of duty might be available under drawback. (*See* "Drawback" §13.5.1 at 122.)

13.4.5. TEMPORARY IMPORTATION UNDER BOND (T.I.B.)

> Drawback should be considered as a possible alternative to a T.I.B. or Carnet because, while it involves advancing duties, there are no Customs penalties associated with a failure to account for goods and failure to export them.

Temporary Importation under Bond, as the name implies, provides for importation for a limited period: Up to one year, with up to two one-year extensions, for a maximum of three years.[107]

The decision that articles will be temporarily imported need not be made until an entry is filed with Customs. Merchandise is eligible for Temporary Importation under Bond only when imported for specific and limited purposes that are set forth in Chapter 98 of the HTSUS. While the importation may only be temporary, it does not exempt the shipment from other requirements, including marking and quota.

Failure to re-export or destroy the imported articles under Customs' custody (if required) will result in penalties in the form of liquidated damages. The penalties are guaranteed by a Customs Bond posted at the time of entry. The penalty for failure to export or destroy, or to do so under Customs' supervision, is either twice the duty that would have been due if imported for consumption, or, if the goods are duty free, then 110% of the duty had they been dutiable.[108]

Proof of the exportation or destruction must be filed in order to cancel the bond obligation.

13.4.6. CARNET

A Carnet (ATA Carnets Admission Temporaire) is essentially a multi-country T.I.B and is available in most countries. In the United States, they are administered through the U.S. Council for International Business, however, can be obtained through a surety acting as your agent under a Power of Attorney. Carnets usually permit faster customs clearance for travelers with accompanying goods, and simpler paperwork for multi-country travel.

A fee is paid for the Carnet, and re-exportation is guaranteed by the U.S. Council for International Business in much the same way that a Customs bond guarantees re-exportation under a T.I.B. The issuing authority may require collateral in return for its guarantee.

A Carnet may include multiple items, but care must be taken as to which articles are combined on a single Carnet or split over multiple Carnets, because, while changes are technically permissible, they can be impracticable.

The United States is not a signatory to all international conventions for Carnets. Most significant, the U.S. does not subscribe to all provisions of the TIR carnet (Transport International Routier), which exempt articles from many local requirements, such as marking.

Use of an ATA Carnet recognized by the United States does not exempt goods from compliance with general import requirements. Just like any other import, they must be properly marked.

13.5. DUTY REFUND

As a general rule, once duty has been paid, refund is only available if specifically authorized in the law; and those authorizations are few.

13.5.1. DRAWBACK

Drawback is a program which provides for a refund of duty when most kinds of goods are exported or destroyed. Drawback has been an essential part of tariff since it was enacted in 1789 providing a relief from duties for U.S. manufacturers who were dependent upon foreign made materials to produce goods for the export market. Upon the exportation or destruction of goods, drawback permits Customs to refund 99% of the duties paid when the goods were imported.[109] It does not, however, cover other import fees or taxes paid on imports.

While statutorily drawback is an entitlement program, Customs has traditionally treated it as a privilege earned only by precise compliance with rules and regulations. The most important procedural requirement is the filing of a drawback application in order to give Customs the opportunity to inspect the shipment, PRIOR TO EXPORTATION.

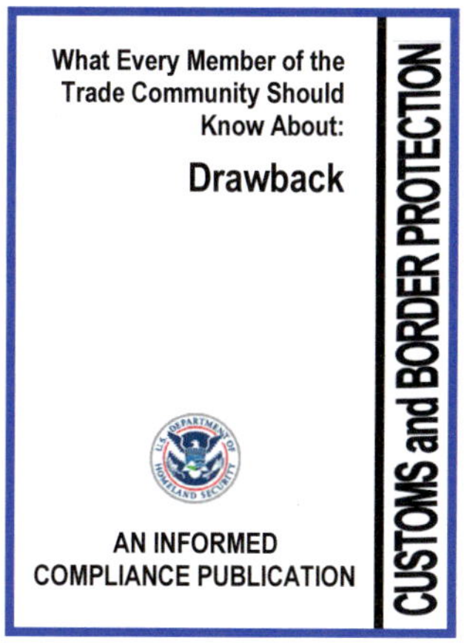

An Exporter Summary Procedure for those frequently exporting with claims for drawback, speeds up export by eliminating most pre-export inspection and permits cumulative filings after exportation. The exporter summary procedure requires prior approval and is dependent, in part, upon a prior good record of drawback claims.[110]

Drawback refunds can sometimes be very slow. Refunds can be accelerated by filing an Accelerated Drawback Bond to provide Customs with recourse should a payment be made to the importer and then a drawback claim ultimately be denied.

An importer or exporter may process a drawback for itself, however more often drawbacks are handled by a Customs Broker who is generally capable of handling routine drawback claims. In addition, there are some Customs Brokers who specialize in handling drawback entries.

There are four (4) commonly used types of drawback. They apply to: merchandise that did not conform to specification at the time of importation, merchandise which has not been used while in the U.S., merchandise manufactured from imported materials, and domestic merchandise substituted for imported goods in the case of 'unused' or manufactured goods drawback.

13.5.1.1. MERCHANDISE NOT CONFORMING TO SAMPLES OR SPECIFICATION [111]

Imported merchandise that was not solicited or did not conform to either samples or specification at the time it was imported may be exported with benefit of drawback provided it is re-exported within five (5) years[112] from the time that the merchandise was released by U.S. Customs.[113] Although this provision specifically provides for rejected merchandise, nonconforming goods may also be exported with benefit of drawback under the provision for 'Unused Goods'.

13.5.1.2. UNUSED MERCHANDISE DRAWBACK[114]

Unused Merchandise drawback permits the exportation of goods which have not been used while in the U.S. with benefit of drawback if exported within three (3) years from the date of importation increasing to five (5) years in 2018[115]. This is essentially a refinement of the Same Condition Drawback which required that, at the time of exportation, the goods are in the "same condition" as when imported, and have not been used. The term "used" has a special meaning, and even though the common sense meaning of the word may be generally applicable, it cannot be relied upon. Changes in Drawback law have made it easier for the exporter, who would normally claim the drawback to transfer that right to either the importer or any intermediate party, which could influence the economics of a transaction.[116]

13.5.1.3. MANUFACTURING DRAWBACK[117]

Manufacturing drawback provides for drawback on imported goods or materials used in the manufacture of new articles of commerce exported within three (3) years increasing to five (5) years in 2018.[118]. A prerequisite to the use of a manufacturing drawback is for the exporter and Customs to enter into a contract that sets forth the manufacturing operations, the way in which material will be accounted for, and what portions will actually be exported with benefit of drawback, and at what rate of duty.

Figure 38 - Manufacturing Drawback Certification 1867[119]

13.5.1.4. SUBSTITUTION DRAWBACK[120]

While referred to as a form of drawback, Substitution Drawback is better thought of as an augment to other forms of drawback. Drawback is normally available only against duty-paid imported goods. Under Substitution Drawback, domestic goods may be exported with benefit of drawback in place of an equivalent amount of the same kind of goods as those that were imported.

Previously, the same kind of goods meant commercial interchangeability which presented a very high barrier to substitution. A 2016 change in the drawback law reduced this barrier by redefining equivalent to generally mean classifiable under the same 8 digit HTS number.[121]

13.5.1.5. PETROLEUM BASED PRODUCTS - 1313(P)

Special rules have been established that provide greater latitude in terms of identification and interchangeability of certain petroleum based products. Under all other drawback provisions, goods are only deemed interchangeable if commercially interchangeable, which is a very hard criteria to meet. However, under 1313(p) products are considered interchangeable if they meet a much lower threshold of merely being classified at the same 8 digit tariff number.

13.6. DUTY ADJUSTMENTS

International Trade is about more than duty and freight rates. It is also about market access and a level playing field.

Temporary Modifications can reduce duties. Presidential Proclamations can reduce or increase duties.

A series of laws intended to protect U.S. industry from unfair competition can result in the imposition of substantial duties.

The most commonly encountered remedies, used to level the playing field by neutralizing the impact of certain predatory practices of foreign sellers or governments, are Anti-dumping and Countervailing duties.

CAUTION

If you are not sure if your products are or could be subject to AD/CVD with duty rates of 200% or more, you should find out.

13.6.1. ANTI-DUMPING DUTIES

Anti-dumping duties are imposed to counter the export of goods to the United States which are sold at prices significantly lower than that at which they are sold in their Country of Origin or comparable third country markets.[122]

Anti-dumping duties are generally imposed upon specific products from specific manufacturers in specific countries. They are imposed only after the International Trade Commission (I.T.C.) has investigated and made a final determination that an industry in the United States has been materially injured, or is threatened with material injury by the practice. Many importers do not have sufficient merchandise at

CAUTION

Scope Rulings are similar to Customs Rulings in that they set forth the treatment of a particular good.

However, they differ dramatically in terms of the process for obtaining them.

Customs Rulings are based primarily upon your submission to Customs.

Scope Rulings are based upon both your submissions as well as all other interested parties who are opposed to your position. In that respect it is more like litigation before a less than impartial judge.

stake to warrant opposing an Anti-dumping proceeding. An importer can, nevertheless, use published information about an investigation or finding to address the problem of potential additional duties by selecting suppliers who are either not subject to Anti-dumping or have their own rate.

13.6.2. COUNTERVAILING DUTIES

Countervailing duties are intended to neutralize reductions in the cost of goods resulting from tax reductions, grants, bounties or any other subsidy bestowed on exported merchandise by a foreign country.[123]

The Countervailing duty is approximately equal to the amount of any subsidy found to exist, and will usually vary according to the commodity, place and circumstances of manufacture.

The amount of countervailing duty is reviewed annually by the Department of Commerce, but will remain in effect until revoked.

Like Anti-dumping determinations, Countervailing Duty investigations and findings are published and available.

> Recent changes in the law have added teeth to the AD/CVD laws by increasing efforts to identify goods that should be included within a current AD/CVD order and to collect those neutralizing duties.
>
> Interim rules seek out whistleblowers and provide for secret deliberations with no opportunity provided for opposition.
>
> If you are a complaining affected domestic party this means an increased possibility of success.
>
> If you are the importer, it means that you might only know about it when Customs hands you the bill.

- Continued on next page -

13.6.3. TEMPORARY LEGISLATION, MODIFICATION AND PRESIDENTIAL PROCLAMATIONS

Duties can also be modified through temporary legislation under special trade bills or protective legislation sponsored by a domestic industry. These modifications can either be duty increases or duty reductions.[124]

Duty additions imposed by Presidential Proclamation are infrequent, usually political in nature, and well publicized. They are based upon a variety of different laws and political motivations.

Harmonized Tariff Schedule of the United States (2013) (Rev. 1)

Annotated for Statistical Reporting Purposes

XXII
99-II-7

Heading/ Subheading	Stat. Suf-fix	Article Description	Unit of Quantity	Rates of Duty 1 General	Rates of Duty 1 Special	Rates of Duty 2	Effective Period
9902.01.78	1/	Bags (provided for in subheading 4202.92.45) for transporting, storing, or protecting goods of heading 9503 or 9504, imported and sold with such articles therein.	1/	8.9%	No change	No change	On or before 12/31/2012

1/ See chapter 99 statistical note 1.

Note: The shaded areas indicate that the provisions have expired.

Heading/ Subheading	Stat. Suf-fix	Article Description	Unit of Quantity	Rates of Duty 1 General	Rates of Duty 1 Special	Rates of Duty 2	Effective Period
9902.24.67	1/	Unicycles (provided for in subheading 8712.00.50).	1/	Free	No change	No change	On or before 12/31/2012
9902.51.11	1/	Fabrics, of worsted wool, with average fiber diameters greater than 18.5 micron (provided for in subheading 5112.11.60, or 5112.19.95)	1/	10%	No change	No change	On or before 12/31/2014
9902.51.13	1/	Yarn, of combed wool, not put up for retail sale, containing 85 percent or more by weight of wool, formed with wool fibers having average diameters of 18.5 micron or less (provided for in subheading 5107.10.30).	1/	Free	No change	No change	On or before 12/31/2014

Figure 39 - Temporary Duty Reduction

Very often, due to a financial impasse within Congress duty remission programs such as GSP or Temporary Duty Reductions expire and it can sometimes be years before renewal is even discussed.

There were no Temporary Duty Reductions for the years 2015 and 2016.

- Continued on next page -

18899

Federal Register
Vol. 77, No. 61
Thursday, March 29, 2012

Presidential Documents

Title 3—

The President

Proclamation 8788 of March 26, 2012

To Modify Duty-Free Treatment Under the Generalized System of Preferences and For Other Purposes

By the President of the United States of America

A Proclamation

1. Section 502(b)(2)(E) of the Trade Act of 1974, as amended (the "1974 Act") (19 U.S.C. 2462(b)(2)(E)), provides that the President shall not designate any country a beneficiary developing country under the Generalized System of Preferences (GSP) if such country fails to act in good faith in recognizing as binding or in enforcing arbitral awards in favor of United States citizens or a corporation, partnership, or association that is 50 percent or more beneficially owned by United States citizens, which have been made by arbitrators appointed for each case or by permanent arbitral bodies to which the parties involved have submitted their dispute. Section 502(d)(2) (19 U.S.C. 2462(d)(2)) provides that, after complying with the requirements of section 502(f)(2) (19 U.S.C. 2462(f)(2)), the President shall withdraw or suspend the designation of any country as a beneficiary developing country if, after such designation, the President determines that as the result of changed circumstances such country would be barred from designation as a beneficiary developing country under section 502(b)(2). Section 502(f)(2) requires the President to notify the Congress and the country concerned at least 60 days before terminating the country's designation as a beneficiary developing country for purposes of the GSP.

18902 Federal Register / Vol. 77, No. 61 / Thursday, March 29, 2012 / Presidential Documents

IN WITNESS WHEREOF, I have hereunto set my hand this twenty-sixth day of March, in the year of our Lord two thousand twelve, and of the Independence of the United States of America the two hundred and thirty-sixth.

Figure 40 - Presidential Proclamation

---

[89] 19 C.F.R. 141.101(b), 19 C.F.R. 144.38(d)
[90] 19 C.F.R. 152.12, 141.69(a)
[91] 19 C.F.R. 144.39(d) - Duty due on withdrawal for consumption.
[92] 19 C.F.R. 144.5
[93] 19 USC 1562, 19 C.F.R. 19.11(d)
[94] 19 C.F.R. 146.41
[95] 19 C.F.R. 146.65(a)(1)
[96] 19 C.F.R. 146.42
[97] H.R. 1295, 114th Cong., 1st Sess. (2015)Trade Preference Act of 2015 (H.R. 1295)
[98] 19 C.F.R. 10.14
[99] 19 C.F.R. 10.13
[100] 19 C.F.R. 10.14(b)
[101] 19 C.F.R. 10.16(b), *See* contra Operations Not Incidental to the Assembly Process, 10.16(c)
[102] 19 C.F.R. 10.23
[103] 19 C.F.R. 10.22
[104] 19 C.F.R. 10.24. Documentation generally
[105] 19 C.F.R. 181 subpart F, 181.62 generally
[106] 19 C.F.R. 181.62(c)
[107] 19 C.F.R. 10.37
[108] 19 C.F.R. 10.39(e)(4)
[109] 19 USC 1313, 19 C.F.R. 191.2
[110] 19 C.F.R. 191.53
[111] 19 USC 1313(c), as amended by Public Law 103-182, 107 Stat 2057
[112] Changed from three (3) years to five (5) years. Trade Facilitation and Enforcement Act of 2015, Public Law No: 114-125, 130 Stat. 122 §906 (2016)
[113] Previously Rejected Merchandise drawback required action within 90 days and consent of the original exporter. 19 U.S.C. 1313(c)
[114] 19 USC 1313(j), 19 C.F.R. 191 subpart N
[115] Changed from three (3) years to five (5) years. Trade Facilitation and Enforcement Act of 2015, Public Law No: 114-125, 130 Stat. 122 §906 (2016)
[116] 19 U.S.C. 1313(j) as amended by Public Law 103-182, 107 Stat 2057 Section 632(j)(1)(B)
[117] 19 USC 1313(a), 19 C.F.R. 191 subpart B
[118] Changed from three (3) years to five (5) years. Trade Facilitation and Enforcement Act of 2015, Public Law No: 114-125, 130 Stat. 122 §906 (2016)
[119] Downloaded about August 24, 2016 from Ebay.com
[120] 19 USC 1313(j)(6)(2); 19 C.F.R. 191.4(a)(2)
[121] Trade Facilitation and Enforcement Act of 2015, Public Law No: 114-125, 130 Stat. 122 §906 (2016)
[122] 19 USC 1673
[123] 19 USC 1671, 1303
[124] Harmonized Tariff Schedules of the United States (1994), Chapters 98 and 99 Generally

– Page intentionally left blank –

14. COUNTRY OF ORIGIN

Executive Briefing

From a commercial/marketing standpoint, the determination of the Country of Origin is a crucial issue.

Consumers are demanding information on a product's Country of Origin so that they may exercise their "preference" or "prejudice" regarding a particular country or based upon a perception of quality, (e.g. Shoes from Italy, or Stainless Steel Kitchen Knives from Bangladesh.)

From a business sourcing and legal standpoint, the Country of Origin may determine if you are eligible for duty-free treatment under a preference program.

Conversely, a wrong determination of the Country of Origin can lead to penalties and delays.

It is, therefore, crucial to make the determination of origin as early as possible, generally at the time that the goods are sourced, and definitely before they are produced or shipped.

Historically, Country of Origin marking was for informational purposes to protect domestically produced goods. In more recent times, however, it is a tool used by consumers to exercise their purchasing power. The nature of the labor used, the factory conditions, women's rights, and local politics all feed consumer opinions, which influence their purchasing decision.

Thus, it is important to understand the mechanism by which Country of Origin will be determined.

14.1. RULES FOR DETERMINING THE COUNTRY OF ORIGIN

If all of the components or parts of a product and all the manufacturing procedures originate in the same country, then that country determination is simple: That country will be deemed the Country of Origin. [125]

In today's world, however, it is rare for a product to be wholly made in only one country, and of all materials originating in that one country. In the case of multiple countries, the method for determining which country is the Country of Origin for Customs rules depends on where certain types of manufacturing processes take place.

Regardless of intent, determinations as to origin can still be subjective and determined on a case-by-case basis based upon a determination of "the most important assembly or manufacturing process".

Historically, there was a very subjective rule applied by Customs known as 'substantial transformation.' This test was based on a change in the name, character or use of the product. Specifically, the product must be transformed into a new and different article of commerce. This rule still applies, but only sporadically.

Later, a more objective set of rules was codified that is more similar to the NAFTA rules of origin. With a few exceptions, such as textile and apparel, when the product is created in more than one country, the Country of Origin is the country in which the most important assembly or the most important manufacturing process occurs.

The origin of Textile and Apparel products is determined by a "tariff-shift" method. [126] This means the product's HTSUS classification needs to move from one provision to another in the Tariff.

(t)	Section XX: Chapter 94 through 96
9501	A change to heading 9501 from any other chapter except from heading 8714 if that change is pursuant to GRI 2(a).
9502.10	A change to subheading 9502.10 from any other subheading, except from skins for stuffed dolls (9502.99.10).
9502.91	A change to subheading 9502.91 from any other chapter except from heading 6111 and 6209.
9502.99	A change to subheading 9502.99 from any other heading, except from subheadings 9503.41 through 9503.49.
9503.10 - 9503.30	A change to subheading 9503.10 through 9503.30 from any other subheading including another subheading within that group.
9503.41 - 9503.49	A change to toys of subheading 9503.41 through 9503.49 from any other heading; or
	A change to toys of subheading 9503.41 through 9503.49 from parts and accessories of subheading 9503.41 through 9503.49; or
	A change to parts and accessories of 9503.41 through 9503.49 from any other heading, except from heading 9502, 6111, or 6209

Figure 41 - Part 102 Origin Determination by Tariff Shift

For yarn, thread, twine, cordage, rope, cable or braiding, the rules for determining the Country of Origin are more complex in that they involve the tracing of the raw materials to their origin, for example, to the Country of Origin in which staple fibers are spun in to yarn.

The Country of Origin of *knit-to-shape* products is the country in which major parts are knitted or crocheted directly to the shape used in the finished product. Minor cutting, trimming or sewing is usually insufficient to qualify a component or garment as *knit-to-shape*.

The expressed desire for the new rules has been, in part, based upon the fact that there have been a substantial number of legal decisions which have led to varied case-specific interpretation. Much of the litigation in this area has resulted in the overturning of Customs positions. It, therefore, appears that more than anything, these new rules attempt to reduce a subjective evaluation to a more clerical function subject to less judicial review.

For the importer, the difficulty which remains is that in those all-important situations where a specific origin is sought either to qualify for duty free benefits or for marketing purposes, the new rules can ultimately be just as subjective as the old, just at a different level of the evaluation.

[125] A "wholly obtained" product that is wholly the growth, product or manufacture of a particular country, is considered as originating in that country. (This applies for non-preferential countries).
[126] 19 C.F.R. 102.21

– Page intentionally left blank –

15. MARKING AND LABELING

Executive Briefing

Virtually every imported or exported article is subject to the marking regulations of one or more agencies.

Incorrect markings can result in having to mark or remark the goods and liquidated damages if the importer cannot redeliver the goods for marking because they have already been delivered. This is in addition to the costs of remarking, delays or potential loss of an order.

Marking which is false, not just inaccurate or in error, can result in seizure, penalties and even criminal sanctions.

Every article imported into the United States, unless specifically exempted, is required to be marked with at least its Country of Origin,[127] and possibly with additional markings and labels.

> The marking laws applicable to imports remain applicable to those goods even when repackaged *after* importation.
>
> *(See* "Repacked Articles Subject to Marking" §15.1.8 at 141.)

Most marking requirements are statutory and rarely change, however, agency interpretations of what the law requires do periodically change.

Marking laws are enforced through physical inspection, usually at the time the shipment is released by Customs, but also after release, through a request to the importer to provide a sample. (*See* "Request for Information (CF 28) §19.2.1 at 180.)

If the determination is made that marking is improper prior to release of the shipment, it will delay release until remarking has been accomplished.

If the determination is not made until after the shipment has been released, Customs will demand return of the shipment for remarking. (*See* "Notice to Mark and/or Notice to Redeliver (CF 4647)" §19.2.3 at 185.) If you are not able to return the goods, you may be subject to liquidated damages.

Marking laws fall into two classes:

- U.S. Customs and Border Protection Country of Origin Marking
- Those of other agencies

Both are enforced by Customs and Border Protection, but the consequences for importing improperly marked goods essentially divide along these same lines.

While correcting deficient marking when directed to do so is obviously the prudent course of action, it is not always possible, especially when the goods have been sold and shipped.

If the importer fails to redeliver the shipment, Customs will make a demand for a penalty in the form of liquidated damages. Liquidated damages can amount to three times the dutiable value of the violating goods. Collection of this penalty is secured through the bond posted at the time of entry.

However, if Customs fails to enforce its own marking requirements within thirty (30) days after release, the penalty is limited to a 10% statutory marking duty on the dutiable value of the goods, which is still a significant amount.

When the marking violation relates to agencies other than Customs and Border Protection, the demand for redelivery can be made any time during the conditional release period. Conditional Release periods vary based upon the law and type of product, but generally are between 30 days for most products, up to 180 days for products subject to the Food and Drug Administration (FDA). (*See* "Notice to Mark and/or Notice to Redeliver (CF 4647)" §19.2.3 at 185.)[128] False certification that marking has been corrected and that the goods are available for re-inspection should be avoided because it can result in both seizure of the shipment and penalties, in addition to the liquidated damages and marking duties.

15.1. U.S. CUSTOMS COUNTRY OF ORIGIN MARKING

U.S. Tariff Act Country of Origin Marking laws require that every article of foreign origin which is imported into the United States must be marked with its Country of Origin, unless specifically exempted.

Regardless of whether an article is exempt from marking, the outer shipping carton must always be marked with the Country of Origin of its content.[129]

Figure 42 - Marking of Shipping Carton

Even if an article is exempt from marking, its product packaging must be marked with the Country of Origin of the article.

The purpose of the marking requirements is to ensure that the "ultimate purchaser" will be able to identify the Country of Origin of an imported product, so that they can assert their preference or prejudice.

The requirements are that the marking must be in a conspicuous place, legible, and as indelible and permanent as the nature of the article will permit to indicate to an ultimate purchaser in the United States the English name of the Country of Origin of the article.[130]

15.1.1. LEGIBLE AND CONSPICUOUS

The ultimate purchaser in the United States must be able to find the marking easily and read it without strain.[131]

Generally, any method of marking, at any location that ensures that the Country of Origin will conspicuously appear on the article, will be acceptable. This would include the use of stickers, labels or tags, according to the type of goods.

What size and type of marking may be considered acceptable will vary, depending upon the nature of the article, the presence of other markings, the use to which the article will be put, and by whom it will be used in its condition as imported.

Marking in a contrasting plain print style avoids questions as to legibility[132].

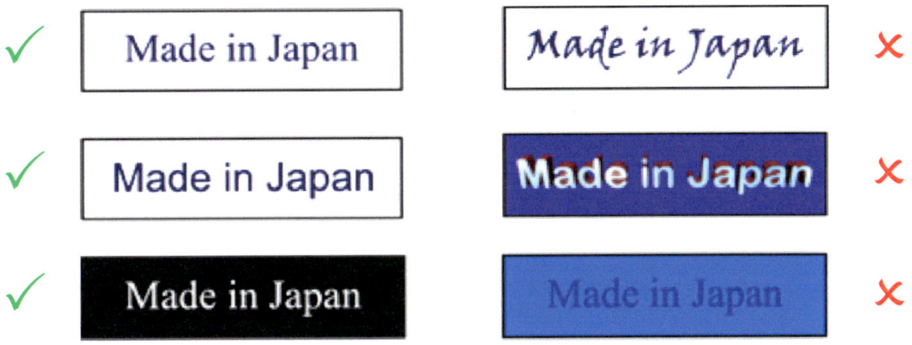

Figure 43 - Marking Font, Style & Color

Acceptability of a font size varies based upon the product.

A height of no less than 1/8 inch (9 point) in height has generally been held to be sufficiently conspicuous.[133]

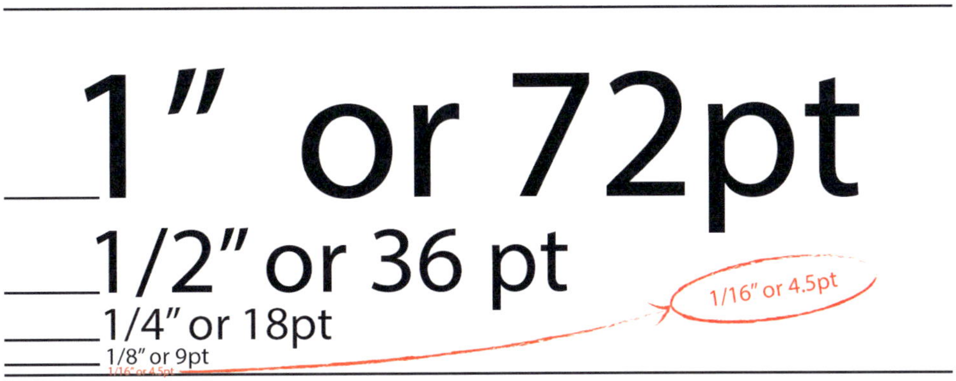

Figure 44 - Marking Size

Under limited circumstances usually relating to products with limited surface areas, font sizes as small 5 or 6 points have been found sufficient.

15.1.2. PERMANENCE

The marking should be as permanent as the nature of the article will permit, but must be at least sufficiently permanent so as to survive normal distribution and handling. It should be permanent enough to ensure that under any reasonably foreseeable circumstance, the marking will remain on the article (or its container) until it reaches the ultimate purchaser.[134]

> A lot of marking problems are simply the result of graphics artists and marketing departments who are not familiar with all of the marking rules, even if they think they are.
>
> Given the cost of having to remark products, it only makes sense to:
>
> 1. Educate them as to the marking rules, and
> 2. If you are contemplating using a more novel approach to placement, color, size, permanence or location of Country of Origin, you should have it reviewed by a professional.

For certain classes of products, there are special rules as to what constitutes "conspicuous," "sufficiently permanent," where a marking must be placed, and to how the marking must be attached. These Customs requirements are in addition to those of other agencies, including the Federal Trade Commission, and the Food and Drug Administration. These special classes of merchandise include:

- Wearing apparel
- Knives
- Luggage
- Watches

For certain classes of products, there are also special rules for permanence. These products include:

- Certain textile furnishings (furniture) – sewn-on labels
- Machinery - placard

15.1.3. ULTIMATE PURCHASER

The "ultimate purchaser" is generally the last person in the United States to receive the article in the form in which it was imported. Who the "ultimate purchaser" is can vary depending upon the product and how it will be used in the United States.[135]

- If an article is to be sold at retail in its imported condition, the retail purchaser is the "ultimate purchaser."
- If the imported article is distributed as a gift, the recipient is the "ultimate purchaser."
- If an imported article will be used in manufacturing, the manufacturer may be the "ultimate purchaser" if the article is going to be substantially transformed.
- If the manufacturing process is merely a minor one that leaves the identity of the imported article intact, the consumer or user of the article who obtains the article after the processing, will be regarded as the "ultimate purchaser."

15.1.4. ENGLISH MARKING

Only the English name for the Country of Origin may be used unless a variant is specifically approved by the Commissioner of Customs.[136]

Abbreviations or variations that clearly indicate the English name are acceptable, but it is ill advised to risk using them without a prior determination that the variation will be acceptable to CBP.

Dual language markings such as "Fabrique/Made in France" are acceptable, provided one set of markings is in English and in proper form.

15.1.5. NAME OF COUNTRY

The name of the country should be the most obvious, however, not only must the name be in English, it has to be the name by which that country is known when exported. Given global changes over the last several decades, even its name should not be assumed.

At times, borders are realigned, which can result in a fundamental change in the name of the Country of Origin.

- Armenia, Azerbaijan, Estonia, Kazakhstan, Kyrgyzstan, Latvia, Lithuania, Moldova, Russian Federation, Tajikistan, Turkmenistan, and Uzbekistan split from U.S.S.R. (1992)
- Former Yugoslav Republic of Macedonia split from Yugoslavia. (1993)
- Czechoslovakia (Czechoslovak Socialist Republic) split into Czech Republic and Slovakia. (1994)
- "Serbia and Montenegro" split into two countries: Serbia and Montenegro. (2006)

At times, countries make a major change in their names which does not affect the Country of Origin of a good produced in that geographic location, but would change the name that must be used when marking the goods.

- Southern Rhodesia changed to Zimbabwe. (1980)
- Burma changed to Myanmar. (1989)
- Zaire (Republic of Zaire) changed to The Democratic Republic of the Congo. (1997)
- Yugoslavia changed to Serbia and Montenegro. (2003)

Sometimes the name changes may seem relatively minor.

- Republic of Yemen changed to Yemen. (1993)
- Democratic Republic of Madagascar changed to Republic of Madagascar. (1993)
- Republic of Hungary changed to Hungary. (2012)

Political ownership of an area does not always identify the proper country for marking purposes.

- Hong Kong is treated as distinct from China.[137]
- Gaza, Gaza Strip and West Bank are all distinct from Israel.[138]

15.1.6. ABBREVIATIONS

The use of an abbreviation or shortened name for a Country of Origin is not generally acceptable even if it conforms to the ISO abbreviations which Customs uses itself.[139] An abbreviation or shortened name will only be acceptable if it "unmistakably identif[ies[the name of a country".[140]

Obtaining prior approval to use an abbreviation that has not been previously ruled on is not required, but is a good practice.

COUNTRY	ACCEPTABLE ABBREVIATIONS	UNACCEPTABLE ABBREVIATIONS
Argentina[141 142]		Argen, Arg, Argtin
Australia[143 144 145]	Austrlia	AU, AUS, Austri
Austria[146]		Austri
Belize[147]		Beliz
Brazil[148 149 150]	Brasil	Braz
Canada[151]		CAN, CDN
China, Peoples's Republic of[152 153]	China	P.R.O.C., PRC
Costa Rica[154]		C Rica
Croatia[155]	Croatia	Croatia (EU), Croatia (European Union)
Czech Republic[156]	Czech Republic, Czech Rep	CZ, CR,
Dominican Republic[157 158 159]	Dominican Republic, Dominican Rep	Dom Rep, DR
Germany[160 161]	Germany	Germ, D, G, Ger
Great Britain[162 163 164]	United Kingdom, U.K., Gt. Britain, Great Britain	GB
Guatemala[165]		Guate
Honduras[166]		Hond
Hong Kong[167]		H.K.
Hungary[168]		Hun, Hung
Indonesia[169 170 171]		Indon, IN, INDO
Italy[172 173]	Italie	
Jamaica[174]		Jam
Luxembourg[175]	Luxemb, Luxembg	
Malaysia[176]		Malay
Mexico[177 178]		MX, Mex
Netherlands[179]	Netherlands, Holland	NL
Philippines[180 181]		Philip, Phil
Poland[182]		Pol
Puerto Rico[183]		P Rico
Russian Federation[184]		RF
Singapore[185]		SINGPR
South Africa[186]		S Afri
Taiwan[187]		Formosa, R.O.C.
Thailand[188]		Thai

Turkey[189]		TR
United Arab Emirates[190 191]		U.A.E
Venezuela[192 193 194 195]		Venez, VZLA, V, Venzla

Figure 45 - Abbreviations of Country of Origin Names

15.1.7. FORM OF MARKING

Generally acceptable forms of marking are:

- ✓ "Product of ..."
- ✓ "Made in ..."
- ✓ "Contents product of ..."
- ✓ "Contents made in ..."

In certain situations, where a product is wholly made in a single country, it is permissible to use the name of the Country of Origin without the preface language, e.g., "China" instead of "Made in China". This option should not be utilized without a full examination and evaluation of the article, its other markings, special marking rules, as well as the requirements of other governmental agencies.

The adjective form of a name, e.g., Swiss Made, can be used provided it is clearly identifies the origin of the product. Care should be taken to ensure that the adjective version of the Country of Origin name remains easily understood.

15.1.8. REPACKED ARTICLES SUBJECT TO MARKING

Your obligations to mark do not necessarily stop once the goods enter the United States.

Not only must the articles and/or their containers be properly marked with the Country of Origin at the time of importation, if the goods are repacked or remarked in the United States, the product packaging container must also be properly marked. Repackaging cannot be used to conceal or obscure the original Country of Origin marking.

If the items are repacked, a "Remarking Certification" is required by the importer and each subsequent re-packer.

15.1.9. CONFUSING ORIGIN MARKINGS

The Country of Origin markings must be clear and not confusing. It becomes confusing when an address, name of any city, locale, or country, either within or without the United States that is not the Country of Origin, appears on an article or its container.[196]

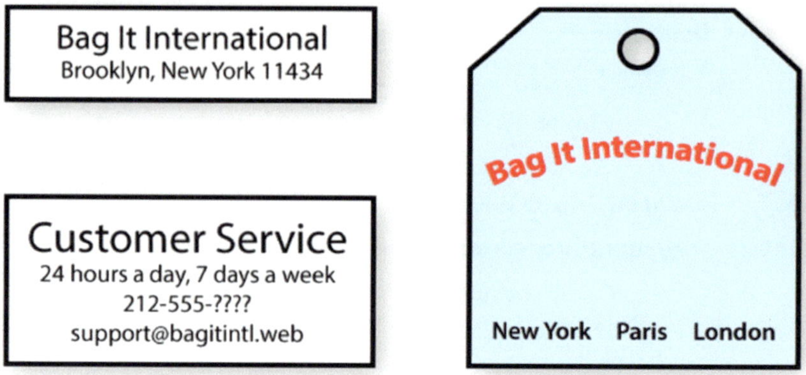

Figure 46 - Confusing Marking

Customs takes the position that use of any geographical locations other than that of the Country of Origin may potentially mislead the ultimate purchaser.

> It is irrelevant that this additional information was required by another law. The corrective marking is still required.

Even the use of an adjective with non-origin references triggers this requirement. For example, the use of the adjectival "fine Italian hand stained and hand finished embossed calf skins" for belts that were made in China, requires corrective marking. [197]

15.1.10. CORRECTIVE ORIGIN MARKING

Where there is use of a location that may cause confusion, there needs to be "in close proximity" and "in lettering of at least comparable size" corrective marking in the form of the name of the actual Country of Origin preceded by the words "made in," product of," or similar phrases.

> The corrective marking is required even if the Country of Origin appears elsewhere on the article or container.

15.1.11. EXCEPTIONS TO MARKING REQUIREMENTS

> Even if the article qualifies for a marking exception, the outermost container in which the article reaches the ultimate purchaser must be properly marked.

Exceptions to the requirement that each imported article of foreign origin be marked with its Country of Origin fall into two categories: those articles exempted because they are inherently incapable of being marked, and those which are accepted because of their use or some other specified reason.[198] The following are examples of available exemptions:

- Articles that are incapable of being marked
- Articles that cannot be marked prior to shipment to the United States without injury
- Articles for which the marking of the container will reasonably indicate the origin of the article contained therein.

- Articles that are crude substances.
- Articles imported for use by the importer and not intended for sale in their imported form or any other form.
- Articles to be processed in the United States by the importer, other than for the purpose of concealing the Country of Origin of such articles, and in such manner that any mark would necessarily be obliterated, destroyed, or permanently concealed.
- Articles for which the ultimate purchaser must necessarily know the Country of Origin by reason of the circumstances of their importation, or by reason of the character of the articles, even though they are not marked to indicate their origin.

> While referred to as an exception in the law, the application of a marking exception is often a matter of a subjective determination on the part of a CBP Import Specialist. Consequently, for practical reasons, an exception should not be viewed as a right, but as a permissive waiver.

If there is a question as to whether the exception will be accepted by Customs, a prior waiver or ruling should be obtained. A one-time waiver may be available when marking is merely questionable or where otherwise justified under one of the marking exceptions. However, these are merely temporary dispensations which are often begrudgingly granted.

15.1.12. OPPORTUNITIES THROUGH TRADEMARK AND DESIGN

There are, however, opportunities for enhanced marketing variations. Due to the inherent risk, such opportunities should be pursued only after some form of advanced opinion.

A reference to any location other than the Country of Origin often requires corrective marking.

The primary issue from a marketing perspective becomes a question of where the corrective marking has to be placed.[199]

> Generally, corrective marking must appear in close proximity to the potentially misleading geographical term. Where, however, a location is part of a trademark, there may be an opportunity to put it in "some other conspicuous location," which is not necessarily in close proximity nor of comparable size.

15.2. OTHER MARKING REQUIREMENTS

Most regulatory agencies whose laws are enforced by Customs and Border Protection have their own marking requirements. A number of these marking requirements provide for Country of Origin markings which either overlap, or are identical to those of Customs and Border Protection.

While Customs may be the front line for enforcement of other agency marking rules, it is that other agency, not Customs, which will have the final word as to what constitutes compliance. The other agency may, very well, also have the final word with respect to any penalties or liquidated damages imposed for violating its own marking requirements.

Unlike improper Customs markings, where the demand for redelivery of the shipment can only be made within 30 days after release of a shipment, when another agency's marking rules are violated, Customs may demand return of the goods any time during the conditional release period which, depending upon the law and type of product, generally runs between 30 days for most products, up to 180 days for products subject to the Food and Drug Administration (FDA).

The most common labeling rules encountered, other than the basic customs origin marking requirements, relate to:

- ✓ Name and Address of the Importer or Distributor of Textile Products (RN#) – Federal Trade Commission (FTC).
- ✓ Fiber Identification of Textile Products – Federal Trade Commission (FTC).
- ✓ Wearing Apparel Care Labeling – Federal Trade Commission (FTC).
- ✓ Safety Warning – Consumer Product Safety Commission (CPSC).
- ✓ Federal Communication Commission (FCC).
- ✓ Foods and Cosmetics, and Drugs - Food and Drug Administration (FDA).
- ✓ Wine and Liquor – Bureau of Alcohol, Tobacco, Firearms and Explosives (ATF).

– Balance of page intentionally left blank –

15.2.1. REGISTERED IDENTIFICATION NUMBERS (RN)

Executive Briefing

As part of the labeling requirements, importers of textile, wool and/or fur products are required to list their name and address on the products.

There may be times when this is not desirable. As an alternative, the importer may register with the Federal Trade Commission and obtain a Registered Identification Number ("RN"). Once obtained, the RN can be used in place of the name and address of the importer on labels or tags.

If the product is imported, the label can identity any of the following:

- ✓ Name of the Foreign Manufacturer
- ✓ Name of the Foreign Distributor
- ✓ Name or RN of the Importer
- ✓ Name or RN of the Wholesaler
- ✓ Name or RN of the Ultimate Retailer (with their consent)

Obtaining an RN number is ministerial; it can be done on-line and there is no fee for registration.[200] You can also look up a company by their RN. Obtaining the RN number also does not preclude you from continuing to use your name and address; it is merely an option.

CAUTION

If for any reason you need to sell any products marked with the name or RN of the retailer to someone else, you will have to obliterate their name or RN and re-label them.

This is a problem similar to selling goods bearing the trademark of the original purchaser when selling those goods to a third party.

SINGLE SIDED LABELS

Made in Mexico RN 00003	55% polyester 45% cotton Size 10 Made in Australia RN 00001	Warm Iron -12- Made in New Zealand Kangaroo Imports, Inc.

DUAL SIDED LABELS

Elegant Lines™ Size 10 Made in USA of imported fabric	100% Silk Dry Clean Only RN 00001
Front of Label	Back of Label

Figure 47 - RN Labels

15.2.2. MADE IN USA

Executive Briefing

Just because goods are manufactured in the USA does not automatically mean they can be marked "Made in USA."

No other origin marking is as fraught with potential problems as is "Made in USA."

Its use is governed by multiple and inconsistent laws and has different meanings and criteria, depending upon what circumstances it is used, including circumstances where:

Sold for consumption in the United States;

Sold in the United States for use in special government programs, such as the Buy American Act;

Sold for export from the perspective of U.S. export laws or;

Sold for export when viewed from the perspective of the foreign purchaser's government.

15.2.2.1. GOODS SOLD IN THE U.S.

The most stringent marking rules apply to goods that are to be sold in the United States where there is a claim that the goods were manufactured in the United States.

Under the Federal Trade Commission rules, in order to be labeled "Made in USA" without qualification, the products must be "all or virtually all" made in the U.S. This "means that all significant parts and processing that go into products must be of U.S. origin."[201] There must be either no foreign content or only a negligible amount of foreign content.

If a product does not meet this criterion, it may be labeled with a qualifier such as "Made in USA of U.S. and Imported Parts." This qualified marking still has a strict standard that must be met. The product must contain a significant amount of U.S. content. For example, it would not be permissible to mark a product "Made in USA of U.S. and Imported Parts" if the major parts of the product were foreign origin, even if, for Customs purposes, there was a "substantial transformation" in the U.S.

If there is no substantial transformation in the U.S. and the product is predominantly made of foreign parts, it is impermissible to mark it with the "Made in USA" or "Made in the USA" with qualified term.

15.2.2.2. GOODS INTENDED FOR USE IN GOVERNMENT PROJECTS

The next level of stringency applies to goods that are intended for use in U.S. Government related projects under the "Buy American Act" which imposes its own threshold for U.S. content. Marking of these goods can be problematic because while meeting a "Buy American Act" standard, they might still bear a foreign origin marking, a fact which U.S. workers may notice.

15.2.2.3. PRODUCTS EXPORTED FROM THE UNITED STATES

The third level of marking stringency is for products that are exported from the United States to foreign markets. For Census purposes, the U.S. will allow "Made in USA" claims even for minimal U.S. content. However, one must pay careful attention to the laws of the importing country with regard to whether it is permissible to be marked in this way.

15.2.2.4. PRODUCTS ORIGINALLY EXPORTED RETURNED TO THE UNITED STATES

Yet another level is for goods that were originally produced for export from the U.S. and appropriately marked at that point as "Made in USA" but are now being returned for the U.S. market. Just because they were properly marked at the time of export does not mean that they are now in compliance for use in the U.S. market.

It makes no difference as to why the goods are being returned.

– Balance of page intentionally left blank –

[127] 19 USC 1304(b); 19 C.F.R. 134.11

[128] Regardless of the Conditional Release period, liquidated damages are contractual and not penal. This means that a liquidated damage claim against the customs bond is not permitted after Liquidation. HQ 222836 (January 30, 1991).

[129] 19 USC 1304(b); 19 C.F.R. 134.11

[130] 19 USC 1304(a), 19 C.F.R. 134.11

[131] 19 C.F.R. 134.41(b)

[132] Ruling 0734523 dated July 24, 1992 - "[L]arge enough to be read without strain."

[133] Ruling 0734523 dated July 24, 1992 - "[L]arge enough to be read without strain."

[134] 19 C.F.R. 134.41(b)

[135] 19 C.F.R. 134.1(d)

[136] 19 C.F.R. 134.45(a)

[137] 19 C.F.R. § 134.1 (a) “Country” means the political entity known as a nation. Colonies, possessions, or protectorates outside the boundaries of the mother country are considered separate countries.

“For purposes of the country of origin marking requirements, Hong Kong is a separate country from China.”, HQ 731701, January 26, 1990.

[138] CSMS# 16-000047 - West Bank Country of Origin Marking Requirements. 01/23/2016 12:13 PM EST

Per Treasury Decisions 95-25 and 97-16 (see attachments), unless excepted by statute (19 U.S.C. §1304) or regulation (19 C.F.R. §134), goods produced in the West Bank or Gaza Strip shall be marked as originating from ''West Bank,'' ''Gaza,'' ''Gaza Strip,'' ''West Bank/Gaza,'' ''West Bank/Gaza Strip,'' ''West Bank and Gaza,'' or ''West Bank and Gaza Strip.'' It is not acceptable to mark the aforementioned goods with the words ''Israel,'' ''Made in Israel,'' ''Occupied Territories-Israel,'' or any variation thereof.

[139] Appendix C – ISO Country Codes.http://www.cbp.gov/document/guidance/appendix-c-iso-country-codes

[140] 19 C.F.R. 134.45 (b) (2014)

[141] Customs Ruling Letter NY R05081 October 31, 2006, Headquarters Ruling Letter 561543 August 21, 2000

[142] Customs Headquarters Letter 733104 March 15, 1990

[143] Customs Headquarters Ruling Letter 562240 February 4, 2002

[144] Customs Ruling Letter 562240 February 4, 2002, Headquarters Ruling Letter 733104 March 15, 1990

[145] Customs Headquarters Ruling Letter 561543 August 21, 2000

[146] Customs Ruling Letter NY R05081 October 31, 2006, Headquarters Ruling Letter 561543 August 21, 2000

[147] Customs Ruling Letter NY R05081 October 31, 2006, Headquarters Ruling Letter 561543 August 21, 2000

[148] Customs Ruling Letter NY R05081 October 31, 2006, Headquarters Ruling Letter 561543 August 21, 2000

[149] Customs Headquarters Letter 561327 June 8, 1999

[150] 19 C.F.R. 134.45(b) (2014)

[151] Headquarters Ruling Letter 731760 December 27, 1989

[152] Customs Ruling Letter N058316 April 28, 2009

[153] Headquarters Ruling Letter W968266 September 19, 2006

[154] Customs Ruling Letter NY R05081 October 31, 2006, Headquarters Ruling Letter 561543 August 21, 2000

[155] Customs Ruling Letter N252458 May 7, 2014

[156] Customs Headquarters Letter 560978 July 24, 1998

[157] Customs Ruling Letter N033436 July 22, 2008, HRL 561543

[158] Customs Ruling Letter NY R05081 October 31, 2006, Headquarters Ruling Letter 561543 August 21, 2000

[159] Customs Headquarters Letter 561028 September 21, 1998

[160] Customs Ruling Letter NY R05081 October 31, 2006, Headquarters Ruling Letter 561543 August 21, 2000

[161] Customs Headquarters Letter 560978 July 24, 1998

[162] Customs Ruling Letter N225356 July 31, 2012

[163] 19 C.F.R. 134.45(b) (2014)

[164] Customs Ruling Letter NY 818111 January 22, 1996

[165] Customs Ruling Letter NY R05081 October 31, 2006, Headquarters Ruling Letter 561543 August 21, 2000

[166] Customs Ruling Letter NY R05081 October 31, 2006, Headquarters Ruling Letter 561543 August 21, 2000

[167] Customs Headquarters Letter 735281 February 24, 1994
[168] Customs Headquarters Letter 733104 March 15, 1990
[169] Customs Ruling Letter NY R05081 October 31, 2006, Headquarters Ruling Letter 561543 August 21, 2000
[170] Customs Headquarters Letter 734443 June 3, 1992
[171] Customs Headquarters Letter 561028 September 21, 1998
[172] Customs Headquarters Ruling Letter 563047 July 22, 2004
[173] 19 C.F.R. 134.45(b) (2014)
[174] Customs Ruling Letter NY R05081 October 31, 2006, Headquarters Ruling Letter 561543 August 21, 2000
[175] 19 C.F.R. 134.45(b) (2014)
[176] Customs Ruling Letter NY R05081 October 31, 2006, Headquarters Ruling Letter 561543 August 21, 2000
[177] Customs Ruling Letter NY R04562 August 30, 2006
[178] Customs Headquarters Ruling Letter 561442 July 19, 1999
[179] Customs Ruling Letter J80994 April 25, 2003
[180] Customs Ruling Letter NY R05081 October 31, 2006, Headquarters Ruling Letter 561543 August 21, 2000
[181] Customs Headquarters Ruling Letter 561543 August 21, 2000, Headquarters Ruling Letter 722566 Sept. 14, 1983
[182] Customs Ruling Letter NY R05081 October 31, 2006, Headquarters Ruling Letter 561543 August 21, 2000
[183] Customs Ruling Letter NY R05081 October 31, 2006, Headquarters Ruling Letter 561543 August 21, 2000
[184] Customs Headquarters Ruling Letter 561543 August 21, 2000, Headquarters Ruling Letter 5959931 July 11, 1996
[185] Customs Headquarters Letter 561306 April 15, 1999
[186] Customs Ruling Letter NY R05081 October 31, 2006, Headquarters Ruling Letter 561543 August 21, 2000
[187] Customs Ruling Letter NY G89369 March 28, 1991
[188] Customs Ruling Letter NY R05081 October 31, 2006, Headquarters Ruling Letter 561543 August 21, 2000
[189] Customs Headquarters Ruling Letter 561008 August 4, 1999
[190] Customs Headquarters Ruling Letter 563047 July 22, 2004
[191] Customs Headquarters Ruling Letter 561997 March 4, 2001
[192] Customs Ruling Letter NY R05081 October 31, 2006, Headquarters Ruling Letter 561543 August 21, 2000
[193] Customs Headquarters Ruling Letter 561543 August 21, 2000, Headquarters Ruling Letter 731799 May 15, 1989
[194] Customs Headquarters Ruling Letter 563047 July 22, 2004
[195] Customs Headquarters Ruling Letter 968034 March 16, 2006
[196] 19 C.F.R. 134.46
[197] HQ 562613 (2003)
[198] 19 USC 1304(a)(3), 19 C.F.R. 134.32
[199] In JBLU, Inc. v. U.S., 15-1509 (Fed.Cir.2016) the Court of Appeals noted that: "Section 134.47 provides more lenient requirements for instances where the location words, letters, or name are 'part of a trademark or tradename' In such a case, the country of origin marking must be legible and permanent; 'conspicuous[]'; and either 'in close proximity [to the location words, letters, or name] or in some other conspicuous location."

Customs acknowledged that the corrective marking shown which would not have satisfied basic marking rules did satisfy the more lenient requirements of section 134.47.

[200] http://www.business.ftc.gov/content/registered-identification-number-database
[201] 62 FR 63756, 63765 (1997)

– Page intentionally left blank –

16. RESTRICTIONS ON DOMESTICALLY PRODUCED GOODS & RE-IMPORTED GOODS

Executive Briefing

Even though there is movement towards more universal standards for products, determining their origin, their marking, labeling and other commercial standards and designations, there are still very often substantial differences from country to country as to quality, composition, construction, health and safety standards and markings.

Consequently, goods produced in the U.S. for a particular export market might not be eligible for sale in the U.S.

16.1. MARKED MADE IN USA

"Made in USA" is a prized origin designation. The circumstances under which it may be used vary, depending upon the country in which goods will be distributed.

The requirements for goods destined for export are governed by the laws of the destination country.

The requirements for goods to be distributed in the United States are governed by U.S. law and the rules of the Federal Trade Commission (FTC). The eligibility requirements for the "Made in USA" designation are stricter for domestic distribution than for export.

There is no law requiring that a product be labeled as made in the USA when it is entirely domestically produced and sold.

The Federal Trade Commission's (FTC) *Made in USA* policy applies to all goods ***advertised*** or ***sold in the U.S.***[202]

Marketing today also includes "new age" platforms including "Facebook" and other social media websites where the FTC is only beginning to address advertising on such mediums.

The advertising implications set forth in the FTC's March 2013 publication "Dot Com Disclosures,"[203] addresses the implications of omissions rather than the affirmative descriptions that are being analyzed herein.

There is no law requiring that a product be labeled as "Made in the USA" when it is domestically produced and the FTC does not mandate use of any particular language when making such a claim.

Rather, the FTC's oversight addresses the ***truthfulness*** of a claim and therefore, when such a claim is made by a manufacturer, compliance with Section 5 of the *Federal Trade Commission Act* (15 U.S.C. 45) (Act) must be ensured.[204]

The Act prohibits "unfair or deceptive acts or practices"[205] which can arise from an ***express statement*** or an ***omission*** that results in misleading consumers in their decision to buy or use a product, and are therefore considered fraudulent marketing.

Claims of U.S. origin can be express or implied, e.g., active or passive, qualified or unqualified.

An example of an express ***unqualified*** statement of U.S. origin is:

Product Is American-Made [206]

An example of an express ***qualified*** statement is:

Product Made in Korea – Packaging Made in USA [207]

16.1.1. USING "MADE IN USA"

The FTC standard for permissible use of a claim of U.S. origin is when a product is "*all or virtually all*"[208] made in the USA.

An implied statement of U.S. origin could include a U.S. symbol such as the U.S. flag, or a geographical reference which may convey a claim of U.S. origin either by itself or in conjunction with other phrases or images.[209]

Express statements which are a truthful representation about the U.S. production of a product meeting the FTC standard can include:

Made in USA

Our Products are American Made

(in reference to an entire product line), or

USA [210]

Using "This Product is American Made" versus "Our Products are American Made," would, therefore, limit the claim of U.S. origin to the product identified as such on a cut sheet.[211]

16.1.2. "*ALL OR VIRTUALLY ALL*" STANDARD (NOT QUITE 100%)

This threshold can be thought of as the "almost all" standard in order to use a statement like "Made in USA."

"All or virtually all" means that all significant parts and processing that go into the product are of U.S. origin, e.g., where this is only a *de minimus* or negligible amount of foreign content.[212]

Three factors should generally be considered when evaluating whether a product is *"all or virtually all"* made in the USA[213] :

1. Whether the final assembly or processing of the product took place in the USA,
2. The portion of the total manufacturing cost of the product that is attributable to USA parts and processing, and
3. How far removed from the finished product any foreign content is.

While the first factor is clear, for the second factor FTC recommends using the cost of goods sold, or finished goods inventory cost, as the measure for calculating manufacturing costs which will generally include (and be limited to), the cost of manufacturing materials, direct manufacturing labor, and manufacturing overhead.[214]

16.1.3. 100% US ORIGIN – USING AMPLIFIED CLAIMS

The "*all or virtually all*" standard, as explained above, means that even where the origin is not 100% of U.S. origin but is almost of 100% U.S. origin, a "Made in USA" statement may be used provided it is ***virtually all*** of U.S. origin.

When 100% of the materials and labor originate within the U.S. however, statements amplifying the nature of the U.S. origin would not be considered deceptive and would therefore be permissible. Examples are:

Made in USA Entirely of U.S. Origin Parts

Made Entirely of U.S. Sourced Materials

Proudly Manufactured in the USA – 100% U.S. Origin Parts

The order in which the statement is made is irrelevant. Therefore, using "*100% US Origin Parts – Proudly Manufactured in the USA*" would be acceptable as well.

16.1.4. "MADE IN CALIFORNIA"

Statements like "Made in California" are regulated by laws of the individual state which often mirror those of the FTC.

Therefore, a statement such as "Made in California – Made Entirely of U.S. Origin Material" would not be considered deceptive at the Federal level and, therefore, would be permissible.

Before usage of this type of state claim, further verification of local laws is recommended.

16.2. GOODS DOMESTICALLY PRODUCED AND DISTRIBUTED

Under the U.S. Federal Trade Commission rules, the type of origin marking required or permitted is dependent upon the origin of the component materials. Historically, in order to be marked "Made in U.S.A." goods must have been composed 100% of U.S. labor and materials.[215] A recent FTC settlement suggests that use of the "Made in U.S.A." designation might be permitted if only "virtually all" of the materials and labor are of U.S. origin.[216]

If an article contains less than 50% of foreign materials there are two options available. The article *may* be marked "Made in U.S.A. of...", and identify the origin of the components; or alternatively, origin marking *may* be totally omitted. If however, the article contains 50% or more of foreign materials, the article *must* be marked "Made in U.S.A. of..." and identify the origin of the components.[217]

Regardless of the markings that may be generally permitted or required under FTC rules, there are also special rules for clothing and automotive products. Other agencies, such as the Federal Communications Commission and the Foods and Drug Administration, also have additional marking requirements.

16.3. GOODS DOMESTICALLY PRODUCED FOR EXPORT

Most countries require that imported articles be marked with the Country of Origin. Fortunately, disclosure of constituent materials is not generally required, and the presence of the disclosure is not fatal. Unfortunately, determining the rules and standards for both marking and origin determinations can be difficult. In some instances certain countries' rules can actually be contradictory with those of another.

> Exporters must learn the rules of each country in which they intend to market or distribute their product because it will be the laws of the importing country that determine how both origin is determined and the type of marking required.

16.4. CONSEQUENCE OF MARKING

The consequence of these differing standards is that an article manufactured for distribution in the U.S. might not be properly marked for export and a U.S. made article marked for export and then re-imported might not be properly marked for U.S. Distribution.

For example:

> In Switzerland and Austria, origin markings are generally only required for certain products, e.g., textiles, military defense materials and certain foods. Thus, many goods could be produced for export without an origin marking. However, if those same goods were re-imported to the U.S., they would be deemed improperly marked if they contained more than 50% of foreign content.

16.5. RE-IMPORT RESTRICTIONS

Inconsistent marking and labeling are not the only problems facing companies exporting products or re-importing products.

16.5.1. DUTY LIABILITY

Goods which are of U.S. origin are generally exempt from U.S. Customs duty upon re-importation, providing certain strict regulations are complied with.

There is no equivalent duty exemption from Customs duty upon the re-importation of previously imported goods. In fact, there are very limited circumstances where re-imported foreign-made goods will not be subject to duty every time they are imported. (*See* "Articles Not Advanced or Improved In Condition" §13.4.1 at 118 and "Articles Advanced or Improved in Condition" §13.4.2 at 119.)

16.5.2. DISTRIBUTION RESTRICTIONS

The fact that a product may be imported or re-imported into the U.S. does not mean that they may be distributed domestically.

Product standards vary from country to country and each is intolerant of the other's standards. A product is normally produced according to the specifications of the country in which it will be distributed. These standards may be inconsistent with those required for domestic distribution. The result is that goods which may be produced domestically for export might not be eligible for domestic distribution.

For example:

> Most heart surgery instruments and respiratory equipment require Food and Drug Administration certification in order to be distributed in the U.S. Goods manufactured for export may never have had to qualify for FDA certification. So, while these goods could be manufactured in the U.S. for export to a foreign country, they might not be eligible for domestic distribution.

Exporters/Sellers should be aware of the risk that, when they produce goods for a foreign market, they might not be able to bring them back to the United States and readily re-sell them domestically.

Importers/Buyers should be aware that just because goods purchased abroad are marked "Made in the U.S.A." it does not mean they are properly marked for, or even eligible for, distribution once re-imported into the U.S.

– Balance of page intentionally left blank –

[202] Federal Trade Commission, Complying with the Made in USA Standard, 3, https://www.ftc.gov/system/files/documents/plain-language/bus03-complying-made-usa-standard.pdf (1998).

[203] https://www.ftc.gov/sites/default/files/attachments/press-releases/ftc-staff-issues-guidelines-internet-advertising/0005dotcomstaffreport.pdf

https://www.ftc.gov/sites/default/files/attachments/press-releases/ftc-staff-revises-online-advertising-disclosure-guidelines/130312dotcomdisclosures.pdf

https://www.ftc.gov/sites/default/files/attachments/press-releases/ftc-staff-revises-online-advertising-disclosure-guidelines/130312dotcomdisclosures.pdf

[204] FTC has three (3) publications which provide guidance related to US Origin claims. Namely, an FTC Enforcement Policy, a 1998 publication entitled, "Complying with the Made in USA Standard," and FTC's "Dot Com Disclosures" updated in March 2013 and focuses on advertising and sales on the internet to address the FTC Act as it relates to mobile marketing and social networking.

[205] 15 USC §45

[206] See, Complying with the Made in USA Standard, 4 (1998)

[207] Id at 12

[208] Id.

[209] Id.

[210] These are two statements cited by FTC as express claims of the US origin of a product. FTC's Publication, "Complying with the Made in USA Standard" (1998), page 4.

[211] Id at 5. The FTC has stated that a manufacturer should not indicate, either expressly or impliedly, that a whole product line is of US origin by stating for example, "Our products are Made in USA", when only some products in the product line are made in the US according to the *all or virtually all* standard. *Id.*

[212] 62 FR 63756, 63765 (December 2, 1997).

[213] 62 FR 63756, 63765 (December 2, 1997). These are the same factors the FTC would use when evaluating the truthfulness of such a claim.

[214] FTC's Publication, "Complying with the Made in USA Standard" (1998), page 37. These terms are used in accordance with generally accepted accounting principles.

[215] FTC Advisory Opinion No. 22.

[216] Agreement Containing Consent Order to Cease and Desist, Hyde Athletic Shoes Inc., File No. 922-3236 (1996) Hyde Athletic Shoes Inc., File No. 922-3236

[217] FTC Advisory Opinions Nos. 381, 255, 315, 224.

17. OBTAINING A FIXED LEGAL OPINION

Executive Briefing

The lack of fixed opinion creates the risk of uncertainty. This risk is most critical where a change in duty or import requirements affects the viability of a transaction. This does not mean, however, that formal requests are the only means, or should be the only means you use when obtaining advice.

17.1. CUSTOMS DECISIONS

There are several ways of obtaining a written and binding opinion from Customs as to Classification, Value, Origin, Marking, Quota, or other laws enforced by the service. The types of opinions available are largely dependent upon the stage of importation at the time those opinions are sought. Although collectively and commercially referred to as rulings, there are significant differences between them.

Opinions obtained **before importation of a particular product** are called rulings. "Rulings" are binding upon all Customs ports for imports of the particular product by the particular importer from a particular supplier and cannot be changed by the government without 60 days prior notice.[218]

Opinions sought for all imports of a particular product **after importation** are referred to as "Internal Advice." An Internal Advice will be binding upon all Customs ports for all importations of the same product.[219]

Opinions sought **after liquidation of an entry on a single importation** are generally referred to as "Protests" and/or "Protest and Further Review." Protest decisions are applicable only to the entry against which they were filed. They are highly persuasive, but not binding upon other Customs ports.[220] (*See* "Protest" §20.2.1 at 198.)

Whether an importer should seek a ruling and how it should be obtained depends on the risks of not having a binding opinion that can be relied upon. Rulings are binding not just on the agency issuing them, but also on the importer. If an importer fails to follow a ruling issued to it, the failure is often viewed by the government as a fraud in the importing process which can result in substantial penalties.[221]

If a binding opinion is needed from Customs, it should be sought as early as possible. Customs will normally issue prospective rulings on classification locally[222] in 30 days. If the matter has to be pursued at Customs Headquarters, a minimum of a 120 day delay can be expected. The following considerations should be part of the evaluation as to whether a ruling is necessary.

If Customs disagrees with your position, will that disagreement prevent you from importing the goods, e.g., if there is a possibility that the goods might be held to have originated in an embargoed country?	**Obtaining a prior ruling is essential.**
If the only issues are monetary, can any downside risk be covered in the price to the end purchaser?	**Not only may it not be necessary to obtain a ruling, but the risk of a negative answer may make it undesirable to seek a ruling.**
If the viability of the product is dependent upon cost differences?	**A ruling may be a necessity even if the answer turns out to be negative.**

Ruling requests can range from very simple and inexpensive inquiries handled by a Customs Broker, or even the importer itself, to full legal presentations requiring the assistance of an attorney specializing in Customs matters. Which way is best is dependent upon the results needed.

If the importer wants or needs a binding opinion, but is not concerned with what that opinion is, so long as it can be relied upon, then a simple ruling merely identifying the details of a product or transaction and requesting Customs' opinion may be sufficient.

In most instances, where an importer wants or needs a ruling, they want a specific answer. They will want to present evidence and legal arguments to persuade Customs that a particular decision should be made. In that case, special counsel should be sought.

Worthy of a special note is a "pre-classification" program, the use of which is encouraged by Customs because the program provides a review and a binding ruling on most of an importer's product line. In practice, it is equivalent to requesting a series of individual rulings where the importer is unconcerned with the specific decision. Once the ruling is issued, the importer is required to enter its goods in accordance with the ruling, whether or not the importer agrees with Customs' determinations.

This program should not be used without first considering the consequences and determining if certain products should be excluded from the review.

17.2. OPINIONS OF OTHER GOVERNMENT AGENCIES

Most other Governments or Government Agencies do not issue prior binding opinions, although there are means by which an opinion can be obtained which can reasonably be relied upon.

---

[218] 19 C.F.R. 177.1(a)(1), 177.1(d)(1)

[219] 19 C.F.R. 177.11

[220] 19 C.F.R. Part 174 Generally

[221] 19 C.F.R. 162.43

[222] 19 C.F.R. 177.2(d)

18. IMPORT PROCESS OVERVIEW

18.1. PRE-SHIPMENT ADVISES

Pre-shipment advices are the principle sources of information used by Customs in making Cargo Release decisions.

18.1.1. 24 HOUR RULE

Known as the 24-hour rule, this advance notification law requires carriers of containerized and certain break bulk ocean freight to present information 24 hours before loading on a vessel making a call on a U.S. port.

Although known as the 24-hour rule, the time frames may be much shorter, depending upon the mode of transportation. The Trade Act of 2002 requires advance transmission of electronic cargo information to Customs for both arriving and departing cargo, which includes air and truck. For truck cargo, information must be received by Customs in its electronic systems at least one (1) hour prior to arrival.

18.1.2. IMPORTER SECURITY FILING (ISF OR 10+2)

Importer Security Filing[223] requires importers of merchandise arriving by ocean vessel to electronically submit certain advance cargo information to Customs *prior* to the importation of the cargo.

ISF importers must provide 8 data elements no later than 24 hours before the cargo is laden aboard a vessel destined to the United States. These data elements are: the name of the seller, name of buyer, importer of record number, consignee number, manufacturer, ship to party, Country of Origin, and 6-digit HTSUS number.

Just as important as the details of the cargo is information about who and where the cargo was loaded into a container. The importer, therefore, also needs to provide the details on the party who loaded the container and where they loaded it.

The carrier is responsible for providing the "+2"

As of 2014, ISF applies only to inbound cargo arriving by ocean vessel, but comparable programs are being tested for use with other modes of transportation.

> The Importer Security Filing can be filed on either the export side or import side.
>
> Unlike the basic filings under the 24-hour rule, here the Importer is directly held responsible for the:
>
> 1. Accuracy of the information,
> 2. Timeliness of the filing, and
> 3. Consistency with the subsequently filed Customs Entry.
>
> The ISF is best thought of as a pre-shipment preview of the Customs Entry. For that reason many importers prefer to have the ISF filed by the same Customs Broker who will prepare their Customs Entry.

18.1.3. SOLAS - VERIFIED GROSS WEIGHT FILINGS

The Safety of Life at Sea or SOLAS is an international treaty that requires ocean carriers to have a verified gross weight for all cargo loaded on board their vessels.

> **CAUTION**
>
> Under SOLAS, cargo without a Verified Gross Mass (VGM) statement on file will not be loaded onboard the ship.

The Verified Gross Mass or weight of a sealed container is in addition to any declaration of weight on the Bill of Lading. The SOLAS requirement to file a Verified Gross Mass (VGM) statement applies regardless of the point of origin or destination. (*See* "SOLAS Verified Gross Weight filings" §3.2 at 16.)

18.1.4. AIR CARGO ADVANCED SCREENING PROGRAM (ACAS)

The Air Cargo Advanced Screening program (ACAS) is an ISF comparable advance notice program for air shipments. During implementation it is voluntary but will ultimately become mandatory.

Unlike ISF, which provides advanced screening information only to CBP, ACAS will provide shipment details to both CBP and Transportation Security Administration (TSA).

18.1.5. OFFICE OF FOREIGN ASSET CONTROL (OFAC)

The Office of Foreign Asset Control (OFAC) prohibits financial transactions with certain persons, companies, entities, or counties.

That prohibition can relate to:

- ✓ Individuals and companies owned or controlled, or acting for or on behalf of a targeted country, and
- ✓ Individuals, groups, and entities, such as terrorists and narcotic traffickers, independent of the country.

A Consolidated Search List which covers all programs can be searched on line: As of the date of publication the URLs are as follows, but do change periodically.

- http://export.gov/ecr/eg_main_023148.asp
- http://apps.export.gov/csl-search#/csl-search

It is relatively easy to check Consolidated Search Lists for details relating to your buyer or seller prior to the time that you undertake a transaction.

> The Consolidated Search List provides a print function. You should maintain copies of both the combined search/results page as well as the detail page for any company you deem to be a potential match to the party you are checking on.

Your risk, however, may come from the status of other parties to a transaction which you may not be aware of, or, who might change during the course of a transaction.

For example:

The buyer or purchaser is acceptable, but the bank they, not you, chose to use for transfer of payments is on the list.

There are over 100 banks, and over 100 shipping and logistics companies on the Consolidated Search, many of which are not even located in a country which is sanctioned.

All of sudden, while the shipment of the goods may be permissible, the financial transaction may not be; and someone is not going to get paid.

You may never know who all the parties are, especially in the case of a Routed Shipment. (*See* Electronic Export Information and Principal Party In Interest, §3.114) but at least you have exercised due diligence.

In most cases, Best Practice would only require you to check the buyer or seller, as appropriate.

However, if you are dealing with companies or destinations that are in the general region of a country subject to sanctions, checking ALL names appearing on documents would be a better practice.

18.2. SHIPMENT ARRIVAL

The arrival of a shipment is what most importers view as the end of the importation process. Procedurally, it is more properly viewed as the beginning of the entry process.

Certain information and documentation is required in order to start the entry process. Most of the consequences associated with different methods of shipment (air, vessel, or ground) have more of a time consequence than anything else. Due to the length of vessel voyages, documentation is usually sent ahead, but it normally accompanies air shipments.[224] The lead time gained by having information and documentation prior to arrival of a shipment not only provides the possibility of some degree of pre-review and/or Customs pre-clearance, but more important, it provides an opportunity to correct errors in documentation that might be critical to importation of the shipment, such as the correct Visa. Most of the procedural distinctions associated with the different modes of transportation can, for entry purposes, be eliminated by the use of fax, email, and express mail services.

18.3. ENTRY

As the speed of trade increased, the ability to review the shipment details prior to their release decreased. Since the 1960s, when the Immediate Delivery of Cargo (CF3461) was first introduced for trucks crossing in from Canada to the United States, the process known as "making entry" was separated into a "Cargo Release" based upon limited information and a promise to follow-up with details (on what is still the CF3461), and an "Entry" declaration and admissibility review of complete shipment details (on what is still most commonly the CF7501.)

While from a legal perspective Entry involves two documents: the Entry (CF3461) and Entry Summary (CF7501), as a practical matter there are really three filings that an Importer needs to be concerned with today:

CAUTION

This separation of operations, however, means that reviews of classification, value and admissibility normally takes place upon filing of the CF7501 with full shipment particulars, and generally takes place days after the Cargo Release.

This necessarily means that all Cargo Releases are conditional pending that review.

The Importer Security Filing (ISF), which is filed prior to and is a condition for loading a cargo on board an exporting carrier destined for the United States,

1. The Customs Entry (CF 3461), which is the primary Cargo Release document which summarizes the shipment details which can be filed around the time of arrival of the cargo at the port of entry, and
2. The Entry Summary (CF7501), which provides transaction details and must be filed within 10 days after the cargo has been conditionally released.

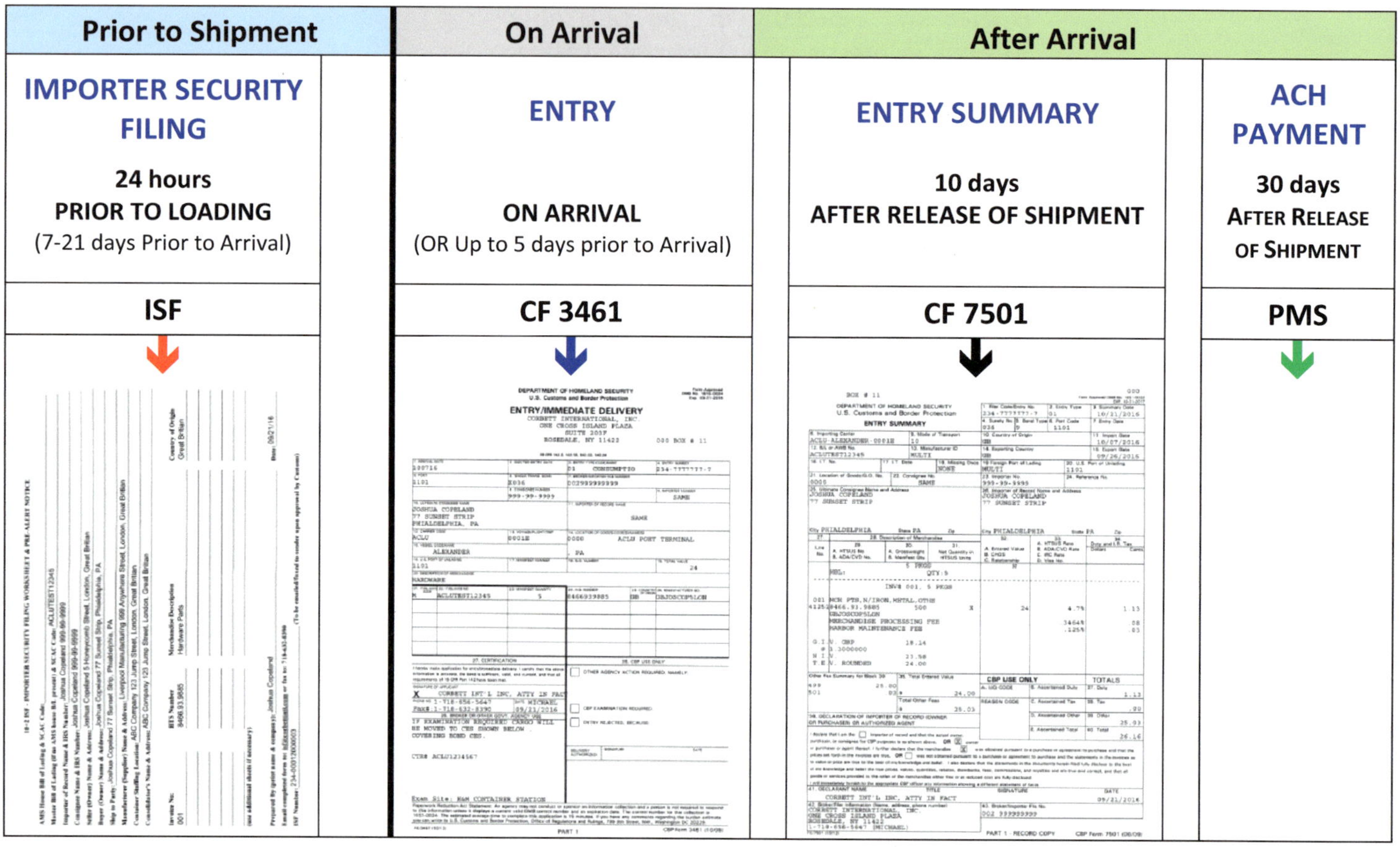

Figure 48 - Current Entry Flow

18.3.1. IMPORTER SECURITY FILING (ISF)

Customs has, for many years, required the filing of advanced information about a shipment through the Automated Manifest System. The Importer Security Filing of ISF requires additional information and requires it with greater specificity and assurances of accuracy.

> **CAUTION**
>
> Failure to timely file an accurate ISF will result in penalties of up to $5,000 per shipment along with delays.

The information is used to identify cargo which poses both a security and compliance threat.

ISF Information	CF 3461	CF7501
24 HOURS BEFORE LADING		
1. Importer of Record Number	✓	✓
2. Consignee Number	✓	✓
3. Seller (Owner) Name and Address		
4. Buyer (Owner) Name and Address	✓ Generally, the Importer of Record	✓ Generally, the Importer of Record
5. Ship to Party	✓ Generally, the Consignee	✓ Generally, the Consignee
6. Manufacturer (Supplier) Name and Address	✓ As MID	As MID
7. Country of Origin	✓	✓
8. Commodity HTS-6 digit level	✓ HTS-10 digit level	✓ HTS-10 digit level
ASAP BUT NOT LESS THAN 24 HOURS PRIOR TO ARRIVAL		
9. Container Stuffing Location		
10. Consolidator (Stuffer) Name and Address		
TO BE PROVIDED BY THE CARRIER		
1. Container stowage plan		
2. Container status		

The Customs Entry, to a large extent, re-states information filed in the Importer Security Filing (ISF) *prior to shipment*.

Any differences between the ISF, Entry (3461) and/or Entry Summary (7501) will result in additional scrutiny of the entry.

This is one reason many importers choose to have their Customs Broker, rather than the shipper or forwarder, file their ISFs.

18.3.2. ENTRY, ENTRY SUMMARY (IMMEDIATE DELIVERY ENTRY)

Today, almost all entry information and forms are filed electronically. That information is loosely divided into two groups: details which are necessary to make a determination as to the preliminary release of cargo, and details required for the assessment and collection of duties and other charges or taxes.

The Entry (CF 3461) or "Immediate Delivery Entry," under new systems referred to as a "Cargo Release," is procedurally the preferable means of making entry. As its common name indicates, it permits a preliminary release of a shipment based upon the filing of partial papers, abbreviated information, and without the assessment or payment of Customs duties or other charges. The information filed to obtain the Cargo Release is essentially a recitation of the information filed under the Importer Security Filing (ISF) prior to the cargo being loaded in the foreign port.

More complete details are then filed under the "Entry Summary" (CF 7501) within 10 days after the release of the shipment.[225] The advantages are speedier release of merchandise by Customs and improved cash flow.

The date that the payment of duty is due will depend upon which systems you use: old or new. Under Customs newest system, the Automated Commercial Environment (ACE) and under the use of Periodic Monthly Statement (PMS) Processing, the payment due date is moved from 10 days after the Cargo Release to the 15th working day of the month following the release.

> As Customs transitions to the Automated Commercial Environment (ACE) Remote Filing and the applicability of the Immediate Release privilege will more generally be applied to all goods, eliminating the last vestiges of local filing requirements.

Immediate Delivery Cargo Release is not available for all classes of goods. The Immediate Delivery procedure is a privilege which can be suspended by the importer's failure to make timely payment of duties or penalties.

Paper entries are generally used only when, for example, Customs demands to see ALL of the supporting documentation rather than relying on electronic information before releasing the goods.

In this sense, from a practical perspective, the entry is being processed as a "live entry."

18.3.3. ENTRY/ENTRY SUMMARY (LIVE ENTRY)

The Entry/Entry Summary or "live entry," requires that complete documents be filed and duty paid prior to the processing of the entry and release of the shipment.[226] While less common today, "live entry" is still required in the case of goods subject to quotas, such as certain cheeses, and when the importer has lost the immediate release privileges because they had not made timely payments to Customs in the past.

18.3.4. ENTRY PROCESSING

There have been significant changes in Customs operations over the last half century, all geared to improve service in the face of increased workloads and reduced staffing. Technology has played a large part in those changes, both in terms of back office operations as well as how it interacts with importers, exporters, Customs Brokers and other logistics providers.

Over the last 50 years, as the volume of cargo has increased and technology has improved, Customs has been constantly restructuring its operations. Customs saw the changes as purely a means of improving operations, while many others, both inside and outside of Customs, saw some of them as politically motivated. Change was nonetheless inevitable or, as expressed by William von Raab, Commissioner of Customs under President Reagan, *Automate or Perish*. It was as true for Customs as it was for the Customs Brokerage industry he was addressing.

- Customs first moved away from the physical review of every entry filed to review of only a sampling of entries as a result of an increase in the volume of imports and limitations on manpower at the ports.
- They then separated consistency of practice controls with respect to the entry of merchandise from the physical processing of the entries. This was accomplished by relocating the National Import Specialists, who were responsible for treatment consistency at a national level, from the teams that processed the entries for their product lines.
- They moved away from the filing of paper entries to the electronic filing of Paperless Entries.
- They redistributed operations by relocating them from the ports at which they were historically centralized, due to the prevalence of a particular product, entry type, or service, to other areas of the country.
- They removed the limitation of filing entries only at the port at which cargo arrived, and at which a Customs Broker was authorized to operate, to permitting remote filing from any location.
- They redistributed workloads by shifting some of the back office entry processing functions, from a purely localized activity to a distributed activity, effectively creating virtual teams.

18.3.5. AUTOMATED COMMERCIAL ENVIRONMENT (ACE)

The Automated Commercial Environment (ACE) became the official gateway for U.S. Customs as well as most other agencies involved in international Trade in mid-2016. It replaces ACS which was built on 80 column punch card design concepts rooted in the 1960's, The change is more than cosmetic in that with it comes significant operational and organizational changes. The most significant change relates to managing uniformity of practice. This time, however, rather than local teams and national specialists, there will be a series of virtual teams known as Centers of Excellence and Expertise (CEEs).

18.3.6. CENTERS FOR EXCELLENCE AND EXPERTISE[227] ("CENTERS" OR "CEES")

There are currently 10 Centers:

1. Automotive & Aerospace
2. Electronics

3. Petroleum, Natural Gas & Minerals
4. Pharmaceuticals, Health & Chemicals
5. Agriculture & Prepared Products
6. Apparel, Footwear & Textile
7. Base Metals
8. Consumer Products & Mass Merchandising (the big-box stores)
9. Industrial & Manufacturing Materials
10. Machinery

These centers are virtual organizations that perform primarily post entry functions such as validation activities, post entry amendment/post entry correction reviews, and the review of prior disclosures.

From a practical standpoint, the means of processing an Entry/ Cargo Release does not change, except that they will be internally assigned to a Center for Excellence, regardless of the port at which the goods arrive.

18.3.7. SINGLE WINDOW PORTAL

Just as significant, but less obvious, are changes affecting other federal agencies having jurisdiction over International Trade. Historically, each Agency had its own gateway for access. That not only presented a problem for importers and exporters but also a coordination problem between those agencies and the creation of a single window portal through the International Trade Data System (ITDS).[228] ACE is expected to eliminate, or at least reduce, these problems.

18.4. CONSEQUENCE OF DELAY

18.4.1. DEMURRAGE, STORAGE, PER DIEM, AND DETENTION

The liabilities associated with international freight include, not only the cost of the international freight, but also, potentially, additional costs related to storage of the cargo and use of equipment, such as Demurrage, Storage, Per Diem, and Detention.

The primary problem with respect to all of these charges, regardless of what they are called, is that while contractually both the shipper and consignee are liable to the carrier for them, more likely, only one of them is responsible for incurring the costs. A carrier may not care who they collect from, but as between buyer and seller (shipper and consignee), they do care.

> These are part of the unforeseen risk. Sellers/Exporters generally do not think past the sale and provision for payment for the goods. They view what happens after delivery as the buyer's responsibility. And they assume that practices abroad are the same as those found domestically; a reasonable supposition perhaps, but not always applicable.
>
> The less valuable the goods are to the buyer (the less they have on the line), or the more problematic the goods are in terms of local rules or restrictions, the more likely they will refuse or abandon the shipment, leaving the liabilities with the shipper.

This is where terms of sale start to make a big difference. Just because you have a contractual right or obligation, does not mean that they can be practically and economically enforced in remote jurisdictions.

So, where payment issues arise between buyer and seller, cargo may remain with the carrier for much longer than expected. As the shipper, you have some degree of control, and you might be able to recall the cargo, although you will remain liable for any charges that have already accrued. If you are using a negotiable bill of lading, control may have already passed to the buyer's bank.

More often than not, however, the delays are on the consignee's side:

1. Delay in payment to the seller,
2. Delay in payment to the carrier,
3. Customs problems on foreign entry,
4. Refusal or abandonment of the shipment, or
5. The consignee decides to make the container his new warehouse.

And all the while it is the shipper, alone, who the carrier will look to for payment.

What is covered under a charge for Demurrage, Storage, Per Diem, or Detention can vary, as between carrier agreements, in terms of when, how, and to what each excess cost applies. Unfortunately, no clarity on these distinctions has been provided by our legal system.[229 230]

As a practical matter, however, the following general descriptions apply.

"Free-Time" is generally recognized as the time allocated by a carrier within your freight agreement for the use of their resources after the cargo has been discharged from the vessel, train, truck, or aircraft, and made available for delivery.

Cargo remaining at the carrier's pier or terminal after the expiration of "Free Time" will be charged a daily fee for storage ("demurrage" at piers) until the cargo is picked up by the importer's designated trucker, or delivered to a Customs General Order Warehouse.

> It should be clear that a number of events, both within and outside of your control, can result in unanticipated expenses.
>
> You can, however, at least make sure that those things that are within your control, including having all the documents needed to make entry, are in proper order when (or preferably before) the shipment arrives.

Space at a carrier's facility is a valuable commodity and so, storage/demurrage can be expensive, almost to the point of being punitive, to encourage prompt removal of goods from the premises and can vary substantially between carriers, types of carriers, air, vessel or rail, and even between ports.

Pier/Terminal demurrage rates vary depending upon whether cargo is containerized, the size and type of container, and the length of time the cargo remains.

The additional charge on air shipments is called "Storage." Storage is usually based upon a minimum weight, plus increments for additional weight.

"Detention," or "Per Diem" both relate to excess costs for your use of resources and/or equipment such as containers and chassis, beyond the time provided for in your freight agreement(s).

18.4.2. GENERAL ORDER[231]

Due to the limited amount of space at piers and airports for storage of cargo, and the need to control un-entered freight, the time during which cargo is permitted to remain at a carrier's premises, regardless of storage or demurrage charges, is often limited. Cargo for which an entry has not been filed and which Customs has not released, will eventually be moved to a Customs General Order Warehouse, often referred to as "G.O."

The cost of storage at the Customs G.O. Warehouse, and the cost of moving the cargo there, is charged to the claimant of the goods. This storage is generally accrued on a monthly basis. While the rate is better than the rates for demurrage and storage, the costs can still be substantial. Like demurrage or storage at a carrier, these charges must be paid before the cargo is delivered.

> Twenty (20) days is an outside number. The number of days before cargo will be ordered into General Order is usually less and is based upon local conditions including, the mode of transportation, and the availability of space at the carrier's facility.

Customs regulations require a carrier to order goods into G.O. no later than 20 days after the shipment has arrived at the carrier's facility when it has not been released or an entry filed.[232]

Several other procedural problems also result from your cargo going into General Order:

- Procedurally, a Live Entry (an entry/entry summary) is required for entry of all cargo held in G.O. even if the goods would have otherwise been eligible for an Immediate Delivery Entry. This will require payment of estimated duties in advance, and release of the merchandise will take longer.
- Any freight or warehouse liens will have to be satisfied before the cargo will be released, even after entry is made and duties paid.

If delays are unavoidable or will be lengthy, a prompt evaluation should be made as to which option will involve the least expense: storage/demurrage, general order, warehouse, or FTZ.

18.5. TYPES OF ENTRY

18.5.1. CONSUMPTION ENTRY[233]

Entry for Consumption is the most common form of entry. It is used when goods are to be entered into the commerce of the United States for general consumption or sale. This procedure requires the presentation of all necessary documents in proper order and payment of estimated duties at the time of entry or within 10 days after release, depending upon how entry is made. (*See* "Entry, Entry Summary (Immediate Delivery Entry)" §18.3.2 at 163 and "Entry/Entry Summary (Live Entry)" §18.3.3 at 164.)

18.5.2. WAREHOUSE ENTRY[234]

Merchandise deposited in a Customs Bonded Warehouse through a Warehouse Entry is not subject to Customs duties until it is withdrawn from the warehouse for consumption. Upon withdrawal from the Bonded Warehouse, duty will be assessed at the rate of duty in effect on the date of withdrawal.

Warehouse entries are commonly used when the merchandise is not to be immediately shipped or consumed, or certain documents necessary for entry are missing. Warehouse entries are also commonly used to delay payment of customs duties or taxes.

18.5.3. RECONCILIATION ENTRY

There will be times when an importer does not possess all of the required information at the time of entry. This happens most often when costs are annualized and the totals not determined until after the close of the accounting year.

> Reconciliation requires both:
>
> Advanced approval from Customs to use the procedure.
>
> Advanced planning with respect to information is essential: what information will be available, when will it be available, and in what form will it be available.

Reconciliation provides a means for an importer to make a timely adjustment to a group of entries at one time rather than having to revise a series of individual entries. Adjustments are most commonly made to tariff classifications (HTS number) and values.

The ability to use Reconciliation is best thought of as a privilege in that prior approval is required for its use. It does not apply to all entry issues. Reconciliation applies to only those entries which are "flagged for Reconciliation". Entries can be flagged on a blanket basis where all entries made under a particular EIN number will automatically be flagged or on selective entries if, for example, the missing data only related to a more limited set of entries or a single project.

Reconciliation Entries must generally be filed within 21 months after the first entry summary was due. Under certain trade agreements, it is only 12 months.

18.5.4. INFORMAL ENTRY

An informal entry is a simplified entry that may be used for certain commercial shipments whose dutiable value is $2,500[235] or less.[236]

Unlike a formal entry, a Customs bond is not required, but neither may one be posted in lieu of missing documents. Liquidation of the entry is immediate.

An importer or broker can use a formal entry in lieu of an informal entry if they choose. Further, Customs has the option of requiring formal entry at any time the local District Director of Customs believes it is necessary to protect the interests of the government.[237]

18.5.5. TRANSPORTATION ENTRY[238]

While still termed an entry, the procedure called an Immediate Transportation Entry or In Transit Entry (I.T.) is primarily a device for moving a shipment from one port to another while it is still within Customs Custody (before release). Another form of Customs Entry must still be made when the shipment reaches its destination port in the United States.

Of great importance is that the date the I.T. is approved at the original port (I.T. date) may affect certain time sensitive requirements, such as the effective date of the rate of duty, which would otherwise be determined by the date Entry was made at the destination port.

An I.T. Entry can be invaluable when trying to beat a specific date, such as when import licenses are expiring, or embargoes are about to go into effect, duty rates are about to go up, or changes in Customs Regulations or procedures will go into effect on a certain date, and there is not enough time to get the shipment to its final destination. In those cases, having the goods arrive at any U.S. port before that date and, depending upon the law involved, having the goods cleared there or re-forwarded under an In Transit (I.T.) bond to the final port, may buy the needed time.

18.6. CUSTOMS BONDS

A Customs Bond must be posted in order to make formal entry of merchandise into the United States.[239] The bond serves to protect the revenue of the United States and guarantee the performance of any other requirements.

Customs bonds are not insurance. A Customs bond is actually a performance bond that protects Customs' interests and guarantees payment of duties, some penalties and liquidated damages. The importer or other principal on the bond remains fully liable for any duty, penalty or liquidated damages. If the surety that provides the bond makes any payment to Customs under a bond it has signed, the surety will look to, and sue the importer, if necessary, to recover its payment.

Customs bonds are available only from companies specifically licensed by Customs to act as a Surety. Customs bonds can be obtained directly from an agent of the surety or, more commonly, through the Customs Broker handling the Customs clearance.

The cost of the bond is based upon the amount of the bond, and the class of goods, or type of bond required. The higher the amount and/or higher the risks involved, the higher the premium will be.

There are two types of bonds:

- Single transaction bonds (STB) also known as an E-Bond under the ACE systems, covers an individual transaction or importation, and
- Continuous Bonds cover all transactions for a given Importer except certain types of additional risks, e.g. anti-dumping or countervailing duties.

Bond amounts are based upon risk. A new importer or foreign importer potentially poses a higher risk to enforcement of U.S. law as do certain products, programs and importer history; consequently, Customs may require higher bond amounts.[240]

18.6.1. SINGLE TRANSACTION BOND (STB)

A Single Transaction Bond is filed to secure a single Customs Entry, or as a supplement to any other bond. There are different formulas used to determine STB amounts, based upon the commodity.[241]

Trade sensitive merchandise and goods subject to other agency review (FDA, EPA, CPSC, BATF, FTC, and TOSCA) require STBs in an amount equal to three times the entered value of the shipment.

Non-trade sensitive merchandise requires STBs in an amount equal to the entered value of the shipment, plus all duties and taxes.

Unconditionally free goods are still subject to bond requirements, but the bond can represent as little as 10% of the entered value of the shipment.

Bond premiums are generally charged as a base fee for a minimum bond with a face value of $10,000, plus additional charges based upon the dollar value of the bond, and the class of merchandise.

Single Transaction Bonds are almost always obtained through your Customs Broker.

18.6.2. CONTINUOUS BOND

A Continuous Bond can be used in lieu of multiple Single Transaction Bonds to secure multiple transactions and becomes economical as the number of imports increase.

The amount of the bond is based upon a percentage of the previous year's duty, the importer's record of compliance, the importer's financial condition, certain port minimums, and the adequacy of the bond to protect the revenue of the U.S. The minimum face amount for a continuous bond is usually $50,000.[242]

A Single Transaction Bond may still be required for individual entries/transactions where the bond either does not cover a specific liability or the amount of the bond is inadequate to secure the revenue or security that is required for obligations not covered by the continuous bond, e.g., antidumping duties.

As the surety's exposure is based upon the volume, frequency, and value of your shipments, the surety may require a financial statement or the posting of some form of security, or both, as a precondition to issuing a continuous bond.

Customs Brokers can arrange for continuous bonds or they can be obtained through an insurance broker.

18.7. INSPECTION / EXAMINATION

All merchandise entering, exiting and even transiting the United States are examined electronically.

All shipments are subject to additional inspections by Customs or other regulatory agencies.

Shipments are inspected when physical examination of the shipment is necessary to confirm the accuracy of documentation and compliance with laws. This includes examinations looking for instances of smuggling and counterfeiting. This does not mean that all shipments will be inspected.

> One hundred percent (100%) of shipments are examined electronically although only about four percent (4%) will actually be physically inspected.
>
> Of course, it always seems as though Customs inspects 100% of your shipments and none of your competitor's.

There are essentially three different types of inspections employed:

- VACIS or Non-Intrusive Inspection (NII), which is essentially a full container X-ray.[243]

Figure 49 - Non-Intrusive Inspection

> **CAUTION**
>
> Few shippers realize that foreign to foreign couriers often use Anchorage Alaska as a way point, giving U.S. Customs authority to examine goods for potential violation of U.S. laws.
>
> This is particularly true of potential violation of U.S. Intellectual Property right including Trademarks.

- A partial examination where a random sample is selected from a shipment, usually from the tail of the shipping container.
- An intensive examination where an entire shipping container or the entire shipment will be devanned (unloaded) so that samples can be randomly selected from within the shipment.

18.8. SELECTION OF CARGO TO BE EXAMINED

The determination as to which shipments will be inspected and which type of examination will be performed is made through an automated system augmented by human judgment. This selectivity is, in large degree, based upon a past record of compliance. If an importer's past record of compliance is good, the probability of inspection is reduced. If the record is poor, or there is no record, then the shipment is more likely to be inspected. The basic factors evaluated by Customs in determining selectivity are: the importer, manufacturer, Country of Origin, classification, port, entry filer, and various other factors, not all of which Customs discloses.

Customs periodically changes the criteria used to determine which cargo will be examined. In addition, Customs also periodically targets for examination particular Harmonized Tariff numbers nationwide, irrespective of any other criteria, as part of a 'Snap Shot' program to determine a benchmark for compliance.

If more than three shipments in a row are set for examination, even though the first three were found to be in order, the importer would be well advised to look into the matter. While the additional inspection may be part of a Snap Shot program, other issues may be involved.

18.9. C-TPAT

Customs Trade Partnership Against Terrorism (C-TPAT) is a voluntary enhanced supply chain security program which offers importers a credit against the chances of their cargo being inspected in exchange for their extra vigilance in securing their supply chain. As a result of the mutual recognition of security programs with other countries, today this program also covers exporters.

Since the program is voluntary, you have a choice as to whether to participate or not. The bottom line in making the decision as to whether to participate comes down to the question: Is C-TPAT worth enough in terms of dollars and cents of profit that I should consider it? Most large importers have considered it to be of significant value. (*See* "Customs Trade Partnership Against Terrorism" §22.5.1 at 229.) The Trade Facilitation and Enforcement Act of 2015 mandates that Customs "provide trade benefits to private sector entities that meet the requirements for participation" in the program.[244] So, if you are not currently a member of C-TPAT, it is time to reconsider it.

18.10. TRUSTED TRADER

Customs Trusted Trader Program can best be thought of as C-TPAT (*See* "Customs Trade Partnership Against Terrorism" §22.5.1 at 229) and Informed Compliance on steroids in that it requires a C-TPAT level 3 certification. Most companies are only level 2. It also requires participation in the Importer Self-Assessment program which, again, generally only larger companies participate in. (*See* "Importer Self-Assessment"§22.1.6 at 215.)

The goal of the program is to enhance entry processing and reduce inspections and other reviews of those who qualify. As a practical matter, it is still in its development stage so there are no clear tangible benefits which would make it a worthwhile goal for a smaller importer.

18.11. BROKER KNOWN IMPORTER

The Broker Known Importer Program can best be thought of as Trusted Trader lite. There is much less overhead involved with participation and is, therefore, well worth the effort.

18.12. LIABILITY FOR EXPENSES

The cost of opening a shipment and/or devanning (unloading) for examination by Customs and repacking the shipment is born solely by the importer. Inspections are usually performed by appointment and may add several days delay to the release of the shipment from Customs custody. In addition to any other expenses, these delays can result in demurrage or storage charges, also borne by the importer.

18.13. DAMAGES AND LOSSES

There is generally no liability on the part of the government for loss or damage to goods during inspection, or when otherwise under Customs custody.[245] While efforts have been made to address the matter, the House Ways and Means Subcommittee on Oversight found that "Customs has little or no incentive to avoid damaging cargo during examination."[246] The Customs Modernization act of 1993 reaffirms Customs' immunity for damage to commercial goods.[247] While most inspection methods generally do not cause damage, certain procedures are, by their nature, invasive, e.g., probing bags of powder with a shaft while looking for drugs.

To a limited extent, that immunity has been waived under the Federal Tort Claim Act (FTCA). If your damages are substantial, it may be worth filing such a claim. The claim is made on form SF95 which is available on-line and generally filed at the port of entry.[248]

In addition to the normal risks of damage, loss, or theft associated with the unpacking and repacking of unsecured cartons or containers, there is at least one costly problem rarely considered. It is not uncommon to find that after inspection the cargo cannot be as efficiently repacked into the same shipping unit, which results in extra charges for local cartage of the leftovers.

Trade Trivia

How much Customs history can you find in the stamp?

The badge number, 7311789, represents the date of July, 31, 1789, on which the first Congress passed the third of three acts dealing with tariff administration which created U.S. Customs. (1 Stat. 29)

The stamped date, February 28, 2003, is that on which the U.S. Customs Service (USCS) ceased to exist when, as a result of its merger into the Department of Homeland Security, it was reborn as U.S. Customs and Border Protection (CBP).

The signature of the Customs Officer is that of the author Herman Melville who was a Customs Inspector at the port of New York in the middle of the 19th Century.

18.14. RELEASE

Release is the technical term used to indicate that U.S Customs has relinquished control over a shipment. The term under Customs Automated Commercial Environment (ACE) is more precisely "Cargo Release" which is also more descriptive of its actual function and is consistent with the historical split between the release of the cargo and the making of formal declarations and payment of duties.

Regardless of the name used, Release from Customs' Custody is what most importers view as the end of the entry process because it is usually the point at which the importer receives delivery of its shipment. It may be far from the end of the actual entry process.

Release signifies only that, as of the date of the release, based upon primarily pre-shipment advises, Customs has no basis to believe that the goods violate any law that would preclude their admission into the stream of commerce.

A more detailed review of classification or admissibility generally takes place after the submission of an Entry Summary (CF7501), which supplies additional details. This can result in, essentially, a revocation of the release.

CAUTION

ALL releases are conditional and shipments subject to a demand for redelivery if found to be inadmissible.

You need to make sure that you have ALL required releases from any other agency involved with your goods PRIOR to distributing the goods.

At any time up until the expiration of any Conditional Release period, or in the worst case, until Liquidation, Customs can reassert control over imported merchandise.

Shipments may be subject to releases by more than one agency. The release by Customs is independent of a release from any other agency. So, while Customs may have conditionally released goods for distribution, they may still be under a hold by another agency.

Customs generally reasserts control either by demanding voluntary redelivery of a shipment to Customs' Custody, or by seizing it. Neither is the outcome that the importer hoped for. Either can result in substantial delays and penalties. (*See* "Notice to Mark and/or Notice to Redeliver (CF 4647)" §19.2.3 at 185, "Seizure Notice" §19.3.2 at 190 and "Liquidated Damages" §21.2.4 at 206.)

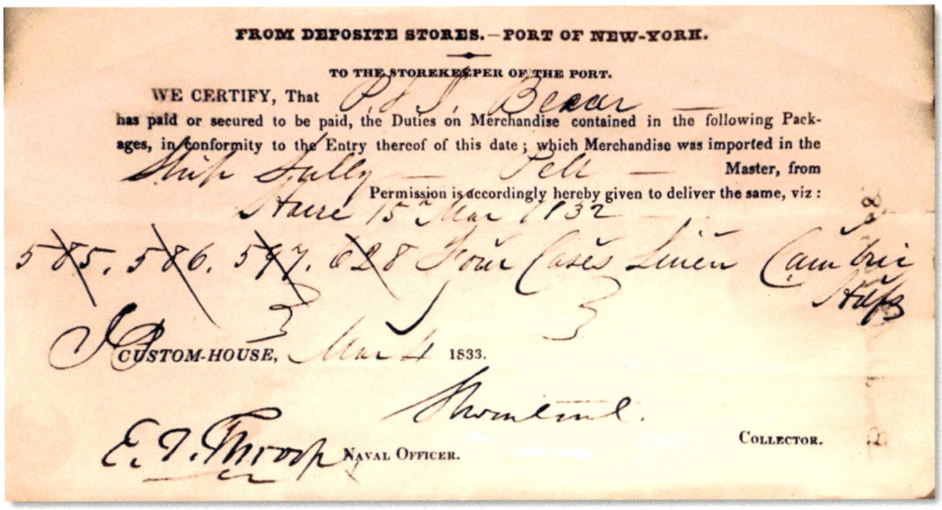
FROM DEPOSITE STORES.—PORT OF NEW-YORK.

TO THE STOREKEEPER OF THE PORT.

WE CERTIFY, That [illegible] has paid or secured to be paid, the Duties on Merchandise contained in the following Packages, in conformity to the Entry thereof of this date; which Merchandise was imported in the Ship [illegible] — [illegible] — Master, from [illegible]

Permission is accordingly hereby given to deliver the same, viz:

585. 586. 587. 628 Four Cases Linen Cambric

CUSTOM-HOUSE, [illegible] 1833.

COLLECTOR.

NAVAL OFFICER.

Figure 50 - Customs Release 1833

---

[223] 19 C.F.R. 149,3

[224] Provisions in the Customs Modernization Act of 1993, which in the future will permit acceptance of electronically communicated documents, will further diminish some of the differences due to lead time.

[225] 19 C.F.R. 142.22(a), 142.23

[226] 19 C.F.R. 142.11(a), 142.6, 142.13

[227] Trade Facilitation and Enforcement Act of 2015, Public Law No: 114-125, 130 Stat. 122 §110 (2016)

[228] Proclamation No. 10655, 79 Fed. Reg. 13659 (Feb. 25, 2014), http://www.whitehouse.gov/the-press-office/2014/02/19/executive-order-streamlining-exportimport-process-america-s-businesses

[229] The comingled nature of these terms is illustrated in the recent case, Elite Logistics Corp. v MOL Am., Inc., Case No., 2013 U.S. Dist. LEXIS 124109 (C.D. Cal. Aug. 29, 2013) *explaining at Footnote 1* that MOL charges a late return fee of the shipping containers containing the cargo as either a "detention charge" or "per diem." In the case of Mediterranean Shipping Co., (USA) Inc. v. Int'l Freight Servs., 2014 U.S. Dist. LEXIS 42075 (S.D.N.Y. 2014), where a container was returned late, e.g., beyond the "free time," the carrier charged a fee for demurrage.

[230] Demurrage has been described as detention itself, e.g., in Mediterranean Shipping Co. v. Cargo Agents, Inc. Case No., 2011 U.S. Dist. LEXIS 144981 (S.D. N.Y. Dec. 16, 2011) stating "demurrage has sometimes been described as stipulated damages for detention." It was similarly described more than 60 years ago such as in the case of The Great Atlantic & Pacific Tea Company v. United States Maritime Commission, et al., (No. 29730, February 14, 1949), wherein the court stated "[w]e have uniformly held that demurrage and storage charges are properly accrued against the shipper where the detention occurred through no fault of the carrier, and even though the shipper also was not at fault."

[231] 19 USC 1490, 19 C.F.R. Part 127

[232] 19 C.F.R. 127.10 and generally19 C.F.R. 127 subpart A

[233] 19 C.F.R. 141.0a(f)

[234] 19 C.F.R. 141.0a(g)

[235] 19 U.S.C. 1498(a)(1)(A) as amended by Public Law 103-182, 107 Stat 2057 Section 662

[236] 19 C.F.R. 143.21(a)

[237] 19 C.F.R. 143.22

[238] 19 C.F.R. 18.11

[239]19 C.F.R. 142.4

[240] Trade Facilitation and Enforcement Act of 2015, Public Law No: 114-125, 130 Stat. 122 § 115 (2016)

[241] 56 FR 12057, March 21, 1991, Customs Directive 3510-03 effective April 15, 1991

[242] 56 FR 12057, March 21, 1991, Customs Directive 3510-03 effective April 15, 1991

[243] Downloaded 06/26/2016 from : at page 3 -
https://www.dhs.gov/sites/default/files/publications/privacy_pia_cbp_nii_jan2014.pdf

[244] Trade Facilitation and Enforcement Act of 2015, Public Law No: 114-125, 130 Stat. 122 §101 (2016)

[245] Kosak v. U.S., 465 US 848, 104 S. Ct 1519 (March 21,1984)

[246] Customs Modernization & Informed Compliance Act: Hearing on H.R. 3935 Before the Subcomm. On Ways And Means On The Judiciary, 102nd Cong. 2 (Mar. 10, 1992)

[247] Public Law 103-182, 107 Stat 2057 Section 670.

[248] Federal Tort Claim Act (FTCA), 28 USC 2671 et seq.

Filing a claim against Customs, https://help.cbp.gov/app/answers/detail/a_id/178/~/tort-claims---claim-for-property-damage-or-loss,-or-personal-injury,-or-death.

Claim form SF95. Download from http://www.gsa.gov/portal/forms/download/116418.

19. POST ENTRY PROCEDURES & PROBLEMS

Executive Briefing

Post entry problems, in most cases, indicate that the risk most often created through a lack of adequate planning and a failure to adhere to Best Practices of Informed Compliance have matured from theory to reality. These risks fall into three basic categories:

Inquiry as to the details of a transaction,

Suspicion that a problem exists, or

Customs notification that a violation exists and a demand for correction.

Failure to adequately address these issues will usually result in additional duties, delays, liquidated damages or other proposed sanctions. Of greater significance, however, is that since facts pertaining to a single transaction usually raise questions regarding similar transactions, it can affect a much larger scope of business.

19.1. LIQUIDATION[249]

Executive Briefing

Why should you care about Liquidation Dates?

Sometimes you want to object to the rate or value at which your shipment was liquidated or reliquidated. The time frame within which to do this is limited and not extendable. The Liquidation date starts the clock running on the filing period.

It is equally important to know that Liquidation has not occurred, because it suggests that there are open issues of which the government is concerned, and consequently, you should be concerned.

Liquidation is the process through which Customs completes its review of an entry and finalizes its position as to duty and all other factors involved in the entry.

Customs' review will include the classification, valuation, and admissibility of the merchandise, whether required documentation or information conforms to the merchandise actually imported, as well as any questions as to the validity of any of these items. An entry can be liquidated in one of three ways:

- ✓ "As Entered" or "No Change," which means that Customs made no changes to the way the goods were declared at entry, or to the duty deposited.
- ✓ As an "Increase" which means that Customs found a basis for increasing the duty owed on a shipment. An increase can result

from a change in classification or valuation (sometimes due to the importer's failure to respond adequately to a Request for Information, or a Notice of Action). If the entry is liquidated with an increase, Customs will send the importer of record a bill for the additional duties.

✓ As a "Refund", which means that Customs found that the duty declared or paid was higher than it should have been.

U.S. Customs and Border Protection
6650 Telecom Drive, Suite 100
Indianapolis, IN 46278

PRINT DATE 06/22/2016

For Bill Inquires Please Contact the Port at (701) 241-8124 or the Revenue Division at (317) 614-4811)

BILL TO:.................................MIXED AADC 840 AA P12 &12
IMAGINARY IMPORTS 4338
1313 MOKINGBIRD LANE
BEDFORD FALLS NY 10999-12341

Importer Number:	13-XXXX567-00
Bill Number:	4XX9298765
Bill Date:	08-19-16
Port of Service/Charge:	33411 FARGO ND

Dear Sir or Madam

This Bill is a notice of debt owed to U.S. Customs and Border Protection (CBP). CBP bill for supplemental duties (increased or additional duties, taxes, and fees assessed upon the liquidation or re-liquidation of an entry) together with interest, reimbursable services, and miscellaneous amounts. The Code of Federal Regulations (19 CFR §24.1(a)(2) requires your remittance to be payable in United States dollars and drawn on a United States bank.

Transaction Date	Transaction Identification (i.e., Entry No./Work Ticket No.)	Reference Name	Type of Charge	Amount
05-26-16	0X0123457		DUTY	3210.09
			INTEREST	26.10
			FORMAL MPF	-13.10
			HMF	
			INTEREST	-4.10
			Interest Accrued to Date	0.20
			Full Amount Due Upon Receipt	3,218.99
			Amount Due After 09-17-16 (including interest)	3330.19

Specimen
Not to Scale
Representative Data

Note: Failure to make payment or provide legal justification of non-payment may result in suspension of immediate Release privileges with 19 CFR §142.26

Sanction Status: ____________ Surety Code 93X

Interest rate Effective 04-01-16 4.00 %

For more information visit cbp.gov/xp/cgov/trade/priority_trade/revenue/ CBP Form 6084 (07/11)

PAYER'S COPY

PRINT DATE 08/22/2016

Enclose this portion with remittance

Bill To: **IMAGINARY IMPORTS**
1313 MOKINGBIRD LANE
BEDFORD FALLS NY 10999-12341

Bil Number: 4XX9298765

Amount Enclosed: ____________

U.S. Customs and Border Protection
P.O. Box 530071
Atlanta, GA 330353-0071

01317270312347168937460819160000432I4168

CBP Form 6084 (07/11)

Figure 51 - Increase Duty Bill

An entry can be liquidated by Customs' action or inaction.

19.1.1. NOTICE AS TO THE LIQUIDATION DATE

The official notice of Liquidation is the Liquidation Bulletin posted or made available at Customhouses.[250]

An invoice or statement of refund will be sent by mail in the case of an "Increase" or "Refund, and their issuance date is normally the Liquidation Date.

No notice is sent with respect to the vast majority of entries, which are liquidated "As Entered" or "No Change"

The Importer is responsible for monitoring its liquidations.

A list of entries and liquidation dates can be extracted from the Automated Commercial Environment (ACE) either yourself, if you have signed up for an account, or through your Customs Broker.

> **It is good practice to periodically make a request from either Customs or your surety for all entries filed under your EIN and their date of liquidation.**
>
> **Since you only have 180 days to file Protests, consider requesting the list once per quarter to determine if an entry has been liquidated.**
>
> **If you have access to the Customs Automated Commercial System (ACE) you already have access to this information.**
>
> **This is also a good way of checking for potential Identity Theft as well as seeing if other Customs Brokers have been signing your name to Customs Entries (*See* "Best Practices" §22 at 211 and "Free From the Authors" §23 at 241.)**

19.1.2. NOT LIQUIDATED

An entry might not be liquidated because the liquidation has been extended either by your choice in using Reconciliation or because Customs deemed that there were open issues. This is very common when there are related cases before the International Trade Commission or other suspensions.

If an entry is not liquidated by Customs' action and no notice of suspension or extension of liquidation has been sent by U.S. Customs to the importer, the entry will be "Deemed Liquidated" By Operation of Law.

Because formal notices of suspension are not provided, it can be difficult to know, without investigation, whether an entry is liquidated by Operation of Law, or suspended.

19.1.3. LIQUIDATION BY OPERATION OF LAW

Most entries liquidate through Custom's inaction by virtue of Operation of Law, also known as "Deemed Liquidated". If an entry is not liquidated by Customs' action and no notice of suspension or extension of liquidation has been sent by U.S. Customs to the importer, the entry will be deemed liquidated by Operation of Law through Customs' inaction within one (1) year from the date of entry or reconciliation.[251]

When liquidated by Operation of Law, it is deemed accepted as entered and is therefore treated the same as a "No Change," "As Entered" liquidation. [252]

No notice is given of this, the most common type of liquidation.

A "No Change" liquidation only means that Customs does not see a reason for change; it doesn't mean that Customs agrees with the way you declared the goods.

19.1.4. LIQUIDATION BY AFFIRMATIVE ACTION

Those liquidations, which are by affirmative action on Customs part, normally result in a change in the entry and result in either an Increase or Refund.

When Customs liquidates an entry by reviewing the entry, official notice of liquidation as No Change, Increase, or Refund, will appear in a "Liquidation Bulletin," and generally, an unofficial "Courtesy Notice" mailed to the importer of record, or the Customs Broker, if so directed.

19.1.5. NOTICE OF THE DATE OF LIQUIDATION

Claims against duty assessments under either an "increase" liquidation or "No Change" liquidation are triggered by the date of liquidation.

It is solely the importer's obligation to request liquidation information.

The government does not issue any formal notice for "No Change" liquidations.

The government will generally issue a courtesy notice as to the suspension of liquidation, which means that they are keeping the file open.

It is the importer's responsibility to monitor its liquidations. Tracking liquidation is important for several reasons, most of which are frequently ignored by importers.

First, unless fraud is involved, liquidation sets forth a final and maximum duty liability on an entry. (Essentially, it clears Customs' file).

Second, the date of liquidation offers a narrow window of 180 days within which to file a Protest against the way in which the entry was liquidated. This time frame cannot be extended.

Finally, if there is no liquidation of one or more entries, it may indicate the existence of major issues affecting a product, class of products, or the particular importer involved.

19.2. NOTICES REQUIRING PROMPT ACTION

19.2.1. REQUEST FOR INFORMATION (CF 28) [253]

A "Request for Information" is the beginning of a process which will affect the immediate entry, and is likely to affect future entries as well.

In order for Customs to determine the correct classification and value of imported goods, or compliance with other requirements, certain information is required. Ordinarily, this information should be available from the commercial invoice and other documents presented at the time of entry. However, Customs may find that the information is incomplete, inaccurate, or insufficient. Customs may then issue a Request For Information, Customs Form

28, to obtain additional information, clarification of existing information, financial information, documentation, product literature, or samples of the imported product. The questions preprinted on the Request For Information are consistent with the information required to determine valuation, classification, marking, and admissibility.

- Continued on next page -

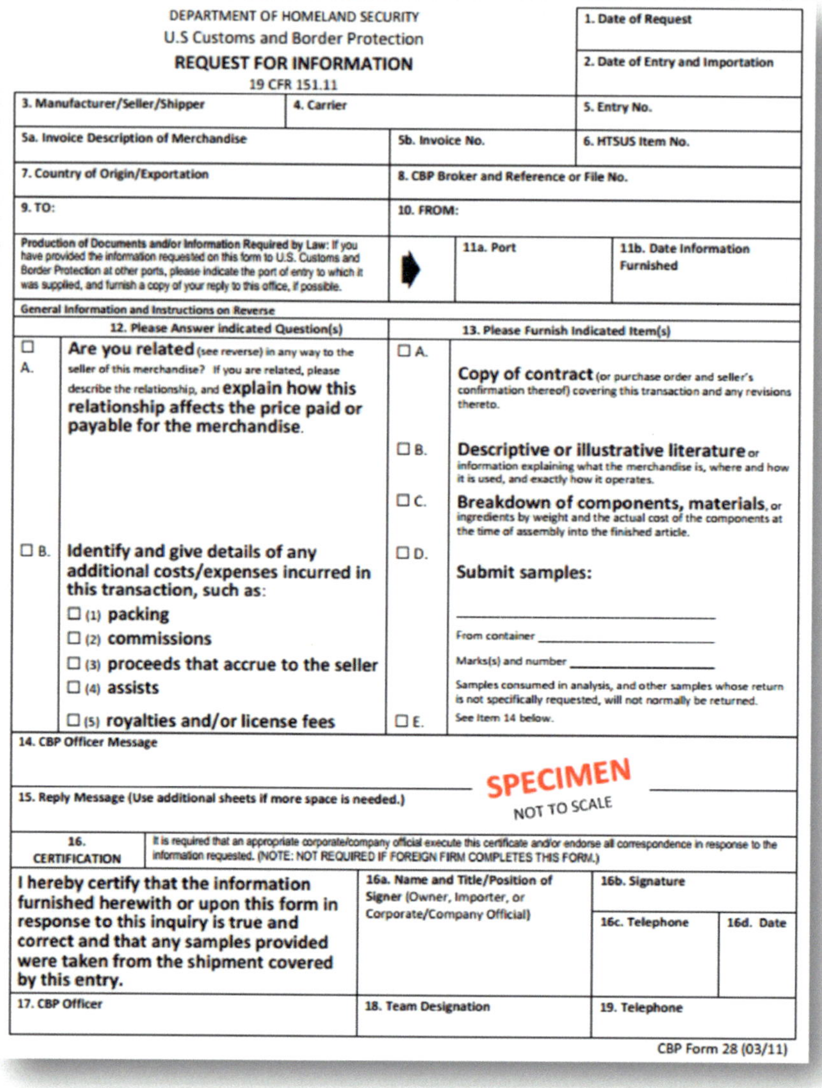

DEPARTMENT OF HOMELAND SECURITY
U.S Customs and Border Protection
REQUEST FOR INFORMATION
19 CFR 151.11

1. Date of Request
2. Date of Entry and Importation
3. Manufacturer/Seller/Shipper
4. Carrier
5. Entry No.
5a. Invoice Description of Merchandise
5b. Invoice No.
6. HTSUS Item No.
7. Country of Origin/Exportation
8. CBP Broker and Reference or File No.
9. TO:
10. FROM:

Production of Documents and/or Information Required by Law: If you have provided the information requested on this form to U.S. Customs and Border Protection at other ports, please indicate the port of entry to which it was supplied, and furnish a copy of your reply to this office, if possible.

11a. Port
11b. Date Information Furnished

General Information and Instructions on Reverse

12. Please Answer Indicated Question(s)

☐ A. **Are you related** (see reverse) in any way to the seller of this merchandise? If you are related, please describe the relationship, and **explain how this relationship affects the price paid or payable for the merchandise.**

☐ B. **Identify and give details of any additional costs/expenses incurred in this transaction, such as:**
☐ (1) **packing**
☐ (2) **commissions**
☐ (3) **proceeds that accrue to the seller**
☐ (4) **assists**
☐ (5) **royalties and/or license fees**

13. Please Furnish Indicated Item(s)

☐ A. **Copy of contract** (or purchase order and seller's confirmation thereof) covering this transaction and any revisions thereto.

☐ B. **Descriptive or illustrative literature** or information explaining what the merchandise is, where and how it is used, and exactly how it operates.

☐ C. **Breakdown of components, materials**, or ingredients by weight and the actual cost of the components at the time of assembly into the finished article.

☐ D. **Submit samples:**
From container ______
Marks(s) and number ______
Samples consumed in analysis, and other samples whose return is not specifically requested, will not normally be returned.

☐ E. See Item 14 below.

14. CBP Officer Message

15. Reply Message (Use additional sheets if more space is needed.)

SPECIMEN
NOT TO SCALE

16. CERTIFICATION
It is required that an appropriate corporate/company official execute this certificate and/or endorse all correspondence in response to the information requested. (NOTE: NOT REQUIRED IF FOREIGN FIRM COMPLETES THIS FORM.)

I hereby certify that the information furnished herewith or upon this form in response to this inquiry is true and correct and that any samples provided were taken from the shipment covered by this entry.

16a. Name and Title/Position of Signer (Owner, Importer, or Corporate/Company Official)
16b. Signature
16c. Telephone
16d. Date
17. CBP Officer
18. Team Designation
19. Telephone

CBP Form 28 (03/11)

Figure 52 - Request for Information –CF28

The issuance of a CF 28 usually indicates that Customs lacks sufficient information upon which to form an opinion as to classification and/or value, or that it may have an opinion, but does not yet have sufficient documentation to act.

> A request usually relates to a single entry, but the importer's response will affect all shipments of the goods at issue. It may also affect an entire class of merchandise, or even the way that the importer itself does business. As a consequence, the response to any Request for Information should be taken seriously, even if it relates to a shipment of minimal value.

Responding to a Request for Information requires more than just responding to simple questions and providing requested documentation.

Prior to responding, an importer needs to make sure that he not only understands the questions, but also that he understands why the questions are being asked, and what might be the effect of the answer on Customs subsequent actions.

This does not mean that a lawyer is necessarily required in order to prepare a response to a Request for Information, but it does mean that care must to be taken in deciding how to respond, and who should respond to the request.

> **CAUTION**
>
> Responding to a CF28 should not be relegated to a clerical function because the response could affect other imports.

A CF 28 should be viewed not just in terms of its down side risk, but also as an opportunity to present a case for the best treatment.

A Request for Information must be responded to within 30 days from the date of its issuance. This is 30 days from the date that appears on the notice, not from the date it was postmarked or received. If it is not possible to respond within 30 days, an extension of time can usually be obtained from the Customs officer who issued the request. Any request for an extension should be followed up in writing so that Customs' file will evidence the extension, otherwise the importer runs the risk that Customs will process the entry as though no response was filed.

If a Request for Information is not responded to, Customs normally presumes the least favorable interpretation of the facts, which usually results in an increase in duty or value.

19.2.2. NOTICE OF ACTION (CF 29)[254]

A "Notice of Action" is Customs' pronouncement of its intentions to change the way in which the current, and possibly future entries will be treated.

U.S. Customs is required to send an importer a written notice of its intention to change a classification or increase a duty assessment more than $25.00 over that asserted by the importer at the time of entry. This document is called a Notice of Action, Customs Form 29. The Notice will indicate either that Customs has already taken the action or that it proposes to act.

ACTION TAKEN

If the Notice indicates ACTION TAKEN, then the issue of increased duties can only be addressed through a Protest or 520 claim after liquidation of the entry.

ACTION PROPOSED

If the notice indicates ACTION PROPOSED, then the importer is afforded a 20-day window within which to convince Customs that the increase or change in classification is unwarranted. If the importer does not respond to the proposed Notice of Action, the entry will be promptly liquidated with the increase as proposed.

DEPARTMENT OF HOMELAND SECURITY
U.S. Customs and Border Protection

NOTICE OF ACTION
19 CFR 152.2

This is NOT a Notice of Liquidation			1. DATE OF THIS REQUEST
2. CARRIER	3. DATE OF IMPORTATION	4. DATE OF ENTRY	5. ENTRY NO.
6. MFR/SELLER/SHIPPER	7. COUNTRY	8. CBP BROKER AND FILE NO.	
9. DESCRIPTION OF MERCHANDISE			
10. TO:		11. FROM	

12. THE FOLLOWING ACTION, WHICH WILL RESULT IN AN INCREASE IN DUTIES,--

☐ IS PROPOSED — IF YOU DISAGREE WITH THIS PROPOSED ACTION, PLEASE FURNISH YOUR REASON IN WRITING TO THIS OFFICE WITHIN 20 DAYS FROM THE DATE OF THIS NOTICE. AFTER 20 DAYS THE ENTRY WILL BE LIQUIDATED AS PROPOSED.

☐ HAS BEEN TAKEN — THE ENTRY IS IN THE LIQUIDATION PROCESS AND IS NOT AVAILABLE FOR REVIEW IN THIS OFFICE.

TYPE OF ACTION
A. ☐ RATE ADVANCE
B. ☐ VALUE ADVANCE
C. ☐ EXCESS ☐ WEIGHT ☐ QUANTITY
D. ☐ OTHER (See below)

13. EXPLANATION (REFER TO ACTION LETTER DESIGNATIONS ABOVE)

SPECIMEN
NOT TO SCALE

14. CBP OFFICER (PRINT OR TYPE)	15. TEAM DESIGNATION	16. TELEPHONE NO.

CBP FORM 29 (20/12)

Figure 53 - Customs Notice of Action – CF29

An importer should, at minimum, presume that if Customs has announced their intention to change the classification, value, or admissibility, and the decision is not reversed with respect to the entry at hand, the same change will be applied to all unliquidated entries as well as all future entries of the same goods.

> A response or non-response to a Notice of Action (CF29), like a Request for Information (CF 28), can have a long term effect on more than just an individual entry.

19.2.3. NOTICE TO MARK AND/OR NOTICE TO REDELIVER (CF 4647)[255]

Notices to Mark and/or Redeliver are demands for the return of goods to Customs. It may affect the ability to distribute the shipment, and the failure to comply with the demand *will* result in liquidated damages.

U.S. Customs has the authority to demand the redelivery to its custody of any imported merchandise that has been released, but subsequently found not to be admissible into the commerce of the United States.

The demand for redelivery can be the result of a violation of the Customs laws **or of any of the other laws that Customs enforces.**

> Even if Customs can no longer demand redelivery of goods for improper marking, it does not mean you are home free.
>
> You might still be liable for an additional "Marking Duty" of 10%.
>
> If a problem is discovered in one shipment, it is important to determine whether similar problems exist in any other shipment.

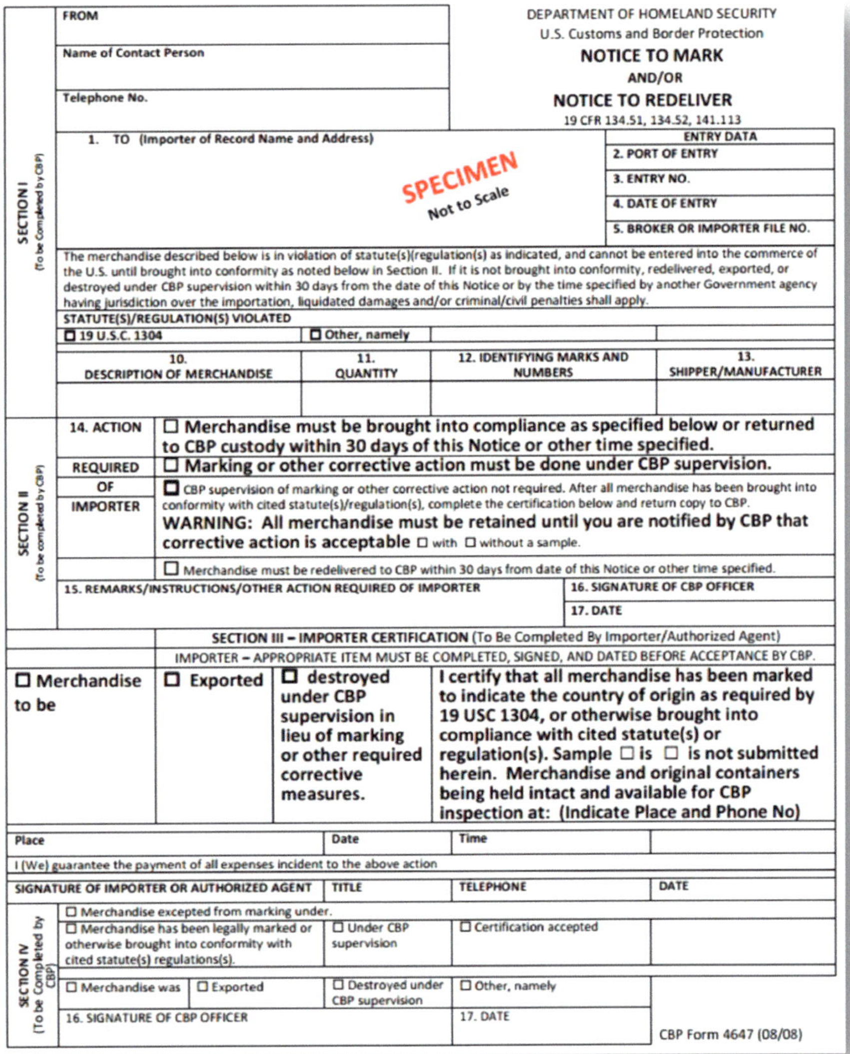

FROM

Name of Contact Person

Telephone No.

DEPARTMENT OF HOMELAND SECURITY
U.S. Customs and Border Protection
NOTICE TO MARK
AND/OR
NOTICE TO REDELIVER
19 CFR 134.51, 134.52, 141.113

SECTION I (To be Completed by CBP)

1. TO (Importer of Record Name and Address)

SPECIMEN
Not to Scale

ENTRY DATA
2. PORT OF ENTRY
3. ENTRY NO.
4. DATE OF ENTRY
5. BROKER OR IMPORTER FILE NO.

The merchandise described below is in violation of statute(s)(regulation(s) as indicated, and cannot be entered into the commerce of the U.S. until brought into conformity as noted below in Section II. If it is not brought into conformity, redelivered, exported, or destroyed under CBP supervision within 30 days from the date of this Notice or by the time specified by another Government agency having jurisdiction over the importation, liquidated damages and/or criminal/civil penalties shall apply.

STATUTE(S)/REGULATION(S) VIOLATED
☐ 19 U.S.C. 1304 ☐ Other, namely

10. DESCRIPTION OF MERCHANDISE	11. QUANTITY	12. IDENTIFYING MARKS AND NUMBERS	13. SHIPPER/MANUFACTURER

SECTION II (To be completed by CBP)

14. ACTION REQUIRED OF IMPORTER
☐ **Merchandise must be brought into compliance as specified below or returned to CBP custody within 30 days of this Notice or other time specified.**
☐ **Marking or other corrective action must be done under CBP supervision.**
☐ CBP supervision of marking or other corrective action not required. After all merchandise has been brought into conformity with cited statute(s)/regulation(s), complete the certification below and return copy to CBP. **WARNING: All merchandise must be retained until you are notified by CBP that corrective action is acceptable** ☐ with ☐ without a sample.
☐ Merchandise must be redelivered to CBP within 30 days from date of this Notice or other time specified.

15. REMARKS/INSTRUCTIONS/OTHER ACTION REQUIRED OF IMPORTER
16. SIGNATURE OF CBP OFFICER
17. DATE

SECTION III – IMPORTER CERTIFICATION (To Be Completed By Importer/Authorized Agent)
IMPORTER – APPROPRIATE ITEM MUST BE COMPLETED, SIGNED, AND DATED BEFORE ACCEPTANCE BY CBP.

☐ Merchandise to be	☐ Exported	☐ destroyed under CBP supervision in lieu of marking or other required corrective measures.	I certify that all merchandise has been marked to indicate the country of origin as required by 19 USC 1304, or otherwise brought into compliance with cited statute(s) or regulation(s). Sample ☐ is ☐ is not submitted herein. Merchandise and original containers being held intact and available for CBP inspection at: (Indicate Place and Phone No)

Place	Date	Time	
I (We) guarantee the payment of all expenses incident to the above action			
SIGNATURE OF IMPORTER OR AUTHORIZED AGENT	TITLE	TELEPHONE	DATE

SECTION IV (To be Completed by CBP)

☐ Merchandise excepted from marking under.
☐ Merchandise has been legally marked or otherwise brought into conformity with cited statute(s) regulations(s). ☐ Under CBP supervision ☐ Certification accepted
☐ Merchandise was ☐ Exported ☐ Destroyed under CBP supervision ☐ Other, namely
16. SIGNATURE OF CBP OFFICER 17. DATE

CBP Form 4647 (08/08)

Figure 54 - Customs Notice to Mark and/or Notice to Redeliver - CF 4647

How long Customs has to demand return of a shipment to their Custody varies depending upon the law involved.

- If a shipment is found to violate only the Customs Country of Origin marking requirements, return may be demanded only up to 30 days after release of the shipment or examination of a sample.

U.S. Customs has gradually expanded this 30-day time limit to 90 days when a sample is requested to determine that the marking is correct[256] and180 days when there is a question as to the origin of textiles and wearing apparel.[257]

- For violation of any other law, Customs can demand redelivery until the end of the conditional release period which, in some cases could be as much as one year after release of the shipment. (*See* "Release" - Conditional Release §18.14 at 174.)

Most demands for redelivery involve violations that can be cured. In those cases, curing the defect within the 30 days provided for in the notice will not only permit cancellation of the demand, but will also avoid a penalty.

- In the case of a marking violation, this means correcting the marking and giving Customs the opportunity to re-inspect and re-release the shipment.
- In the case of *prohibited* merchandise, such as unsafe foods, endangered species, drugs, or embargoed products of certain countries, e.g. Cuba, no cure is possible. Actual physical redelivery into Customs Custody is not necessary in most instances. However, at least re-export or destruction under Customs Supervision will be required.

Failing to comply with a Notice of Redelivery will result in the institution of a case for liquidated damages up to the value of the entry bond. (*See* "Penalties & Liquidated Damages" §21 at 203.)

The importer has the right to petition for mitigation of the Customs' assessment, but mitigation is highly dependent on the nature of the violation giving rise to the demand, the particular facts, and the importer's history of prior violations.

✓ Because of time pressures, importers have been known to sign off on a Notice to Mark or Redeliver, thereby signifying that the goods have been remarked, ***before the marking is complete***. Customs has been known to appear at the importer's premises for inspection of the shipment within hours after the certification of remarking is filed. If the shipment is not present or not marked, the shipment may be seized and/or a penalty case initiated for falsely declaring that re-marking has been completed. (*See* "Fraud (19 U.S.C. 1592)" § 21.2.2 at 204.)

19.2.4. NOTICE OF DETENTION [258]

When questions arise as to the admissibility of goods into the United States, Customs has the authority to detain a shipment until satisfied as to its admissibility.

1100 Raymond Boulevard
Newark, NJ 07102

U.S. Customs and Border Protection

2009

ZYX Distributing
1313 Round Road
Somewhere, NY 11434

Dear Sir or Madam:

Pursuant to Customs Regulation 151.16(c) and 19 USC 1499, the following shipment is detained in order to determine admissibility.

DETENTION ENTRY NO.: XXX-00123456

MANUFACTURER: XYZ MAMUFACTURING CO. LTD.

MERCHANDISE: SHOES

QUANTITY: Cartons

TESTS OR INQUIRES TO BE CONDUCTED: Review

ANTICIPATED LENGTH OF DETENTION: 30 days

SPECIMEN
Information altered for Confidentiality

If you have any questions or concerns, please contact John team 602 at (973) 368-

Sincerely,

Louis
Supervisory Import Specialist

CC: Customs Brokers, INC.

Shipments may be detained for up to 30 days, unless statutory authority or interagency mandates a longer period of time is required, or the importer/broker requests a longer detention period through the port director.

Figure 55 - Customs Notice of Detention

As a practical matter, detention is best thought of as a temporary seizure. During the period of detention, an importer who acts promptly has the opportunity to resolve any issues as to admissibility, avoiding the detention maturing into a rejection or seizure.

Formal Notice of detention must be given within 5 days, but most importers will know about the detention long before that through their Customs Broker. While Customs must render a decision within 30 days after detention, its inaction is treated as a rejection.

19.3. NOTICES REQUIRING IMMEDIATE ATTENTION

In order to determine what, for a particular importer, will constitute compliance with the laws enforced by U.S. Customs, Customs first needs to have an understanding of the nature and scope of the importer's business and how it operates. Written Requests for Information (CF 28s) generally seek information with respect to individual shipments or entries. Focused Assessments and/or Audits, on the other hand, seek to examine all import activities initially through sampling.

19.3.1. FOCUSED ASSESSMENTS AND AUDITS

In order to determine compliance, Customs has shifted its emphasis from evaluating entries to auditing an importer's books and records.

Books and records include, in addition to those records maintained by the importer, records maintained by a third party record keeper, such as a Customs Broker. (*See* "Importer's Responsibilities & Liabilities" §4 at 19.)

The incidence of audits has increased substantially over the last several years. An audit can be triggered by the appearance of a problem with the importer, exporter or supplier. Audits can also be scheduled on a random basis. For many long time importers or larger importers, the question is not whether there will be an audit as much as when there will be an audit.

An audit by U.S. Customs deserves no less attention than does an audit by the I.R.S.

An importer facing an audit must deal with several realities:

- ✓ As with the IRS, standard commercial practices may have far reaching implications that were not foreseen, and all too often, importers are unaware of the Customs implications of their business practices.
- ✓ It is unlikely that a business will know, or be in compliance with, every rule and regulation.
- ✓ No one's records are perfect,

> While procedurally there is a distinction between a Focused Assessment and an Audit in terms of their scope and consequences, from a practical standpoint, they are both what a business would term an Audit.

> Customs expects a 99% compliance rate. Even if you are confident that your records are all in order from a business standpoint, are you 99% sure that they are complete for Customs purposes AND that they show you are substantively in compliance with ALL of the Customs Laws?
>
> A pre-audit assessment by your trade counsel is really the only way to know what you are getting into, how to prepare for it, and what preemptive options are available to you.

> **CAUTION**
>
> Some importers have been heard to say that they can handle these matters themselves, without professional and adequate preparation.
>
> Those who are inclined to think so should consider whether their response would be the same if the IRS, wanted to come in and *"just ask some questions about how you do business"* or *"just take a look at books and records."*

or, at least, so the auditor believes.

Problems found as a result of an audit can result in additional liability for duties, penalties or even criminal sanctions. Because the audit commonly covers a period of more than one year, the risks can be enormous.

Effective preparation for an audit or even for an official visit from Customs involves identifying potential problems before the government does, so that the risks can be evaluated and decisions made as to how to approach them. If the importer finds a problem before the government does, there are provisions under the law which may enable an importer to address the problem, or at least mitigate the consequences. However, certain options to mitigate a potential problem, such as a Voluntary Disclosure, exist only if undertaken as a preemptive strike, and are foreclosed once Customs begins to investigate the problem. (*See* "Voluntary Prior Disclosure - The Preemptive Strike" §21.2.1 at 204.)

CAUTION

It is not uncommon to discover potential problems during preparation for a Focused Assessment or Audit.

If issues are suspected, you may need to consider a Prior Disclosure and/or assistance from Counsel.

For some importers facing a focused assessment, there may be a silver lining. In many instances, the internal examination conducted in preparation for an audit may not only permit correction or mitigation of a problem, but may also identify cost saving opportunities that had not previously been recognized.

Periodic internal audits can be an important part, not just of risk management, but opportunity management as well. (*See* "Establishing the Informed Compliance Program" §22.1.8 at 216 and "The Spiral Implementation Approach"§22.1.9 at 217.)

- Balance of page intentionally left blank -

19.3.2. SEIZURE NOTICE

Seizure amounts to the arrest of a shipment. Seizures are normally authorized by the government when some paramount risk would result if the shipment was not seized. Unfortunately, the determination as to what constitutes paramount risk is made by the enforcing agency and can be as minimal as a risk that Customs will not otherwise be able to collect a penalty.[259] Moreover, expanded authority permits seizure for violation of any import law enforced by U.S. Customs without consideration of risk, or how slight the default may be.[260]

6747 Engle Road
Middleburg Heights, OH 44130

March 16, 2014

U.S. Customs and
Border Protection

NOTICE OF SEIZURE AND INFORMATION TO CLAIMANTS FORM AF

SPECIMEN
Information Altered
for Confidentiality

New Port, NY 10063

Re: Port of Cleveland Case Number 2014-4003-100281

Dear Sir/Madam:

This is to officially notify you that U.S. Customs and Border Protection (CBP) seized the property described below at Indianapolis, IN, on March 14, 2014, as bearing counterfeits of the registered U.S. trademark:

50 counterfeit branded watches.

Description of Trademark: Word Mark
U.S. Customs Recordation Number: TMK 05-09728
U.S. Patent & Trademark Office Registration Number: 1491924

The appraised domestic value of the property is $20,000.00.

The property was seized and is subject to forfeiture in accordance with 19 CFR § 133.21, Customs Regulations (Title 19, Code of Federal Regulations), implementing Section 526 of the Tariff Act, as amended, Title 19, United States Code, Section 526 (19 U.S.C. § 1526(e)), articles bearing counterfeit trademarks are subject to seizure and forfeiture.

The facts available to CBP indicate that you might have an interest in the seized property. The purpose of this letter is to advise you of the options available to you concerning this seizure. An important document is enclosed with this letter. Please do not ignore it. This document is the "Election of Proceedings" form. You should choose one of the options outlined below, indicate your choice on the "Election of Proceedings" form, and return it and any other necessary documents to CBP within the allotted time frame. Even if you are abandoning the property, you should complete the "Election of Proceedings" form and return it to CBP.

Your options are as follows:

Figure 56 - Customs Seizure Notice

In substance, Seizure Notices haven't really changed that much.

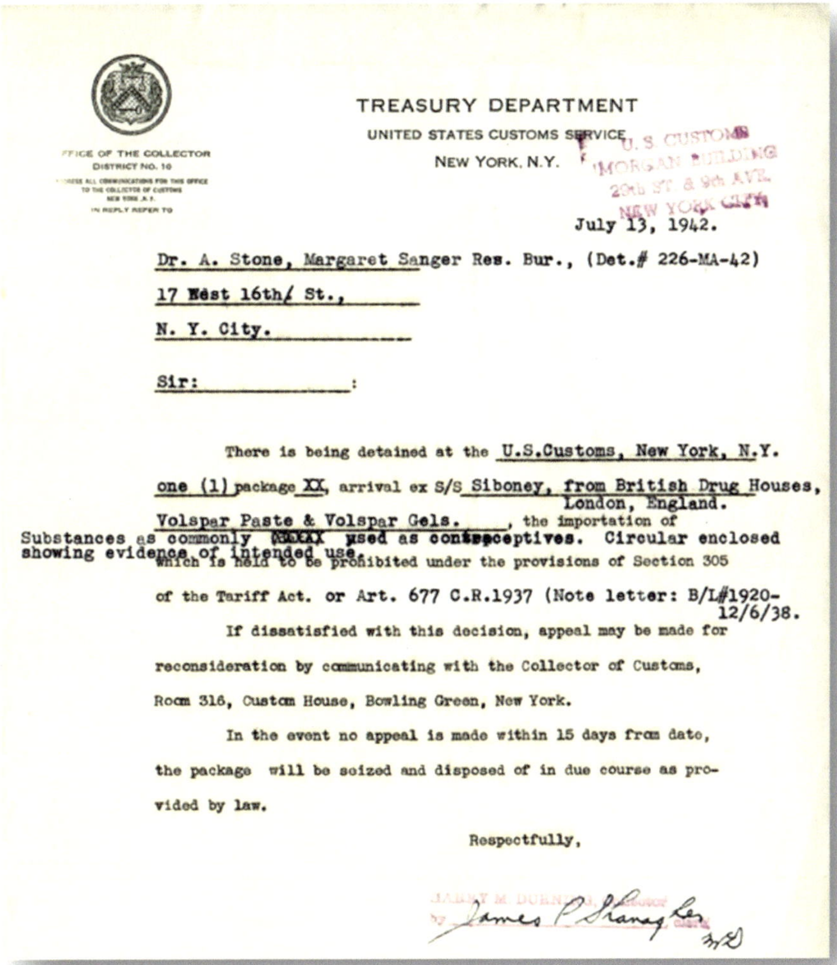

TREASURY DEPARTMENT

UNITED STATES CUSTOMS SERVICE

NEW YORK, N.Y.

U.S. CUSTOMS
MORGAN BUILDING
29th ST. & 9th AVE.
NEW YORK CITY

OFFICE OF THE COLLECTOR
DISTRICT NO. 10

IN REPLY REFER TO

July 13, 1942.

Dr. A. Stone, Margaret Sanger Res. Bur., (Det.# 226-MA-42)

17 West 16th St.,

N. Y. City.

Sir:

There is being detained at the U.S.Customs, New York, N.Y. one (1) package XX, arrival ex S/S Siboney, from British Drug Houses, London, England. Volspar Paste & Volspar Gels. , the importation of Substances as commonly XXXXX used as contraceptives. Circular enclosed showing evidence of intended use. which is held to be prohibited under the provisions of Section 305 of the Tariff Act. or Art. 677 C.R.1937 (Note letter: B/L#1920-12/6/38.

If dissatisfied with this decision, appeal may be made for reconsideration by communicating with the Collector of Customs, Room 316, Custom House, Bowling Green, New York.

In the event no appeal is made within 15 days from date, the package will be seized and disposed of in due course as provided by law.

Respectfully,

James P. Shanagher

Figure 57 - Customs Seizure Notice circa 1942

Whenever Customs seizes property, it is required to promptly issue a Notice of Seizure to all persons known to have an interest in the property. In most instances, the importer of record or the ultimate consignee identified in the Customs' entry are the only parties notified. The seizure notice must identify the merchandise seized, the date of the seizure, the basis for the seizure, and the laws allegedly violated. As a practical matter, Customs' description of the basis for the seizure provides no more than a statutory citation. Consequently, one of the first tasks after seizure is to identify the real nature of the problem. The importer must respond to the seizure notice within twenty (20) days. The claimant, usually the importer of record, has options to have the matter handled administratively or to have the matter referred to a U.S. Attorney, forcing the government to immediately move for forfeiture in a U.S. District Court.

The importer may petition both for the remission of the

forfeiture and for early release of the seized goods. Early release may be available after any violations are cured and after deposit of an amount sufficient to secure any penalties: in other words, bail for the shipment. If the shipment is to be granted early release, it is in part in consideration of execution of an agreement holding the government harmless for its action, even if it is found to have made an unwarranted seizure.

Seizures are relatively rare compared to the number of imports and penalty cases, but the impact of a seizure is sizeable.

19.3.3. ADMINISTRATIVE SUMMONS

Requests for Information (CF 28), Focused Assessments and Audits are administrative tools generally used to determine compliance with Customs and related laws as well as to determine revenue loses.

The Administrative Summons is the investigator's tool. Its issuance is usually a warning of things to come.

> **CAUTION**
>
> The issuance of an Administrative Summons suggests that Customs perceives there to be a significant problem.
>
> While this is a Civil summons, there is no guarantee that the problem will remain Civil.

An Administrative Summons is not a subpoena or a search warrant. It is a formal request, usually for a large quantity of documents, although it can call for the appearance of an individual for questioning. An Administrative Summons will specify the date and place at which production is to take place.[261] As a practical matter, immediate response can never be required, regardless of the date set forth in the summons. If the administrative Summons is served on a third party record keeper, such as a Customs Broker, the minimum response time prescribed by regulations is at least 10 days. [262]

> **CAUTION**
>
> Response to an Administrative Summons should never be made without advice of counsel.

The essential feature of the administrative summons is that Customs can seek enforcement of the summons by a Federal District Court if the importer fails to comply voluntarily. Failure to comply with a court ordered production demand, not only constitutes contempt, but is also one of the few times where an importer's right to import can be suspended.[263]

- Continued on next page –

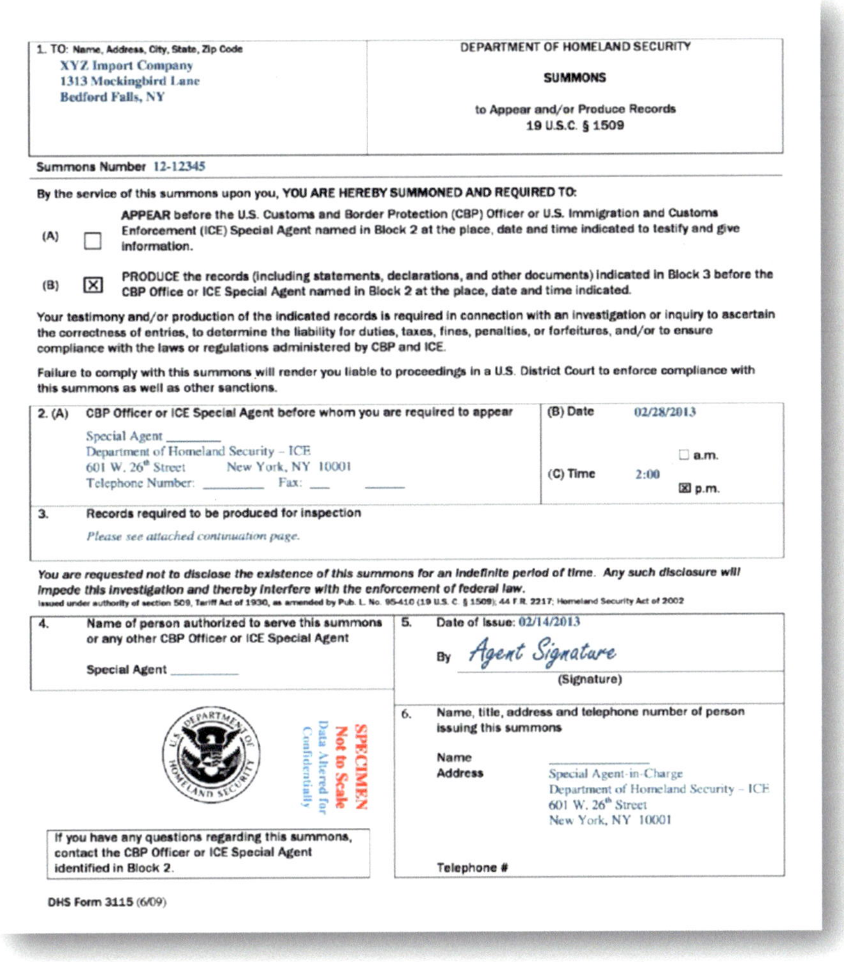

1. TO: Name, Address, City, State, Zip Code
XYZ Import Company
1313 Mockingbird Lane
Bedford Falls, NY

DEPARTMENT OF HOMELAND SECURITY

SUMMONS

to Appear and/or Produce Records
19 U.S.C. § 1509

Summons Number 12-12345

By the service of this summons upon you, YOU ARE HEREBY SUMMONED AND REQUIRED TO:

(A) ☐ APPEAR before the U.S. Customs and Border Protection (CBP) Officer or U.S. Immigration and Customs Enforcement (ICE) Special Agent named in Block 2 at the place, date and time indicated to testify and give information.

(B) ☒ PRODUCE the records (including statements, declarations, and other documents) indicated in Block 3 before the CBP Office or ICE Special Agent named in Block 2 at the place, date and time indicated.

Your testimony and/or production of the indicated records is required in connection with an investigation or inquiry to ascertain the correctness of entries, to determine the liability for duties, taxes, fines, penalties, or forfeitures, and/or to ensure compliance with the laws or regulations administered by CBP and ICE.

Failure to comply with this summons will render you liable to proceedings in a U.S. District Court to enforce compliance with this summons as well as other sanctions.

2. (A) CBP Officer or ICE Special Agent before whom you are required to appear
Special Agent ________
Department of Homeland Security – ICE
601 W. 26th Street New York, NY 10001
Telephone Number: ________ Fax: ___ ______

(B) Date 02/28/2013

(C) Time 2:00 ☐ a.m. ☒ p.m.

3. Records required to be produced for inspection
Please see attached continuation page.

You are requested not to disclose the existence of this summons for an indefinite period of time. Any such disclosure will impede this investigation and thereby interfere with the enforcement of federal law.
Issued under authority of section 509, Tariff Act of 1930, as amended by Pub. L. No. 95-410 (19 U.S.C. § 1509); 44 F.R. 2217; Homeland Security Act of 2002

4. Name of person authorized to serve this summons or any other CBP Officer or ICE Special Agent
Special Agent ________

5. Date of Issue: 02/14/2013
By *Agent Signature*
(Signature)

SPECIMEN
Not to Scale
Data Altered for Confidentiality

6. Name, title, address and telephone number of person issuing this summons
Name ________
Address Special Agent-in-Charge
Department of Homeland Security – ICE
601 W. 26th Street
New York, NY 10001
Telephone #

If you have any questions regarding this summons, contact the CBP Officer or ICE Special Agent identified in Block 2.

DHS Form 3115 (6/09)

Figure 58 - Customs Administrative Summons

19.3.4. GRAND JURY SUBPOENA

The issuance of a Grand Jury Subpoena puts the recipient on notice that there is a criminal investigation underway. The subpoena, which can be for either production of documents, or appearance of a person, or both, is a device used by the government to obtain relevant documents and testimony for use in its investigation.[264]

Regardless of whether you or your company has been identified as a target of the investigation or not, no action should be taken without advice of counsel. Even if it is initially represented that you or your company are only being looked to as a source of information or as a potential witness, the government has no qualms about broadening its sights to include a new target: You.

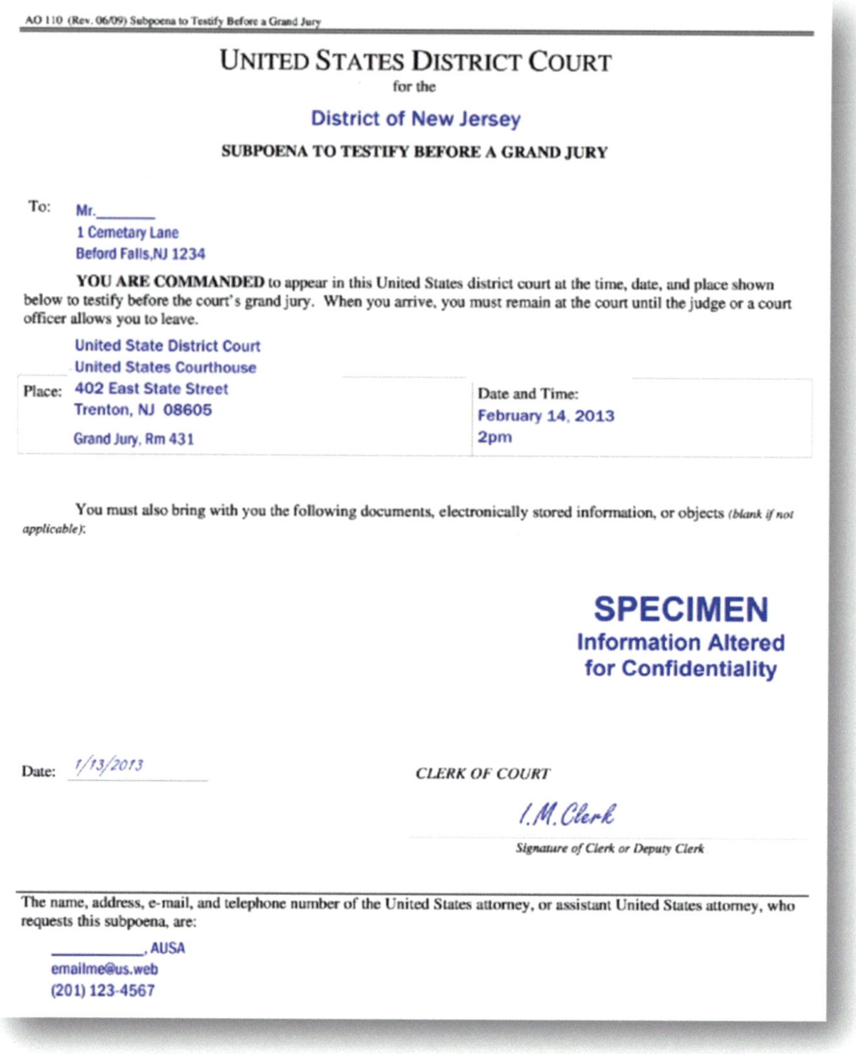

AO 110 (Rev. 06/09) Subpoena to Testify Before a Grand Jury

UNITED STATES DISTRICT COURT
for the
District of New Jersey

SUBPOENA TO TESTIFY BEFORE A GRAND JURY

To: Mr.______
1 Cemetary Lane
Beford Falls,NJ 1234

YOU ARE COMMANDED to appear in this United States district court at the time, date, and place shown below to testify before the court's grand jury. When you arrive, you must remain at the court until the judge or a court officer allows you to leave.

Place: United State District Court, United States Courthouse, 402 East State Street, Trenton, NJ 08605, Grand Jury, Rm 431	Date and Time: February 14, 2013 2pm

You must also bring with you the following documents, electronically stored information, or objects *(blank if not applicable)*:

SPECIMEN
Information Altered for Confidentiality

Date: 1/13/2013

CLERK OF COURT

I.M. Clerk

Signature of Clerk or Deputy Clerk

The name, address, e-mail, and telephone number of the United States attorney, or assistant United States attorney, who requests this subpoena, are:

__________, AUSA
emailme@us.web
(201) 123-4567

Figure 59 - Federal Court Grand Jury Subpoena

19.3.5. SEARCH WARRANT

A search warrant is an order issued by a Court to search premises for evidence of a crime and to remove items. The problem is that in repetitive commercial transactions, such as imports and exports, this usually includes all of the importer's records, computers, fax machines, calendars, diaries and financial records, including check books. Sometimes, all that is left are the desks and chairs and the expressions on the faces of the employees.

Search warrants are based upon affidavits by a government agent setting forth probable cause, usually based upon some investigation and various confidential and undisclosed informants.

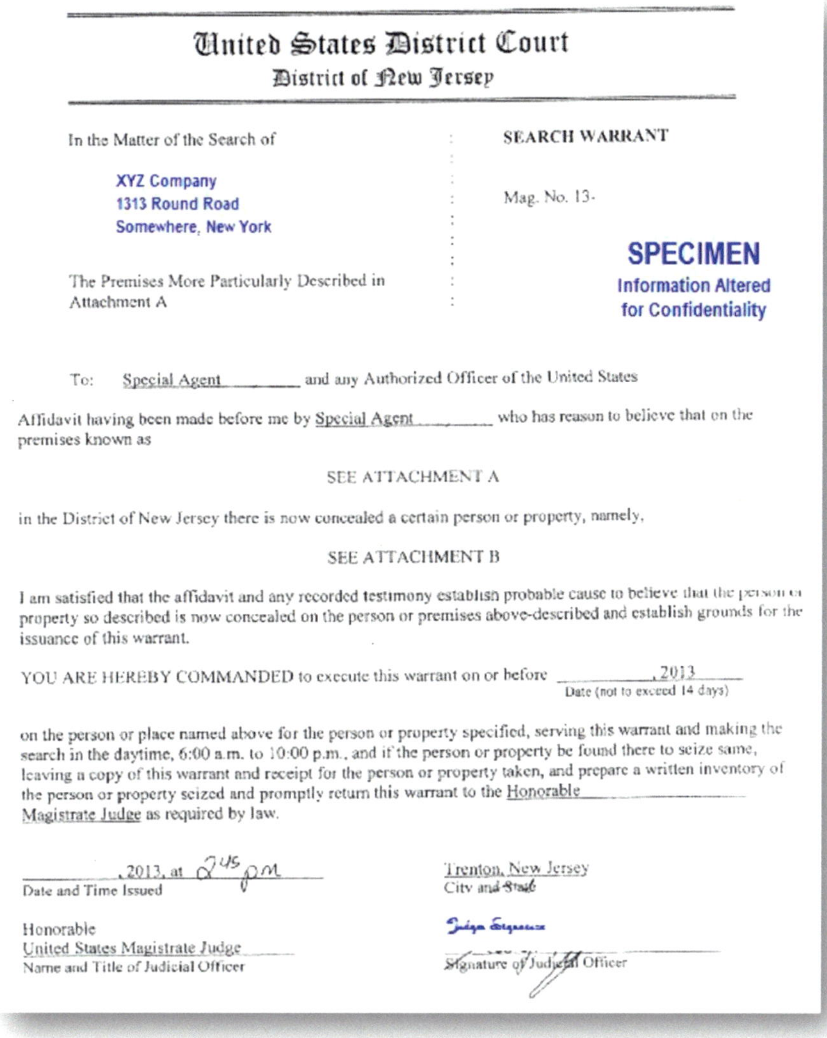

United States District Court
District of New Jersey

In the Matter of the Search of

XYZ Company
1313 Round Road
Somewhere, New York

The Premises More Particularly Described in Attachment A

SEARCH WARRANT

Mag. No. 13-

SPECIMEN
Information Altered
for Confidentiality

To: Special Agent ______ and any Authorized Officer of the United States

Affidavit having been made before me by Special Agent ______ who has reason to believe that on the premises known as

SEE ATTACHMENT A

in the District of New Jersey there is now concealed a certain person or property, namely,

SEE ATTACHMENT B

I am satisfied that the affidavit and any recorded testimony establish probable cause to believe that the person or property so described is now concealed on the person or premises above-described and establish grounds for the issuance of this warrant.

YOU ARE HEREBY COMMANDED to execute this warrant on or before ______, 2013
Date (not to exceed 14 days)

on the person or place named above for the person or property specified, serving this warrant and making the search in the daytime, 6:00 a.m. to 10:00 p.m., and if the person or property be found there to seize same, leaving a copy of this warrant and receipt for the person or property taken, and prepare a written inventory of the person or property seized and promptly return this warrant to the Honorable ______ Magistrate Judge as required by law.

______, 2013, at 2:45 pm
Date and Time Issued

Trenton, New Jersey
City and State

Honorable
United States Magistrate Judge
Name and Title of Judicial Officer

Judge Signature
Signature of Judicial Officer

Figure 60 - Federal Court Search Warrant

Nothing can be done to stop the search, and interfering with the search can lead to arrest. But there are things that should be done immediately to minimize the effect.

- ✓ Contact counsel immediately, Customs/Trade and/or Criminal, is the obvious first step.
- ✓ Equally important is keeping careful track of what is being taken, how it can be identified, and in what carton it was placed since the receipt that the government will issue is too general to enable rapid location of any records that may be needed to continue in business.
- ✓ Communication with the agents executing the search warrant should be kept to an absolute minimum.

Counsel will usually make every effort to be present during a search. The presence of experienced counsel cannot stop the search, but it can make it more survivable. As with a medical emergency, speed and a clear head are the keys to survival.

---

[249] 19 USC 1500; 19 C.F.R. part 159, in general

[250] 19 C.F.R. 159.9(a)

[251] 19 U.S.C. 1504 as amended by Public Law 103-182, 107 Stat 2057 Section 641

[252] 19 C.F.R. 159.11

[253] 19 C.F.R. 175.2

[254] 19 C.F.R. 152.2

[255] 19 C.F.R. 141.113

[256] HQ Ruling 224566, dated August 3, 1993 - *See* earlier cites

[257] TD 94-95 October 24, 1994, Effective January 3, 1995, 59 FR 61798 December 2, 1994

[258] Public Law 103-182, 107 Stat 2171 Section 613(a)

[259] 19 USC 1592(c)(6), 19 C.F.R. 162.75

[260] 19 USC 1595a(c)

[261] 19 C.F.R. 162.1e

[262] 19 C.F.R. 162.1g(b)

[263] 19 C.F.R. 162.1i

[264] In Re April 1977 Grand Jury Subpoenas General Motors Corporation v. United States, 573 F.2d 936

20. IMPORTER'S REMEDIES

20.1. PETITION

Petitions are written presentations, sometimes supplemented by oral presentations, submitted in response to a government claim for a penalty, liquidated damages, or notice of seizure. A petition seeks to convince the government to cancel or mitigate its claim.

Both penalties and procedures are set forth in statutes, regulations, and penalty and mitigation guidelines. While mitigation guidelines are intended to act as a guide for reducing a penalty, they often create an excuse for agency intransigence instead.

If the government has instituted a penalty case or claim for liquidated damages or affected a seizure, it has already made a preliminary finding that the importer is guilty of violating some law. Consequently, as a practical matter, these cases operate under a system of Napoleonic justice where the burden is on the accused to establish its innocence.

Mitigation is based, not on just the facts and circumstances of an individual case, but also on the importer's prior record. Cumulative violations may increase initial penalties or impair the ability to obtain mitigation, and sometimes make it necessary to actively pursue an individual case, even though economics might warrant merely paying the fine. In most cases a competent petition will result in some degree of mitigation of the government's demand.

Most claims for penalties, liquidated damages or seizures resulting from an import or export are affected under Customs laws even though the underlying violation involves the laws of other agencies which are enforced by Customs.

Significant problems arise when discretion for mitigation does not rest with U.S. Customs, but with the agency whose laws Customs is enforcing. In those instances, Customs merely refers the petition to the other agency. Most other agencies are purely regulatory and have no authority to assess penalties. As a consequence, agencies often view petitions in black and white terms, violation or no violation, which is not conducive to mitigation, only to assessment of the full penalty or cancellation.

Regardless of the mitigation or how many supplemental petitions are permitted, in most cases, a time will come when further efforts on the part of the importer yield diminishing returns, and paying a mitigated penalty may be prudent as well as practical.

Petitions or payment are usually due 30 or 60 days after the date of the notice, not the date of mailing or date of receipt.[265]

The failure to submit a petition will result in the government's insistence on full payment.

The failure to pay a mitigated penalty on time revives the original penalty or claim.[266]

The failure to pay a penalty results in the suspension of Immediate Delivery Entry procedures,[267] which may affect cash flow and will affect the time that it takes to obtain release of a shipment. It will not, however, preclude further imports.

20.2. PROTEST AND CLAIMS

Executive Briefing

There will be times when you will disagree with some decision which Customs has made regarding your transactions. The law provides various means of disputing those decisions. What they all have in common are short filing deadlines which cannot be extended.

Claims can be made against a Customs' decision at various times.

- ✓ Before Liquidation - Post Entry Amendments
- ✓ After Liquidation – Protests – All Issues
- ✓ After Liquidation – Section 520 Claims – Special Issues

Keep in mind that just as you have to right to challenge a Customs Liquidation, Customs also has an opportunity to change that liquidation.

Customs may, on its own initiative, within 90 days of the original liquidation liquidate or reliquidate an entry "to correct errors in appraisement, classification, or any other element entering into the liquidation or reliquidation, including errors based on misconstruction of applicable law." [268]

20.2.1. PROTEST

A Protest is the only means of registering an importer's objection as to how an entry was finalized/liquidated by Customs. Virtually any issue as to classification, value or admissibility or any other decision relating to an entry can be raised after the original liquidation.[269]

A protest must be filed within 180 days after liquidation of the entry[270] or within 180 days after the issuance of any other decision if a liquidation is not involved.[271] (Prior to 2004, the Protest Period was 90 days).

CAUTION

A Protest must be filed within 180 days of liquidation.

And there are no extensions of the time to file.

A protest is usually filed on a pre-printed form, CF 19, which calls for certain identifying information, but which should be supplemented by a further statement and documentation supporting the importer's claim.

Generally, a protest will cause a review by local Customs officials, very often by the same person who made the decision of which the importer is now complaining.

A review of the protest at Customs Headquarters, technically a review of the local port's decision, can be obtained by including in the protest a "Request for Further Review." If the Request for

Further Review is approved, the protest will be reviewed at Headquarters, if the protest is denied at the local level.[272] There is no need for Headquarter's review if local Customs agrees with the importer's position and approves the protest.

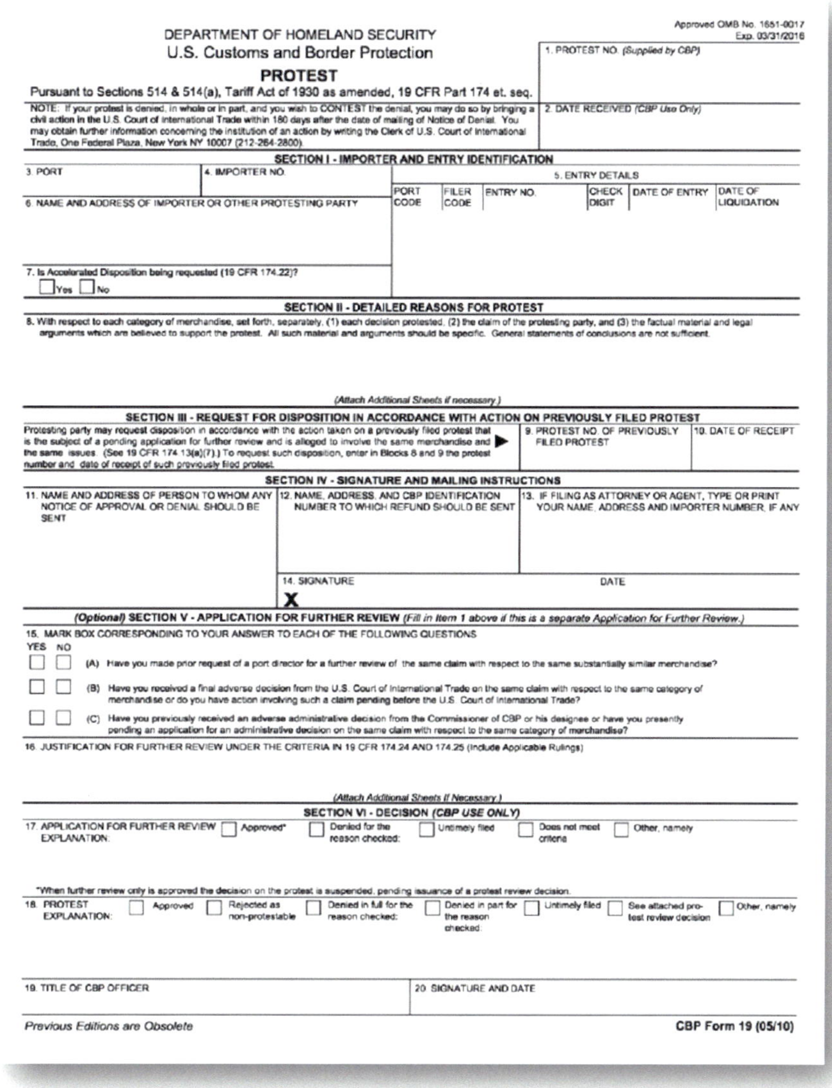

Approved OMB No. 1651-0017
Exp. 03/31/2016

DEPARTMENT OF HOMELAND SECURITY
U.S. Customs and Border Protection
PROTEST
Pursuant to Sections 514 & 514(a), Tariff Act of 1930 as amended, 19 CFR Part 174 et. seq.

1. PROTEST NO. *(Supplied by CBP)*

NOTE: If your protest is denied, in whole or in part, and you wish to CONTEST the denial, you may do so by bringing a civil action in the U.S. Court of International Trade within 180 days after the date of mailing of Notice of Denial. You may obtain further information concerning the institution of an action by writing the Clerk of U.S. Court of International Trade, One Federal Plaza, New York NY 10007 (212-264-2800).

2. DATE RECEIVED *(CBP Use Only)*

SECTION I - IMPORTER AND ENTRY IDENTIFICATION

3. PORT
4. IMPORTER NO.
5. ENTRY DETAILS: PORT CODE | FILER CODE | ENTRY NO. | CHECK DIGIT | DATE OF ENTRY | DATE OF LIQUIDATION
6. NAME AND ADDRESS OF IMPORTER OR OTHER PROTESTING PARTY
7. Is Accelerated Disposition being requested (19 CFR 174.22)? ☐ Yes ☐ No

SECTION II - DETAILED REASONS FOR PROTEST

8. With respect to each category of merchandise, set forth, separately, (1) each decision protested, (2) the claim of the protesting party, and (3) the factual material and legal arguments which are believed to support the protest. All such material and arguments should be specific. General statements of conclusions are not sufficient.

(Attach Additional Sheets if necessary.)

SECTION III - REQUEST FOR DISPOSITION IN ACCORDANCE WITH ACTION ON PREVIOUSLY FILED PROTEST

Protesting party may request disposition in accordance with the action taken on a previously filed protest that is the subject of a pending application for further review and is alleged to involve the same merchandise and the same issues. (See 19 CFR 174.13(a)(7).) To request such disposition, enter in Blocks 8 and 9 the protest number and date of receipt of such previously filed protest. ▶

9. PROTEST NO. OF PREVIOUSLY FILED PROTEST
10. DATE OF RECEIPT

SECTION IV - SIGNATURE AND MAILING INSTRUCTIONS

11. NAME AND ADDRESS OF PERSON TO WHOM ANY NOTICE OF APPROVAL OR DENIAL SHOULD BE SENT
12. NAME, ADDRESS, AND CBP IDENTIFICATION NUMBER TO WHICH REFUND SHOULD BE SENT
13. IF FILING AS ATTORNEY OR AGENT, TYPE OR PRINT YOUR NAME, ADDRESS AND IMPORTER NUMBER, IF ANY
14. SIGNATURE X DATE

***(Optional)* SECTION V - APPLICATION FOR FURTHER REVIEW** *(Fill in Item 1 above if this is a separate Application for Further Review.)*

15. MARK BOX CORRESPONDING TO YOUR ANSWER TO EACH OF THE FOLLOWING QUESTIONS

YES NO

☐ ☐ (A) Have you made prior request of a port director for a further review of the same claim with respect to the same substantially similar merchandise?

☐ ☐ (B) Have you received a final adverse decision from the U.S. Court of International Trade on the same claim with respect to the same category of merchandise or do you have action involving such a claim pending before the U.S. Court of International Trade?

☐ ☐ (C) Have you previously received an adverse administrative decision from the Commissioner of CBP or his designee or have you presently pending an application for an administrative decision on the same claim with respect to the same category of merchandise?

16. JUSTIFICATION FOR FURTHER REVIEW UNDER THE CRITERIA IN 19 CFR 174.24 AND 174.25 (Include Applicable Rulings)

(Attach Additional Sheets If Necessary.)

SECTION VI - DECISION *(CBP USE ONLY)*

17. APPLICATION FOR FURTHER REVIEW EXPLANATION: ☐ Approved* ☐ Denied for the reason checked: ☐ Untimely filed ☐ Does not meet criteria ☐ Other, namely

*When further review only is approved the decision on the protest is suspended, pending issuance of a protest review decision.

18. PROTEST EXPLANATION: ☐ Approved ☐ Rejected as non-protestable ☐ Denied in full for the reason checked: ☐ Denied in part for the reason checked: ☐ Untimely filed ☐ See attached protest review decision ☐ Other, namely

19. TITLE OF CBP OFFICER
20. SIGNATURE AND DATE

Previous Editions are Obsolete **CBP Form 19 (05/10)**

Figure 61 - CBP Form 19 Protest

If the protest is approved, the protested entry will be reliquidated and if a refund is due, a check sent.[273] Only the entry(ies) protested are affected retroactively by Custom's action on the protest, but the decision on a protest can act as precedent affecting future entries. Generally, if a protest is denied, filing a summons in the Court of International Trade is the next step. Recent changes to the law may permit some limited correction of erroneous denials of protests or application for further review.[274]

The filing of a protest does not suspend the liability for Customs duties, but it will suspend collection of any additional duties that were called for at liquidation.[275]

If duties have been paid and the protest is approved, the government will pay interest from the date the duty was paid. If the duty has not been paid and the government position is sustained, it is the importer who pays the interest from the date the duty was originally due.[276]

All outstanding amounts due, including interest, must be paid before an action on a denied protest can be taken to court.[277]

20.2.2. 520 CLAIMS – REFUNDS FOR ERRORS

Claims under section 520 appear to be an attractive alternative to a Protest because you have one year to make a claim as compared to only 180 days under a protest.

However, unlike claims for refunds under a Protest (19 U.S.C. 1514), which can be very broad, claims under section 520 apply only to very specific issues.

It is important to be on the lookout for the Liquidation Date as the one year limitation on filing a claim under 520 could coincide with the liquidation date.

A Protest can only be filed after Liquidation but 520 claims are generally filed prior to liquidation.

20.2.2.1. 520(C) CLAIM

It used to be possible to make some limited claims based upon "clerical *errors or mistakes of factor other errors not amounting to errors in construction of law*" for up to one year after liquidation.

That option was eliminated in exchange for increasing the ability to file a Protest, which allows for broader claims, from 90 to 180 days.

20.2.2.2. 520 (A, B, D) CLAIM

Certain claims may still be filed under 520 within 1 year, but they should be treated as exceptions.

20.2.3. POST ENTRY AMENDMENT

- *Prior to liquidation*—Whenever an importer determines that they made a mistake on their entry and deposited excess duties, fees, charges, or exactions, the importer does not have to wait until after Liquidation to make a claim for a refund. Instead the entry can be amended by filing a Post Entry Amendment (PEA) or Post Summary Correction (PSC) procedure. [278]
- *Excess deposits*—Whenever, upon liquidation, re-liquidation, or reconciliation it was determined that more money had been deposited or paid as duties than required by law, and it had not been refunded.[279]
- *Fees, charges, and exactions*—Whenever it is determined that any fees, charges, or exactions, other than duties and taxes, have been erroneously or excessively collected.[280]

- *Fines, penalties, and forfeitures*—Whenever more money was deposited with Customs or Treasury in contemplation of a fine, penalty, or forfeiture that which is finally determined as due. (19 U.S.C. 520(a)(3))
- *Goods qualifying under a Free Trade Agreement – not claimed at entry.* (19 U.S.C. 520(d))

Regardless of whether a protest is filed, if goods qualify under the rules of origin of one of the following free trade agreements and reduced duty benefit was not claimed at the time the Entry Summary was filed, for whatever reason, a claim may still be made for that benefit after the fact.

- United States-Chile Free Trade Agreement
- United States - Oman Free Trade Agreement
- United States-Peru Trade Promotion
- United States – Panama Trade Promotion Agreement
- United States–Korea Free Trade Agreement
- United States – Columbia Trade Promotion Agreement
- NAFTA
- Certain other Free Trade Agreements

20.3. JUDICIAL REVIEW

Judicial review of an agency decision may be available, but only after all administrative remedies have been exhausted.

20.3.1. COURT OF INTERNATIONAL TRADE

This is a specialized Federal Court empowered to review Customs actions. The jurisdiction of the Court of International Trade ("C.I.T.") and Court of Appeals for the Federal Circuit are very narrow and only specific actions on the part of Customs or the importer will allow these Courts to exercise jurisdiction.

> In order to obtain a review in court you must first exhaust your administrative opportunities for review.
>
> Care needs to be taken to build a record for a potential Court review at that administrative level, because, at least in the case of classification and value, Customs' opinion will be given deference, meaning that you have to not only prove you are right, you also have to prove that Customs is wrong.

The most common means by which an importer can have a Customs' action or decision reviewed in the Court of International Trade is through the filing and denial of a protest. You cannot get into the Court of International Trade directly through the denial of a 520 claim, but you must file a formal protest against its denial. (*See* "Protest" §20.2.1 at 198.)

The C.I.T. has jurisdiction and an expedited procedure to hear challenges to certain other actions by Customs such as the exclusion or detention of merchandise. Challenges to a seizure must be brought in U.S. District Courts, not the C.I.T.

The C.I.T. also has jurisdiction over Customs actions against an importer for non-payment of duties, liquidated damages, or penalties.[281]

20.3.2. U.S. DISTRICT COURTS

Certain matters involving agencies or law other than U.S. Customs may be reviewed by a U.S. District Court sitting in the district in which the cargo is located.

20.3.3. APPELLATE COURTS

The Court of Appeals for the Federal Circuit is the Appellate Court for the Court of International Trade as well as for certain other Federal Courts. The Circuit Court of Appeals remains the Appellate Courts for the District Courts.

The Court of final review is the U.S. Supreme Court but, in over 200 years, very few Customs or trade cases have been accepted for review.

---

[265] 19 C.F.R. 171.12

[266] 19 C.F.R. 171.32

[267] 19 C.F.R. 174.13

[268] 19 USC 1501 as amended. 19 C.F.R. 173.3

[269] 19 USC 1514; 19 C.F.R. 174.13

[270] 19 USC 1514(c)(3)(A), 19 C.F.R. 174.12(c)(1)

[271] 19 USC 1514(c)(3)(B), 19 C.F.R. 174.12(e)(2)

[272] 19 C.F.R. 174.23

[273] 19 USC 1515(d), 19 C.F.R. 174.29

[274] 19 U.S.C. 1515 as amended by Public Law 103-182, 107 Stat 2057 Section 617

[275] Pursuant to Congressional legislative history, while Customs may issue a bill and continue billing the importer for an increased duty assessment, "[t]he increase duties need not be paid on liquidation and need not be deposited in order to protest their assessment before the Customs Service." (Congressional Legislative History of the Omnibus Trade Tariff Act: H.R. Rep. No 1015, 9th Cong., 2nd Sess. 68 (1984))

[276] 19 USC 1677(g), 19 C.F.R. 24.36, T.D. 85-93

[277] 28 USC 2637(a)

[278] 19 USC 1520(a)(4)

[279] 19 USC 1520(a)(1)

[280] 19 USC 1520(a)(2)

[281] 26 USC 1582

21. PENALTIES & LIQUIDATED DAMAGES

Executive Briefing

Penalties, civil or criminal, are the ultimate realization of risk. Whether they were the product of known risks undertaken as a part of doing business, or a mistake, neglect, lack of attention or planning, or "arrogance", they are things to be avoided.

If importers always made plans, and every shipment proceeded as planned, there might not be a reason for this section. The reality is, however, that even with careful planning, there are things beyond an importer's control; details are sometimes overlooked and, in the end, there is Murphy's Law and its corollaries.

There are both civil and criminal penalties which are applicable to import and export transactions. Criminal prosecutions, although far less common than civil penalty cases, are on the increase and are initiated for what are normally considered purely commercial transactions. The exact nature of the problems that will arise cannot be predicted. Through planning and prompt and appropriate remedial action, when problems are discovered, the likelihood of encountering the more draconian penalties can be reduced and the consequences of such problems as they arise can be minimized.

21.1. CONFIDENTIALITY AND PRIVILEGE

Confidentiality laws or contractual terms do not afford the same level of protection from disclosure as does Attorney-Client Privilege. That does not mean that you need an attorney involved in everything.

Many of the laws licensing service providers have rules governing the confidentiality of your information. Confidentiality protects your information from use or disclosure to a third party without your permission. Whether established by law or contractual terms, that confidentiality does not rise to the level of a privilege, and your information and communications remain discoverable by the government.

CAUTION

If you are not sure whether you need this level of protection, don't guess: Ask a Customs and Trade attorney for a consultation.

Confidentiality, once lost, cannot be revived.

A broader level of confidentiality protection is afforded under Attorney-Client Privilege, which protects virtually all communications between you and your attorney. It does not, however, necessarily protect transactional documents or information from governmental reach.

You can lose that privilege by your disclosure of privileged information to third-parties, verbally or in writing. Classically, this can happen by talking about an issue with others, or by including non-essential people in communications with your attorney and, as is all too common, in email communications. Third-parties can include certain people within your own business, consultants, and even those governed by confidentiality rules, such as FMC licensed Freight Forwarders, NVOs, and Customs Brokers.

21.2. CIVIL

21.2.1. VOLUNTARY PRIOR DISCLOSURE - THE PREEMPTIVE STRIKE

> Mistakes will be made. For your business the concern has to be with what is the financial consequence of that mistake.
>
> How Customs views your mistake will depend, in part, on what compliance programs you are involved in and what your history of compliance has been.
>
> *A Prior Disclosure is your opportunity to get ahead of penalties.*

A voluntary prior disclosure is the preemptive strike which, if available, can provide an importer with an invaluable opportunity to correct a mistake before Customs finds it and makes it a problem. A voluntary disclosure permits an importer to make a clean breast of the matter, correct its mistake, and thereby cut off its liability for Customs penalties.[282] Unless fraud is involved, potential penalties can be virtually eliminated.[283] Even in the case of fraud, penalties can be substantially limited.[284]

Voluntary disclosures require complete disclosure of the facts and circumstances of a violation, including a full financial accounting. Statutorily, the benefits of a voluntary disclosure are not available once Customs has begun an investigation into the matter. As a practical matter, making a disclosure after an investigation has begun is equivalent to drawing Customs a map to the violation.

Recent changes to the law put an even greater emphasis on prompt action by the importer. Customs must document the time when it came into possession of sufficient information to commence an investigation but, having done so, it then puts the importer in the unenviable position of proving that, at the time of its disclosure, it did not know that a formal investigation had been commenced.[285]

Voluntary disclosures ***do not*** foreclose the possibility of criminal sanctions.

Voluntary disclosures should never be made without advice of counsel, after a thorough examination of the issues to determine whether a disclosure is available or appropriate, and, if so, what should be its scope.

Periodic internal audits are an important part of this evaluation.

21.2.2. FRAUD (19 U.S.C. 1592)

Customs, as well as other agencies, are dependent upon the accuracy of information provided with an entry to enable them to assess duty, determine admissibility of merchandise and compliance with various laws. The law, therefore, provides penalties for presentation of any document, written or oral statement, or act that is material and false, or any omission which is material, made while entering or attempting to enter merchandise.[286]

The amount of the penalty is based upon whether or not the violation is considered a 'revenue' or 'non-revenue' violation, and how culpable or intentional the act was. Whether it is treated as a revenue loss or non-revenue loss violation is dependent upon the theoretical objective of the act rather than on the intent of the violator.

REVENUE LOSS VIOLATIONS are those where the filing of false documents results in the payment of less duty. This would include the failure to disclose assists or commissions, or misrepresenting total or unit pricing.

NON-REVENUE LOSS VIOLATIONS are generally those where the false documents influence the admissibility of goods. A revenue loss violation may be secondary to the non-revenue loss violation. Typical of non-revenue violation would be using a wrong classification to avoid antidumping duties or other restrictions.

	Penalty Level			For Example		
	Revenue Loss	Non Revenue Loss	VOLUNTARY DISCLOSURE	Revenue Loss	Non Revenue Loss	VOLUNTARY DISCLOSURE
	Multiple of Revenue Loss	Percentage Of Value	Multiple Revenue Loss	Duty Rate 5%	Value $20,000	
Negligence	2	20%	0	$ 2.000	$ 4,000	$ 0
Gross Negligence	4	40%	0	$ 4,000	$ 8,000	$ 0
Fraud	8	100%	1	$ 8,000	$20,000	$ 1,000

Figure 62 - Customs Maximum Statutory Penalties

While these are maximum penalties for each category of violation, which may ultimately be reduced through mitigation, penalty notices are issued for the maximum amount provided for by law.

Rarely, after having opened a case, does Customs concede that there was no violation, or that the violation constituted only a clerical error.

Customs' initial notice provides the importer with the opportunity to show why Customs should not commence a penalty case at all. Like liquidated damage cases, the importer may petition Customs to mitigate the penalties. Should the importer not respond, or Customs not agree with the importer's position, a penalty case will be instituted. The importer may then file a petition in response to the penalty notice (a second bite at the apple) and a supplemental petition (a third bite), and/or make an offer-in-compromise to mitigate the penalty.

Trade Trivia

Being a U.S. Collector of Customs used to carry with it the perk of sharing in the penalties collected.

It being recognized that this provided too much of an incentive for "creating" penalties rather than enforcing the laws, the practice was discontinued in 1876 by the Anti-Moiety Act.

Before that, however, while Chester A. Arthur was the Collector of Customs at the Port of New York, his share of the penalties resulted in him having earned as much as the President of the United States.

21.2.3. IMPORTATION IN VIOLATION OF LAW (19 U.S.C. 1595A(C))[287]

A few laws provide for seizure of violative merchandise and for the imposition of penalties. Laws such as Section 1595a(c) of the Tariff Act provide very broad seizure authority for goods imported in violation of the law. This provision is merely seizure and forfeiture authority. Its authority can be invoked only if there is first a violation of some other law. The underlying violation can be of any law that relates in any way to importation.

This statute was originally enacted as part of a major anti-crime bill to give Customs an additional weapon against drug smuggling, but Customs quickly appropriated the provision for use against commercial violations. In fact, for several years it virtually usurped all other bases for seizure because of its low threshold for seizure. It made seizures so much easier to justify.

Penalties can often be imposed both for the underlying violation and for remission of forfeiture of the seized goods. Repetitive violations within a three year period substantially reduce the opportunity to mitigate penalties under 19 U.S.C. 1595a(c).

21.2.4. LIQUIDATED DAMAGES[288]

Liquidated damages are predetermined penalties to which the importer has agreed to be bound upon breach of the terms of the Customs Bond.

By the terms of the bond and regulations, the liquidated damages on an entry are limited to the face value of the bond which may be up to three times the entered value of the shipment. (*See* "Customs Bonds" §18.6 at 170.)

Liquidated damage, claims arise when the importer fails to comply with Customs regulations or Customs' requests made in accordance with those regulations. An importer most commonly becomes liable for liquidated damages because it failed to redeliver into Customs' custody items originally released by Customs, but which Customs had subsequently demanded return. (*See* "Notice to Mark and/or Notice to Redeliver (CF 4647)" §19.2.3 at 185.)

21.2.5. OFFERS-IN-COMPROMISE

In addition to the ability to petition Customs for mitigation of any penalty or liquidated damages, there is the ability to subsequently try to resolve a liability through an Offer-in-Compromise[289]. The offer is usually supported by some new argument or evidence that Customs did not consider in the original mitigation determination.

Offers-in-Compromise can be used to reduce liability for penalties and/or liquidated damages.

However, Offers-in-Compromise cannot be used to reduce the liability for Customs Duties or other duties or taxes.

DEPARTMENT OF HOMELAND SECURITY U.S. CUSTOMS AND BORDER PROTECTION NOTICE OF PENALTY OR LIQUIDATED DAMAGES INCURRED AND DEMAND FOR PAYMENT 19 USC 1618, 19 USC 1623	**CASE NUMBER** **20120901200#####** **PORT CODE AND NAME** **4601 NEWARK, NEW JERSEY** **INVESTIGATION FILE NO.** **ID: 5218####**
Your Name 0001 Cemetery Lane Pleasantville, VA 10413	SPECIMEN Not to Scale Representational Data ONLY

DEMAND IS HEREBY MADE FOR PAYMENT OF $121,945.00 REPRESENTING LIQUIDATED DAMAGES ASSESSED AGAINST YOU FOR VIOLATION OF LAW OR REGULATION, OR BREACH OF BOND, AS SET FORTH BELOW:

ENTRY NUMBER: 23#####0676 ENTRY DATED: 07/##/2012

SUMMARY DUE: 07/##/2012 BUT HAS NOT BEEN FILED. NBR DAYS LATE: 0000

AMOUNT DUE: $.00 (DUTY + ADD/CVD + TAXES + FEES)

FAILURE TO FILE ENTRY SUMMARY AND FAILURE TO PAY ESTIMATED DUTIES, FEES, TAXES AND CHARGES.

MITIGATION WILL NOT BE CONSIDERED UNTIL THE ENTRY SUMMARY HAS BEEN ACCEPTED WITH ESTIMATED DUTIES, FEES, TAXES AND CHARGES ATTACHED.

LAW OR REGULATION VIOLATED		BOND BREACHED	
19CFR142.12 19CFR113.62(B)		BOND TYPE: 1 BOND #: 109#####6	
DESCRIPTION OF BOND: IMPORTER BROKER	FORM NUMBER: 109#####6	**AMOUNT:** **$2,000,000.00**	DATE: 04/##/2010

NAME AND ADDRESS OF PRINCIPAL ON BOND: **YOUR NAME**

NAME AND ADDRESS OF SURETY ON BOND	SURETY NO.
FEDERAL INSURANCE COMPANY P.O. BOX 1615, PLAINFIELD, NJ 07601	269

IF YOU FEEL THERE ARE EXTENUATING CIRCUMSTANCES, YOU HAVE THE RIGHT TO OBJECT TO THE ABOVE ACTION. YOUR PETITION SHOULD EXPLAIN WHY YOU SHOULD NOT BE PENALIZED FOR THE CITED VIOLATION. WRITE THE PETITION AS A LETTER OR IN LEGAL FORM; SUBMIT IN (DUPLICATE) ADDRESSED TO THE COMMISSIONER OF CUSTOMS AND BORDER PROTECTION, AND FORWARD TO THE FP&F OFFICER AT: U.S. CBP / ATTN: FP&FO, 1313 MOCKING BIRD LANE, BEDFORD FALLS, NY 14###

UNLESS THE AMOUNT HEREIN DEMANDED IS PAID OR A PETITION FOR RELIEF IS FILED WITH THE FP&F OFFICER WITHIN THE INDICATED TIME LIMIT, FURTHER ACTION WILL BE TAKEN IN CONNECTION WITH BOND OR MATTER WILL BE REFERRED TO US ATTORNEY.

TIME LIMIT FOR PAYMENT OR FILING PETITION: 60 DAYS FROM DATE OF THIS NOTICE

SIGNATURE	TITLE	DATE
BY	FP&F OFFICER	07/##/2012

Figure 63 - Notice of Penalty or Liquidated Damages

Liquidated damages can often be reduced or mitigated by petitioning Customs Office of Fines, Penalties & Forfeitures. The degree of mitigation is dependent upon Customs' own mitigation guidelines and on the individual facts. In certain cases, the mitigation guidelines do not provide leeway for much mitigation. And rarely has an importer found that its idea of a reasonable penalty and that of the government are even remotely the same.

21.3. CRIMINAL

Customs, as well as other agencies, use criminal prosecutions in addition to civil actions to aid in their enforcement efforts,

There has, over time, been a significant increase in the use of criminal prosecutions. These prosecutions are not limited to cases involving drugs or smuggling. There are also criminal prosecutions that involve the types of problems associated with commercial transactions which, in the past, would have been addressed as a purely civil problem.

> In Trade, the line between Criminal and Civil can sometimes be very thin and often times the result of any proceedings in one will set the ground work for Customs to pursue you under the other.
>
> If the government pursues you criminally for a Trade transaction, it is good practice to engage both Criminal and Trade Counsel to avoid the situation whereby a good settlement of the Criminal Case results in what can essentially be considered an admission of guilt in a subsequent Customs civil action.

Criminal fines range from five thousand to hundreds of thousands of dollars and also provide for substantial terms of imprisonment. Each entry can constitute a separate violation.

U.S. Customs has been known to use undercover agents who have obtained employment at an importer's premises, former or current employees, as well as customers and the competitor, who is sure that you could only be doing better in business than they are by doing something illegal.

Business entities are not the only targets of these prosecutions. Invariably, the principals, executives and operational people in the company are also targeted. And Customs DOES arrest people.

Two things may account for the increase in these criminal prosecutions, at least by Customs. The first is the shift to an approach more akin to that used by its sister agency, the IRS. The other is their deterrent effect on other importers.

The second, and perhaps a more important reason has to do with the often ignored interplay between the judgment in the criminal proceedings and the civil penalties. Civil penalties are, in addition to and, independent of any criminal sanctions. Perhaps the most significant reason for Customs to urge a criminal prosecution is that it improves its ability to impose substantial penalties by giving them two bites at the penalty apple. Defendants and legal practitioners often fail to realize that a civil penalty case will survive even after the criminal proceeding has been terminated, and that a guilty determination in a criminal case constitutes a predicate to a case for civil penalties. Thus, resolution of a criminal matter, even by plea bargain, and even one which results in no jail time or penalty, can result in substantial civil penalties, unless great care is taken to coordinate the resolution of both the criminal and civil cases.

Whether the government wins or loses the criminal case, it still has the option of pursuing civil penalties through administrative proceedings within Customs, where it is less likely to lose. This is not barred by notions of double jeopardy because the penalties are civil. Moreover, evidence presented in either the criminal or civil proceeding will be used by the government in the other case, again, requiring careful coordination of the two cases.

Traditionally, most Customs criminal prosecutions arise under one of several provisions:

ENTRY BY MEANS OF FALSE STATEMENT - 18 U.S.C. 542 prohibits the entry of goods by means of a false statement. As a practical matter, this allegation is made where entry of goods has been accomplished by means of false statements in documentation, such as misdescribing goods or other characteristics of the transactions, e.g., value, origin or even the very right to make the entry. The maximum penalty is a fine of $5,000 or imprisonment for up to two years, or both.

SMUGGLING - 18 U.S.C. 545 prohibits smuggling. Somewhat surprisingly, commercial importers are not charged very often with smuggling. Although in commerce, wrong goods or additional goods may often be shipped and this could be considered smuggling. This is most likely because commercial importers can and do run afoul of a myriad of other laws and regulations. The maximum penalty for smuggling is a fine of $5,000 or imprisonment for up to five years, or both.

FALSE STATEMENTS - 18 U.S.C. 1001, a common criminal allegation relates to the making of false statements or representations to a government official, usually a Customs officer, agent, or inspector. Due to its breadth, it will almost always be made as a second charge to some other violation. The maximum penalty is a fine of not more than $10,000 or imprisonment for up to five years, or both.

Actual penalties are set out in Sentencing Guidelines and usually depend upon the monetary loss to the Government or other victims.

More recently, Customs has added a new statute to their enforcement arsenal which makes the sanctions of the other criminal provisions pale in comparison.

MONEY LAUNDERING - 18 U.S.C. 1961. Originally enacted to aid prosecution of organized crime and drug dealers, Customs has begun to employ the Money Laundering statute, 18 U.S.C. 1961. The Money Laundering statute gives the government the authority to seize all of an importer's assets, *prior to even obtaining an* indictment, let alone affording the importer a trial. The ability to seize all assets at such an early stage strengthens the government's hand because it threatens to put the defendant importer out of business long before there is any determination of guilt or innocence.

Beyond the long term implications of a criminal investigation, immediate attention must also be paid to the day-to-day business affairs. While resolution of the criminal matter may be months or years away, Customs will have already made determinations as to how it expects an importer to conduct its import business in the future. These determinations will not be in the best interest of the importer and if not addressed immediately, may make continued business impractical, if not impossible.

FOREIGN CORRUPT PRACTICES ACT ("FCP") - 15 U.S.C. ss78dd et seq.

Certain business practices that are the norm in other cultures are illegal under U.S. law. The FCP prohibits payment, directly or indirectly, of anything of value to government officials to obtain a benefit.

In certain countries, where potential problems can be created specifically for the purpose of soliciting payments, importers and exporters can unintentionally be ensnarled by this law which can complicate trade transactions.

---

[282] Generally *See* 19 USC 1592(c)(4), 19 C.F.R. 162.74, NAFTA *See* 19 USC 1592(c)(5)

[283] 19 USC 1592(c)(4)(B), 19 C.F.R. Part 171, Appendix B (E)(1), (3)

[284] 19 USC 1592(c)(4)(A), 19 C.F.R. Part 171, Appendix B (E)(2), (4)

[285] 19 USC 1592(c)(4) as amended by Public Law 103-182, 107 Stat 2057 Section 621

[286] 19 USC 1592

[287] 19 USC 1595a(c)

[288] 19 USC 1623(c); 19 C.F.R. Part 172

[289] 19 USC 1617

22. BEST PRACTICES

"Best Practices" is an often used and rarely defined term. It has been defined as everything from:

> A method or technique that has consistently shown results superior to those achieved with other means, and that is used as a benchmark.[290]

to

> Commercial or professional procedures that are accepted or prescribed as being correct or most effective.[291]

Unfortunately, Best Practices have often times become the vehicle by which government and management lay down, not just good practices, but goals of perfection by which they transfer the responsibility for quality and performance. With regards to Customs, they are frequently set out as factual illustrations rather than rules.

Best Practices, in the context of Risk Management for Importers and Exporters, as presented here, refers to:

- ✓ Written practices and procedures that facilitate compliance with the existing trade laws,
- ✓ Provide for continuity of practice during the absence or change in personnel, and
- ✓ A means for review and correction of problems that might arise.

While a company can seek certification from standard industries such as International Standards Organization (ISO), those certifications do not necessarily address issues that are peculiar to International Trade.

The following programs make up what your authors believe are the core areas of Best Practice in International Trade:

- ✓ Informed Compliance (§22.1 at 212)
- ✓ Known Importer (§22.2 at 220)
- ✓ Recordkeeping (§22.3 at 222)
- ✓ Identity Theft Protection (§22.4 at 227)
- ✓ Supply Chain Security (§22.5 at 229)

---

[290] http://www.businessdictionary.com/definition/best-practice.html

[291] http://www.oxforddictionaries.com/definition/english/best-practice

22.1. INFORMED COMPLIANCE

Executive Briefing

What every business really wants to know about implementing an Informed Compliance Program is why they should invest the time, effort, and resources necessary to create this program. You might ask yourself, "If Customs hasn't complained about what we are doing so far, we must be doing things correctly".

There are three (3) reasons:

1. The law requires it.

2. Implementing a program can help to minimize the exposure associated with problems which inevitably will show up. And no company is perfect.

3. Customs reviews are not based upon single transactions as much as annual reviews. When covering an entire year, any problem discovered is likely to be systemic and therefore pose a greater financial risk.

The fact is, you don't have a choice as to whether you create one. You will. The only issues are as to when and whether you do it voluntarily on your own schedule or as a result of government compunction under their time constraints.

"Informed Compliance" is defined as "A shared responsibility wherein Customs effectively communicates its requirements to the trade, and the people and businesses subject to those requirements conduct their regulated activities in conformance with U.S. laws and regulations."[292] In practice, importers are tasked with knowing the details of the rules and regulations and complying with them.

Though defined as a shared responsibility between Customs and the business community, the concept of Informed Compliance places a greater burden on the importer to be compliant and have a broad understanding of Customs Rules and Regulations.

This is an area where the help of your Customs Broker or Trade Counsel may be necessary to develop a comprehensive and usable compliance program.

The very nature of both Compliance and Enforcement is always evolving. In 2005, Customs' view of Informed Compliance had definitely shifted from cooperation to enforcement. One Customs Regulatory Audit Regional Field Director expressed the new priority as: "We're going after penalties rather than just saying we'll take the loss of revenue."[293]

From Customs' Perspective:

> A program of internal controls goes beyond drawing up a compliance manual with the normal buzzwords designed to impress auditors. The program should be tailored to the products being imported and should include documentation and records proving Country of Origin and compliance with duty preferences under U.S. trade agreements.

The internal compliance manual should be updated when new products are imported. Companies should demonstrate that employees have undergone compliance training and that managers are closely monitoring all import activities.

22.1.1. FAILURE TO ESTABLISH AN INFORMED COMPLIANCE PROGRAM

Customs cannot easily determine if you have a viable compliance program in place if it is not in writing. It will be presumed that you do not have one and that you are not in compliance. (*See* "Establishing the Informed Compliance Program" §22.1.8 at 216.)

The program has to be reduced to writing to allow for a review of your practices in comparison to what you actually do.

If you establish an Informed Compliance Program, evidenced by written corporate policies, and you diligently undertake to comply with your own policies, then you will, at least to some extent, be rewarded for your efforts even if you do not fully succeed in these compliance efforts. In many areas of U.S. regulatory, civil and criminal law involved in trade an opportunity exists for reduced penalties in exchange for diligent effort. In the case of U.S. Customs, the reward can be assistance in designing and implementing revisions to your policies and procedures in time to implement those changes and possibly foregoing or mitigating a penalty.

> **CAUTION**
>
> The 2014 Court of Appeals for the Federal Circuit in U.S. v Trek Leather addressed officer individual liability based upon the degree of direct involvement in import transaction as opposed to more removed supervision.
>
> In smaller companies where the distance between management and operations is shorter, this could affect traditional notions of officer immunity.

If you have not established a program on your own, or you have no formal written compliance policy, or you are not diligent in following your own policies, the government presumes that you are not likely to be very diligent in following their rules and you will be given *No Quarter*. Your chances of being subject to full compliance review and audit will increase as well as your chances of a significant penalty.

In the end, you will need to invest the time and effort to comply. The only question is under what circumstances you will make that investment: voluntarily, under your control as Informed Compliance, or involuntarily, under government threat of penalty after the *knock on the door* as *Enforced Compliance*.

22.1.2. FAILURE TO ADHERE TO AN ESTABLISHED INFORMED COMPLIANCE PROGRAM

The only thing worse than not have a written compliance manual, is having one that you don't follow.

If you don't follow your own compliance procedures why would Customs believe that you are following their rules?

One of the sources of this problem is using a canned Informed Compliance Program. They look good. They are inexpensive. But they reflect some perfect model of what you should do. They do not reflect what you actually do.

The best way to make sure you have an Informed Compliance Manual that you can follow is to start with documenting what you do, and then making as few changes as possible to correct any deficiencies.

22.1.3. COMPLIANCE EVALUATION

Customs evaluates your compliance initially through a Focused Assessment. Essentially, a Focused Assessment is a mini audit evaluating business systems, business and transaction records, as well as a sampling of import transactions. Typically, the initial review is of about 20 entry transactions. For each type of transaction or program you utilize, evaluations are graded on each program separately. So, if you import paying full duty, and duty free under NAFTA and Oman Free Trade Agreement, you will be subject to 3 reviews. If issues arise during the initial review the number of entries reviewed may also rise.

It is important to understand that multiple errors in a single transaction are not viewed as a single failure, but as multiple failures, which is why reaching a required compliance rate is often difficult.

22.1.4. FAILURE TO ACHIEVE COMPLIANCE LEVELS

Achieving compliance levels of 99%, which is what Customs considers a passing grade, in every area of your business is not a practical expectation. In most areas, at best, it is a goal to be strived for.

There are, however, certain areas where you should be able to more easily meet those goals.

- ✓ Ensuring that the value of goods declared matches to what was actually paid. This includes the cost of any additional amounts related to the imported products that you paid to third parties and/or were provided to the manufacturer free of charge or for less than their fair market value – (*See* "Additions to Transaction Value Appraisement" §11.2 at 75.)
- ✓ Ensuring that you can locate supporting records
- ✓ Ensuring that management understands what compliance rules apply to them
- ✓ Ensuring that management actually knows what goes on in this end of the business.

If you fall below the 99% compliance level in any area, but are in general compliance elsewhere, Customs will give you an opportunity to submit and implement an Improvement Plan. They will then, most likely, want to review the implementation to make sure they were effective.

If there appears to be a revenue loss and you cannot provide documents to allow a determination of the amount based upon smaller samplings of books and records, then you are headed for an Audit.

22.1.5. SUPPORT FOR ESTABLISHING A COMPLIANCE PROGRAM.

Establishing an Informed Compliance Program need not be overly burdensome. The problem in getting a program in place is that for any compliance program to work it is essential that top management support the effort.

This support can be difficult to obtain if management cannot see the justification or return on the investment of the time, effort, and expense. Businesses evaluate the need for resource-consuming compliance programs based upon its perception of expected return or the cost of non-compliance.

Management's evaluation of any non-compliance is likely based upon the expectation that their staff knows what it is doing, perceived tangible evidence such as delays in shipments, an increase in duty or other costs, penalties, or the proverbial Government *knock on the door*. Unlike years past, when every document submitted to Customs was reviewed, and most shipments were inspected, the years of transaction-by-transaction review have given way to post importation/exportation reviews after extended periods of time. Today, examination of a shipment's paperwork is rare and, in many cases, like an income tax return, no supporting documents are ever filed. These *after the fact* reviews sometimes occur a year or more after the fact, which means that potential problems are allowed to accrue in silence under the mistaken belief that the absence of a complaint by the government means that there are no problems. *In reality, it just means that Customs hasn't looked for them* ***yet****. Well, now they are very likely to do so.*

While most companies believe that it is their conduct alone that triggers a Customs' review, it can also be the result of an industry review of certain types of transaction, problems with types of goods, the vendors from which they are sourced or "...originate from referrals from other CBP disciplines utilizing risk management principles to identify specific companies involved in certain types of transactions."[294]

This means that your compliance review, whether it is through a Request for Information or a Focused Assessment, may not be the result of your conduct. You can be doing everything correctly. Nevertheless, your transaction may have something in common with others that are not so correct.

22.1.6. IMPORTER SELF-ASSESSMENT

Importer Self-Assessment, also known as ISA, is another voluntary program that offers certain benefits to members such as removal from Regulatory Audit's pool for Focused Assessments and additional leeway with prior disclosures.

If you are a C-TPAT member in good standing, your level of imports is significantly large and you have internal auditors who will, in lieu of Customs, perform an annual audit on your transactions, you may want to consider this program.

22.1.7. SARBANES-OXLEY (SOX)

Customs and Trade Compliance can also impacts regulatory programs not normally considered in the context of international trade.

Sarbanes-Oxley was introduced in 2002 to impose on directors of publicly traded companies an affirmative obligation to ensure accurate financial management and reporting. To some extent it also applies to privately held companies, when they submitted financial statements, to publicly traded companies such as banks. Even though not required, some larger privately held companies nevertheless employ comparable financial compliance standards as part of their best practices.

> Even if your company is not publically traded it might still follow SOX type protocols.
>
> Check with your chief financial offer or financial controller to determine whether your company operates under a Sarbanes-Oxley type compliance program and how it affects operations and documentation.

International purchase and sales fall directly within the purview of SOX and although often times ignored, financial payment practices being very different than those employed in domestic transactions can easily run afoul of corporate guidelines.

If your company does adhere to SOX protocols you should consider coordinating your trade compliance activities with your company's finance department.

22.1.8. ESTABLISHING THE INFORMED COMPLIANCE PROGRAM

There are many ways to set up and maintain an Informed Compliance program. However, regardless of the scale of the program you choose to implement, or how you chose to implement it, certain things remain constant.

What Every Member of the Trade Community Should Know About:

Reasonable Care

(A checklist for Compliance)

AN INFORMED COMPLIANCE PUBLICATION

CUSTOMS and BORDER PROTECTION

1. *The process starts with authority, commitment, and a mandate from senior management.*
2. *You cannot entirely outsource either your responsibility or your liability to an outside consultant. It requires your direct involvement.*
3. *This is not a process that you can do totally on your own. Independent expertise is needed.*
4. *This cannot be just another project. It, like quality, has to become part of the corporate culture.*
5. *It will require a commitment of time and resources to get started but it must become part of the daily routine and, eventually, it will.*
6. *During the process you will uncover problems that were either not recognized, ignored, or were even hidden. But it is better that you find them (and remedy them) than the Government find them.*
7. *Opportunities to reduce duty expenses or improve operations are also often discovered during the process and sometimes even the opportunity to recover past duties from the government as well.*

8. *The benefit clock only starts when your effort starts. There is no retroactive tolerance or leniency offered if you start an Informed Compliance Program late.*
9. *Change is inevitable. Businesses change and your compliance program must adapt.*

The goal of any good Informed Compliance Program is obviously to prevent problems from developing in the first place, and if they do (and some inevitably will) to be able to find them and address them while they are small and before the government does, all with as little additional overhead as possible.

Since each business is as different as are their transactions and management styles, a cookie cutter or off the shelf approach to either implementing or maintaining an Informed Compliance Program is generally inefficient, impractical, and, in the long run, more expensive. Cookie cutter and off-the-shelf programs rarely reflect what you are actually doing and that makes you look like you are ignoring even your own procedures, which will do more harm than good.

One efficient method for implementing and maintaining an Informed Compliance Program is through a Spiral Approach.

In a Spiral Approach, rather than viewing implementation as an isolated and all-consuming project where all areas and all issues are addressed simultaneously, the process starts with an understanding of the systems that exist through limited sampling, and then to establish a program that progresses in incremental stages based upon exigencies, issues, volume, and time since last review.

The Spiral Approach focuses on *Best Practices* aimed at avoiding problems. It focuses on the use of small samplings to rapidly identify problems while they are small, resolving those problems and revising systems to avoid them in the future.

It views compliance and quantification and resolution of past problems as related but separate activities. It attempts to avoid large-scale samplings traditionally associated with compliance reviews since it is not usually necessary to quantify a problem in order to recognize that one exists. Quantification deals with history that we cannot change. It is expensive, time consuming and often undertaken at the expense of a rapid correction of the problem. You cannot avoid the consequence of past mistakes and a more in-depth review may be necessary to file a Prior Disclosure in order to mitigate penalties, but you cannot change the past. (*See* "Voluntary Prior Disclosure - The Preemptive Strike" §21.2.1 at 204.) You can, however, change the present and future.

22.1.9. THE SPIRAL IMPLEMENTATION APPROACH

The Spiral Approach presumes that you are doing most things correctly. What is needed is to reduce those practices to writing and to fix only those areas which are deficient.

The Spiral Approach recognizes that the easiest way to develop Best Practices that work is not to superimpose new systems on overly worked staff, but rather to take the systems that already exist, reduce those Best Practice rules to writing, make as few adjustments as is possible to improve compliance, and to implement those changes in prioritized stages until they become part of the daily routine. Experience shows that trying to implement too many changes at one time will not result in sustainable improvement

The Spiral Approach to implementing an Informed Compliance Program is divided into eight (8) phases. You get to set the time for each phase which will depend upon the size of the company and the nature of your business.

> The number one enemy of all compliance programs is procrastination.
>
> The second is assuming that you are in compliance just because no one has said anything, yet.

Most important is to start, set reasonable target deadlines, and KEEP THE PROCESS MOVING.

A full copy of the Spiral Implementation Approach, along with all worksheets, is available free by contacting the authors. (*See* "Free From the Authors §23 at 241.)

THE EIGHT PHASES OF THE SPIRAL APPROACH

Phase 1 – Preliminaries – Getting Ready

Understanding who needs to be involved – who has answers and authority.

Phase 2 – Familiarization with Existing Systems and Records

Based upon discussion with staff who are supposedly involved with the identification and maintenance of the records and where and how to find these records

- ✓ DRAFT - Transaction Flow Memorandum explaining what type of transactions the business undertakes and the flow of communications with respect to each one.
- ✓ DRAFT - Records Memorandum explaining what documents are maintained, how they are identified, where they are maintained, and who is responsible for their maintenance and retrieval.

Phase 3 – Documenting Existing Systems and Records

(One File Review - One file for each type of transaction, e.g., Import Transaction, Export Transaction, FOB Shipment vs DDP Shipment, or one where you're importing under a special program, such as NAFTA.

- ✓ DETERMINE - If the documents pulled match what the staff reported in the discussion referenced in Phase 2.
- ✓ DRAFT - Recordkeeping Memorandum with examples from each file(s) pulled.

Phase 4 – Preliminary Record Test

(Two File Review - Two for each of the transaction types identified in Phase 3)

- ✓ COMPLETE - General Company Questionnaire.

- ✓ UPDATE - Transaction Flow Memorandum or Memorandums if processes are substantially different.
- ✓ UPDATE - Records Memorandum or Memorandums if processes are substantially different.

Phase 5 – Preliminary Review of Substantive Matters

- ✓ COMPLETE - Valuation Questionnaire(s). If goods are purchased on a different basis or there are different relationships between the buyer and seller, then a separate Valuation Questionnaire might be required for each.
- ✓ COMPLETE - Classification Questionnaire(s). A different questionnaire might be required for different classes of products.
- ✓ COMPLETE - Shipping and Receiving Questionnaire.

Phase 6 – Detailed Review of Identified Issues

- ✓ DRAFT - Corrective Action Memorandum which identifies issues which need to be addressed along with their priority and who will be responsible for implementing the corrections.
- ✓ CALENDAR. After prioritizing corrective actions, identify reasonable timelines for implementation.
- ✓ DETERMINE - If there is a need for a Prior Disclosure to address past problems.
- ✓ DRAFT - The Informed Compliance Memorandum. To the extent possible, by copying or referencing any of the other memorandums and or questionnaires.

Phase 7 –Implementing Fixes

- ✓ IMPLEMENT Corrective Actions.
- ✓ UPDATE - Transaction Flow Memorandum.
- ✓ UPDATE - Informed Compliance Memorandum.
- ✓ CALENDAR - Follow-up for 30, 60, and 120 days to determine if corrective measures are being implemented and proving effective or require further changes. Following up on corrections is the hallmark of good compliance. It demonstrates your attention to detail and is looked upon favorably by Customs

Phase 8 – Periodic Follow-up

(Three File Review – Three for each of the transaction types identified in Phase 3 PLUS any new types of transactions.)

Business is not static. Employees are not static. Review to see what if anything has changed. How frequently follow-ups are performed will be determined based upon the issues identified. Problem areas should be reviewed more frequently than general operations.

- ✓ CALENDAR - Periodic Follow-up,
- ✓ ACTUALLY - Perform the Periodic Follow-up.

Return to Phase 3. ↩

[292] House Ways and Means Committee Report, H.R. Rep. No. 3450, 103d Cong., First Sess. 120. (1993)

[293] "The Journal of Commerce" (Nov. 9, 2005) (quoting regional field director Robert E. Allen).

[294] *Quick Response Audits*, Customs and Border Patrol (Jan. 17, 2006); *See* http://www.customs.gov/xp/cgov/import/regulatory_audit_program/rad_program/focused_assessment/quick_response.xml

22.2. KNOWN IMPORTER

22.2.1. TRUSTED TRADER

The Trusted Trader program, introduced in June 2014 is an effort by Customs to unify several compliance programs, creating a more holistic and efficient approach to shipment processing and increased importer benefits.

Ultimately, it is intended to coordinate with comparable programs in other countries as part of a global initiative under the Security Framework.

Unfortunately, the program came with a very high cost of participation, which effectively limited availability of Trusted Trader benefits to only the largest importers. Participation is limited to those importers who are C-TPAT Tier 3 (most smaller importers are only validated as Tier 2) and who also participated in the Importer Self-Assessment program (ISA), which essentially requires an annual internal audit of import compliance.

22.2.2. BROKER KNOWN IMPORTER PROGRAM (TRUSTED TRADER LITE)

The Broker Known Importer Program (BKIP), introduced in May 2015, with its lower cost of entry, holds the promise of bringing some of the Trusted Trader benefits within reach of smaller importers.

While touted as a new program, in many ways it merely formalizes what many good brokers have been doing with their clients for decades, except that now the Customs Broker and the importer actually get some tangible benefit for the effort.

Precisely what benefits will come from participation in the BKIP is not yet known, but it is clear that it is intended to provide some[295] to be an essential part of a more global and integrated approach to an importer's Informed Compliance and Customs shipment processing.

The object of the BKIP is to create an impetus for the Customs Broker who is filing importer information to take affirmative steps to confirm a client's identities, better understand their client's

> Nothing is ever free, but in international trade this is a close as it gets.
>
> It is a relatively painless way to improve operations and to identify weaknesses in your current practices.

> To make your participation as easy as possible, ask your Customs Broker if they have access to the BKIP functions of Trade-ID.
>
> The BKIP functions of Trade-ID provides for password protected online access to the BKIP questionnaires, which is obviously faster and easier than handling paper, provides for the ability to update information in the future rather than completing new questionnaires, and to easily upload any supporting documents.

import operations and practices and, where necessary, to educate them about their responsibilities.

From a Customs' perspective, it is hoped that it will improve importer compliance allowing Customs to better focus its resources *elsewhere*.

For the importer perspective, if you qualify, it is expected that it will allow Customs to improve the processing of your entries.

From the Customs Broker's standpoint, it enhances ability to maintain client communications and better service the client.

You can expect that the broker will:

- ✓ Ask you a lot of questions about every area of your import and business practices that affect your compliance with the Customs rules;
- ✓ As necessary, ask you for supporting documentation,
- ✓ Discuss with you any areas of concern;
- ✓ Provide you with information and publications needed to improve your knowledge and compliance activities;
- ✓ Update the information with you periodically; and
- ✓ Maintain the information and make it available to Customs to support the benefit that comes from designating an Importer as "Known."
- ✓ From a compliance standpoint many of the questions your broker will ask and issues they will review will serve as a good starting point for establishing an Informed Compliance program or identifying issues within your existing program.

---

[295] Trade Facilitation and Enforcement Act of 2015, Public Law No: 114-125, 130 Stat. 122 §**101** (2016)

22.3. RECORDKEEPING

Executive Briefing

Customs has the right to evaluate and/or re-evaluate your transactions at any time.

Customs expects that you will be able to support any claims you make through documentation.

Unlike recordkeeping for tax purposes, which focuses primarily on financial transactions, under Customs law, documentation is also required to substantiate other details about your product, its development, usage and your eligibility for every duty remission program you used.

An effective Customs Recordkeeping program is not difficult to maintain, if properly set up. The setup may, however, require assistance from either your Customs Broker or an attorney experienced in Customs matters to determine which of the over 200 types of documentation and information you are required to maintain.

22.3.1. OBLIGATION TO MAINTAIN RECORDS

Importers are required to keep records tracing a transaction from the time the product is purchased until the disposition of the products. It is essential to be able to trace the entire transaction using these documents as Customs may make requests for these documents. The importer is responsible for maintaining these records even if it uses a Customs Broker who retains copies in fulfillment of their own recordkeeping compliance obligations.

22.3.2. DOCUMENTS TO BE MAINTAINED AND HOW

With some limited exceptions, trade related documents must be kept for five (5) years.[296]

Many of the trade related documents are also revenue documents. Care needs to be taken not to dispose of revenue documents prematurely by relying on the Customs Recordkeeping timelines without taking into consideration recordkeeping rules of other agencies with which you might be involved.

> Creating a sample document package with annotations (highlighting and colored pens work exceedingly well) as to what information connects records together and where they are generally filed in the office is a low cost but highly efficient means of documenting your record retention system. (*See* "The Spiral Implementation Approach", §22.1.9 at 217.)

The documents need to be maintained in a secure location and be readily accessible. Readily accessible can be a major problem if not addressed in advance.

- As records get archived and time passes it can become

more difficult to locate specific documents with the archive.

- In many smaller companies the precise location of records rest almost exclusively within the memory of
- employees who may no longer be there.
- Cross referencing information which would allow someone to find financial records relating to a trade transaction, too often is not on the documents and is based upon the experience of employees who may have left.

Maintaining documentation as to how records are archived, where and how to find them, and who to contact for assistance can avoid the problem.

22.3.3. OBLIGATION TO PRODUCE RECORDS

Customs can make a demand for these records at any time during the retention period in the form of a Request for Information or in a more formal audit process. When requested as part of a Request for Information, the importer will generally have 30 days to produce the documents. Time frames for other demands will be different and usually shorter.

22.3.4. FAILURE TO MAINTAIN OR PRODUCE RECORDS

The inability to provide documentation can lead to an increase in duty on your importation or all future importation of similar articles, or a review of all of your import practices through a Focused Assessment or a full blown Audit.

> **CAUTION**
>
> You are NOT required to maintain every record listed in the "(a)(1)(A)" list; only those that apply to your product and transaction.
>
> Your answers to the Broker Known Importer questions will help identify which documents relate to your transactions.
>
> Your Customs Broker and/or Trade Counsel can assist you in identifying which documents you need to retain.

The documentation which you are required to maintain is commonly referred to, probably for lack of a better term, as the "(a)(1)(A)" list referring to its Tariff Act citation – 19 U.S.C. 1509 (a)(1)(A)[297], (19 C.F.R. 163, T.D. 96-1)

The following is a representative extract of the types of documentation generally required of all importers to maintain and those that would be unique to your particular business:

Figure 64 - Documentation supporting each declaration made in your Customs Entry

Bond information (§142.4)
Bond information (except if 10.101 or 142.4(c) applies) (§142.4)
Bond Number, Bond Type Code and Surety code (§142.3)
Broker/Importer Filer Number (§§141.61, 142.3a)
Country of Origin
Declaration of entry (usually contained on the entry summary or warehouse entry). (§ 141.19)
Description of Merchandise (§142.6)
Entered Value, Charges, and Relationship (§ 141.61)
Entry Date (§141.61)
Entry Number (§§ 142.3, 142.3a)
Entry Summary Date (§141.61)
Evidence of right to make entry (airway bill/bill of lading or carrier certificate, etc.) when goods are imported on a common carrier. (§§141.11 through 141.15)
Exporting Country and Date Exported (§141.61)
Foreign Port of Lading
Foreign Trade Zone Designation and Status
Foreign Trade Zone Transfers. Supporting documents to CF 214 (§146.32)
Gross Weight (§141.61)
HTSUSA Number (§142.6)
I.T. (In-bond) Entry Date (for IT Entries only)
Import Date and Line Numbers
Importer of Record Name and Address (§141.61)
Importer of Record Number (§141.61)
Importing Carrier Name (§141.61)
IT/BL/AWB Number and Code (§141.11)
Manifest Quantity (§142.6)
Manufacturer ID Number (for AD/CVD must be actual mfr.)
Mode of Transportation (MOT Code)
Net Quantity in HTSUSA Units (§141.61)
Packing list (where appropriate) (§142.3)
Port Code
Power of attorney (when required by regulations). (§ 141.32)
Reference Number
Signature of Declarant, Title, and Date (§141.61)
Total Value
U.S. Port of Unlading
Ultimate Consignee Address (§142.3)
Ultimate Consignee Name and Number/street address of premises shipment is to be delivered (§§141.61, 142.3)
Vessel, Vehicle or Air Manifest (filed by the carrier) (Parts 4, 18, 122, 123)
Warehouse entry information (§144.12)

Figure 65 - Documents required to support reduced duty liability claims under other tariff act rules

Documents required for entry of articles exported and returned. (Part 10)
Foreign shipper's declaration or master's certificate, declaration for free entry by owner, importer or consignee. (§§10.1 through 10.6)
Certificate from foreign shipper for reusable containers. (§10.7)
Declaration of person performing alterations or repairs. (§10.8)
Declaration of processing. (§10.9)
Declaration by assembler Endorsement by importer. (§ 10.24)
Documents required for Temporary Importations Under Bond. (§§ 10.31, 10.35)
Declarations for articles exported and returned. (§§ 10.66, 10.67)
Documents for commercial samples, tools, theatrical effects. (§§10.68, 10.69)
Actual User Declaration (when classification involves actual use). (§10.134)
End Use Certificate. (§10.138)

Figure 67 - Documents required when importing certain products.

Additional invoice information required for certain classes of merchandise including, but not limited to: (§141.89)

Alcohol Declaration of non-beverage ethyl alcohol, ATF permit. (§10.99)

Automotive Products Certificate. (§10.84)

Beef Certificate of fresh, chilled or frozen beef. (§ 10.180)

Boat declarations (CG-5096) and USCG exemption. (§ 12.85)

Certificate of legal exportation

Cheese. European Community cheese affidavit. (§ 12.6)

Civil aircraft parts/simulator documentation and certifications. (§10.183)

Coffee Form O (currently suspended) (19 U.S.C. §1356k)

Copper fluxing material. Declarations for copper fluxing material (§10.98)

Cotton invoice information, additional documents (Part 151, subpart F)

Cultural property declarations, statements and certificates of origin (§§12.104 through 12.104i)

Drugs, Animal. Permit animal viruses, serums and toxins (§12.17)

Drugs, Human. HHS license for viruses, toxins, antitoxins, etc. for treatment of man (§12.21)

Drugs, New. Notice of claimed investigational exemption for a new drug (§12.23)

Electronic Products. Form 2877 and required declarations for electronics products (§ 12.91)

Evidence of exemption

Goods under lease. Lease Statement (§10.108)

Jadeite and Rubies. Documentation supporting importer's certification on jadeite, rubies, or articles of jewelry containing jadeite or rubies, including an exporter's certification. (§12.151)

Knives, switchblade. Declarations for switchblade knives (§12.99)

Lumber, kits. Softwood Lumber Importer Declaration Supporting Documentation, Softwood Lumber Home Packages and Kits Documentation. (§12.142)

Lumber. Canadian-issued Export Permit, Certificate of Origin issued by Canada's Maritime Lumber Bureau. (§12.140(b) and (c))

Metal articles. Declaration by importer of use of certain metal articles (§54.5)

Milk or Cream. HHS permit for milk or cream importation (§12.7)

Motor vehicle declarations (§§12.73, 12.80)

Otter skins. Shipper's declaration, official certificate for seal and otter skins (§ 12.61)

Pesticides, etc. notice of arrival (§12.110)

Petroleum imports sampling/lab information Out turn Report 24. to 25—Reserved (Part 151, subpart C)

Petroleum. Certificate of importer of crude petroleum (§10.179)

Plants. Notice of arrival for plant and plant products (§12.11)

Pre-Columbian monumental and architectural sculpture and murals (§§12.105 through 12.109)

Professional Equipment. Lists for samples, professional equipment, theatrical effects (§ 10.36)

Purebred breeding certificate (§§10.70, 10.71)

Quota goods. Acknowledgment of delivery for mailed items subject to quota (§132.23)

Scientific and Educational Apparatus. Requirements for entry of scientific and educational apparatus (15 CFR part 301)

Steel Entries: Ordering specifications, including but not limited to, all applicable industry standards and mill certificates, including but not limited to, chemical composition.

Sugar imports sampling/lab information (Chemical Analysis) (Part 151, subpart B)

Toxic substances: TSCA statements (§§12.118 through 12.127)

Trademarked goods. Consent from trademark or trade name holder to import otherwise restricted goods (§§133.21(e), 133.22(c)(3) and 133.23€)

Wool and Hair invoice information, additional documents (Part 151, subpart E)

Figure 68 - Documents required under trade agreements and similar programs

AGOA Textile Certificate of Origin and supporting records. (§10.216) ATPDEA Declaration of Compliance for Brassieres. (§10.248) ATPDEA Non-textile Certificate of Origin. (§10.256) ATPDEA Textile Certificate of Origin. (§10.246) BFTA records that the importer may have in support of a BFTA claim for preferential tariff treatment, including an importer's declaration. (§10.805) BFTA TPL certificate of eligibility. (§10.820) BFTA TPL declaration. (§10.821) CAFTA-DR records that the importer may have in support of a CAFTA-DR claim for preferential tariff treatment, including an importer's certification. (§10.585) Carnets (serves as entry and bond document where applicable). (Part 114) CBI Documents, etc. required for duty-free entry of spirituous beverages produced in Canada from CBI rum, declaration of Canadian processor (plus supporting information). (§ 10.199) CBI Documents, etc. required for entries of CBI merchandise, CBI declaration of origin (plus supporting information). (§§10.191 through 10.198) CBTPA Declaration of Compliance for brassieres. (§ 10.228) CBTPA Non-textile Certificate of Origin and supporting records (§10.236) CBTPA Textile Certificate of Origin and supporting records (§10.226) FTA TPL Certificate of eligibility. (§10.522S) GSP Documents, etc. required for entries of GSP merchandise, GSP Declaration (plus supporting documentation) (§§10.171 through 10.178)	HOPE Act Declaration of Compliance. (§10.848) MFTA records that the importer may have in support of a MFTA claim for preferential tariff treatment, including an importer's declaration. (§10.765) NAFTA Certificate of origin and supporting records. (§ 181.22) NAFTA textile requirements. (§102.25) OFTA records that the importer may have in support of an OFTA claim for preferential tariff treatment, including an importer's declaration. (§10.865) OFTA TPL certificate of eligibility. (§10.883) OFTA TPL declaration. (§10.884) PTPA records that the importer may have in support of a PTPA claim for preferential tariff treatment, including an importer's certification. (§10.905) SFTA records that the importer may have in support of a SFTA claim for preferential tariff treatment, including an importer's supporting statement if previously required by the port director. (§10.512) UKFTA records that the importer may have in support of a UKFTA claim for preferential tariff treatment, including an importer's certification. (§10.1005) US-CFTA Certification of origin and supporting records. (§10.410) US-JFTA records that the importer may have in support of a US-JFTA claim for preferential tariff treatment, including an importer's declaration. (§10.704)

296 19 C.F.R. 163.4

297 19 USC 1509 (a)(1)(A), (19 C.F.R. 163, T.D. 96-1)

22.4. PROTECTING YOUR BUSINESS FROM IDENTITY THEFT IN INTERNATIONAL TRANSACTIONS

Executive Briefing

Identity theft is not just for individuals, credit cards and bank accounts. In International Trade, the theft of identity has spread to businesses where it has been the good reputation that the business has with government agencies which is being stolen as a vehicle for circumventing interdiction.

You cannot stop it. But you can take steps to protect against it, identify it in its infancy, and garner cooperation from the government in doing so.

Your authors consider the risk to be significant enough that we want to help you help yourself. (*See* "Free from the Authors" §23 at 241.)

22.4.1. PROTECTING AGAINST IDENTITY THEFT

Identity theft is as much a problem for service providers as it is for importers and exporters. Just as you will want to know the *bona fides* of those you authorize to act as your agent, e.g., Customs Brokers, NVOs, Forwarders, you can expect that they will want to confirm your *bona fides* as well.

Mutual verification of identities is as much for your protection as it is for your service providers.

This mutual verification of identity and authority is an essential part of protecting against Identity Theft in international trade transactions.

If both you and your service providers are assured as to the legitimacy of those with whom they are dealing, it can eliminate at least one known source of identity theft. Unfortunately, this will not totally protect against identity theft. The best that can be hoped for is early identification.

22.4.2. IDENTITY THEFT AND THE POWER OF ATTORNEY

Customs used to require a certificate of authority from every importing company to prove that the person signing a Power of Attorney actually had the authority to bind their company, but that practice was abandoned in the 1970's.

With the passage of the Trade Facilitation and Enforcement Act of 2015[298] Customs Brokers are once again required to obtain certain information and documentation and to verify it in order to confirm authority and identity, changing what was merely a good practice into a legal requirement.

CAUTION

If a Customs Broker is satisfied with you merely filling in a Power of Attorney and signing it, you should probably be as concerned about them as they would be about you if you refused to provide them information and documentation requested or refused to cooperate in verifying it.

Some importers are not going to like the additional requirements, but in this case the law actually serves to protect the legitimate importer.

The Broker Known Importer Program can be viewed as an extension of that process of getting to know you. The difference, of course, is that participating in BKIP should have tangible benefits in terms of how Customs processed your entries.

22.4.3. FERRETING OUT THEFT OF YOUR IDENTITY IN IMPORT TRANSACTIONS

Your Customs Broker can provide you with a list of all of the entries it has handled on your behalf. This list will not reveal information filed by other authorized Brokers at other ports, couriers, nor those filed by those who have stolen your identity.

A good practice is to, at least annually, obtain a complete list of entries associated with your EIN number regardless of who made the filing. This will allow you to track all of your entries as well as provide you with the opportunity to identify in stances of corporate identity theft.

> Comparing these comprehensive reports of entries or export sales to a list of known transactions will help you identify any improper use of your EIN.
>
> Look for the *Free Offer* for help in obtaining these reports . (*See* "Free From the Authors" §23 at 241.)

These same reports can also be used to confirm the liquidation dates on any transactions that you need to Protest. If you are going to make dual use of the reports you should consider requesting the list more often: once per quarter rather than just once per year.

There are several reports that can be requested from different entities, each accessing the same Customs Entry database.

- ✓ If you have access to the Automated Commercial Environment (ACE), then you already have access to that list. Keep in mind that not all ACE reports are created equal. Your access gives you the full list of entries filed in your name regardless of the filer, while the report a Customs Broker can provide will only identify the entries they filed on your behalf.
- ✓ If you have Continuous Customs Bond, your Surety may be able to provide you with a list of entry numbers and dates.
- ✓ Customs Office of Financial Management can provide a report identifying basic entry information regarding liquidated entries and detailed information about only unliquidated entries.
- ✓ Customs can also provide a more comprehensive list known as "ITRAC" or Importer Trade Activity Report which contains detailed information about both liquidated and unliquidated entries through the Freedom of Information Act, which will take a few weeks to process.

22.4.4. FERRETING OUT THEFT OF YOUR IDENTITY IN EXPORT TRANSACTIONS

Electronic Export Information (EEI)s are filed with Census for all exports.

In the same way that Customs can provide a list of import transactions undertaken under your EIN, Census can provide an extract of the records in the Automated Export System which were filed under your EIN.

Comparing this list to your transaction logs can help to both:

- ✓ Identity transactions which are not yours, and
- ✓ Confirm proper filings on Routed Shipments

[298] Trade Facilitation and Enforcement Act of 2015, Public Law No: 114-125, 130 Stat. 122 §116 (2016)

22.5. SUPPLY CHAIN SECURITY

The United States implemented as part of the post 9-11 security enhancements, a joint industry and trade program called Customs-Trade Partnership Against Terrorism ("C-TPAT"). This program rewards participating companies with reduced costly inspections in exchange for implementation of enhanced and verifiable security practices.

Today, other countries have implemented similar security programs paralleling C-TPAT and, under Mutual Recognition, those programs grant reciprocity.

22.5.1. CUSTOMS TRADE PARTNERSHIP AGAINST TERRORISM

The United States implemented as part of the post 9-11 security enhancements, a joint industry and trade program called Customs-Trade Partnership Against Terrorism ("C-TPAT"). This program rewards participating companies with reduced costly inspections in exchange for implementation of enhanced and verifiable security practices.

Today, other countries have implemented similar security programs paralleling C-TPAT and, under Mutual Recognition, those programs grant reciprocity.

C-TPAT is a voluntary enhanced supply chain security program. It is a great program, but it may not be right for everyone.

> C-TPAT originally only applied to Imports. It now also applies to exports.

For importers, it offers significant benefits in the form of reduced level of inspection.

For exporters, it means helping your clients receive the benefits of any security programs they are members of.

For many other companies in the supply chain, such as Customs Brokers and Freight Consolidators, there is no direct benefit and they only participate because their clients require them to.

For still other companies in the supply chain, such as foreign based suppliers and/or freight consolidators, domestic based warehouses and truckers, they are not even eligible to participate.

Since the program is voluntary, as an importer you have a choice. The bottom line in making the decision as to whether to participate comes down to: Is C-TPAT worth enough in terms of dollars and cents of profit that I should consider it?

The program requires more than merely establishing good practices; it requires persistent effort and the ability to prove that your procedures are actually effective.

As part of Validation, Customs will visit both your domestic facilities and at least one of your foreign facilities. And not just once: under the Safe Port Act this first Validation occurs within the first year of membership and then every three years thereafter.

Being dropped from the program for non-performance does not merely put you in the same position as other non-participants; it paints you as high risk.

The following are matters that you should consider in making the determination to participate:

- ☐ JUST-IN-TIME vs. LARGE INVENTORIES

  If you carry large inventories for domestic distribution there is less of a benefit from participating in C-TPAT. If you rely on Just-in-Time deliveries, do drop shipments from the piers, or your ocean container carries time sensitive or perishable merchandise, a delay due to a Customs inspection might be a deal breaker.

  So, if your business relies on fast releases then you do need to consider joining C-TPAT.

  Even if your supply chain has built in delay contingencies, you should nonetheless evaluate the total annual cost of those inspections.

- ☐ CUSTOMS INSPECTIONS

  If you have low import volumes and you are not receiving a lot of inspections, then it might not be economically practical for you to join C-TPAT.

  Inspection costs include more than just fees related directly to the inspection. Though often not considered part of the inspection costs, there are additional Per Diems or Detention Charges as well as Demurrage and Storage charges that can accrue while waiting for the inspection as well as the cost of cartage from the inspection station.

  As your volume increases and the number of inspections increase, resulting in more costs, then joining C-TPAT should be a consideration.

- ☐ FOREIGN VENDORS

  If your company uses an ever changing selection of small volume vendors, then the overhead for C-TPAT can become prohibitive.

On the other hand, if your company has a more stable source of suppliers or high volume vendors, then the program might be worth considering.

- ☐ FC VS LCL CARGO

  If the majority of your imports are Less then Container Load (LCL), and moves along with other companies' cargo, the ocean container is going to be inspected according to the lowest level of security within the container and you will not receive any substantial C-TPAT benefits.

  If you are moving full containers or you consolidate your own containers, then you may be able to benefit from C-TPAT membership.

- ☐ EXPORT AND IMPORT

  If you are importing and exporting only to countries that do not have any mutually recognized security programs with the U.S., the foreign country will not treat your cargo better than anyone else.

  If you are importing but also exporting volumes to a country with Mutual Recognition with the United States then your participation in C-TPAT can be of mutual benefit to you as well as your customers where they are located in countries with which the U.S. has Mutual Recognition and if they are members of their local security program. (See Cooperative Security Programs "WCO International Security Framework and Mutual Recognition" §22.5.2 at 232.)

- ☐ CANADA AND MEXICO MANUFACTURERS

  If you are a foreign manufacturer in Canada or Mexico only, you too can join C-TPAT.

  If you ship only in response to an order from a U.S. based company, you are not going to benefit from C-TPAT membership.

  If you are actively marketing your products for sale to U.S. based companies, then your customers, who are themselves members of C-TPAT, will benefit from your membership.

- ☐ 3 PL DOMESTIC DISTRIBUTOR

  Customs has expanded its membership in C-TPAT to now include certain Third Party Logistics Provider (3PL). Membership is limited to 3PLs that are, what is termed, Asset Based, which essentially means they own their facilities and/or equipment. By definition, it therefore excludes many smaller 3PLs that prefer to rent, lease, engage, or purchase resources and services on an as-needed basis rather than incurring fixed overhead.

- ☐ NOT IMPORTER OF RECORD

  If all of your purchases are on a "landed duty paid basis" and you are not the importer of record because you have no control over your supply chain, you cannot join

C-TPAT.

- ☐ INFORMED COMPLIANCE

  If you have an informed compliance program in your company, C TPAT would be a natural extension of your existing program. Today, in fact, even if you are not a member of C-TPAT, when Customs reviews your import practices under a Focused Assessment, they will review your Supply Chain Security under very similar criteria as that applied to participants in the C-TPAT program.

- ☐ INTERNATIONAL ORGANIZATION FOR STANDARDIZATION ISO

  If your company has International Organization for Standardization Certification for ISO 9000, ISO 14000, ISO 27000, ISO 22000 or any other international management standards, coordinating C-TPAT with it can be very effective.

22.5.2. WCO INTERNATIONAL SECURITY FRAMEWORK AND MUTUAL RECOGNITION

Many countries, starting with the United States, having recognized the limitations of their resources in securing International Trade, created programs which encourage joint effort between industry and government in enhancing supply chain security. These programs are, for the most part, voluntary and the increased obligations assumed by importers and exporters are generally balanced by a reduction in cost and delays resulting from cargo inspections.

The need for better supply chain security has resulted in the incorporation into the international trading conventions of a framework for Mutual Recognition between countries of their respective security programs. For example, if a company is approved under the Authorized Economic Operator (AEO) program, they will be viewed as being in compliance with the U.S. Customs-Trade Partnership Against Terrorism (C-TPAT). The goal is to eliminate redundant activities and avoid conflicting requirements. As of this date, the following countries have executed mutual recognition agreements under this Framework with the United States:

COUNTRY	PROGRAM NAME	EFFECTIVE
New Zealand	Secure Export Scheme	June 2007
Canada	Partners in Protection	June 2008
Jordan	Golden List	June 2008
Japan	Authorized Economic Operator	June 2009
Korea	Authorized Economic Operator	June 2010
European Union	Authorized Economic Operator	May 2012
Taiwan/Taipei	Authorized Economic Operator	November 2012
Israel	Authorized Economic Operator	June 2014
China	Classified Management of Enterprises Program	Pending (TBD)

Switzerland	Swiss Federal Customs Administration	Pending (TBD)
Mexico	New Scheme of Certified Companies (Nuevo Esquema de Empresas Certificadas or NEEC)	October 2014
Singapore	Secure Trade Partnership	December 2014
Dominican Republic	Authorized Economic Operator	December 2015

Figure 69 - Mutual Security Programs under WCO SAFE Framework.

22.5.3. TRANSPORTATION SECURITY ADMINISTRATION (TSA) KNOWN SHIPPER PROGRAM

The Known Shipper Program under the Transportation Security Administration (TSA) applies only to Air Freight. It focuses on whether certain cargo is permitted to be transported on aircraft that also carries passengers or must be moved on freight-only aircraft.

While it affects shippers, it does not provide for direct shipper participation. It is essentially a verification program implemented through Carriers and Freight Forwarders who are approved as Intermediary Air Carriers (IAC).

Regardless of whether cargo is moving on a passenger or freight-only aircraft, 100% of cargo is subject to screening and inspection.

While also addressing Supply Chain Security, IAC rules are independent from C-TPAT and under present TSA guidelines may not be comingled; interagency cooperation at its best.

22.6. SOURCES OF ASSISTANCE

Executive Briefing

There is little reason or excuse for importers or exporters to act without information or assistance. The type of information and the need for it to be accurate and reliable will determine the sources that should be sought out and the cost of the information.

22.6.1. GOVERNMENT SOURCES

Government agencies can be a good source of information with several provisos:

Finding the right person and getting to speak to them can often be exceedingly difficult.

Everyone that you will speak to is likely to sound knowledgeable, if for no other reason than the fact that they are supposed to know more than you. That does not mean that they know enough to give an answer that can be relied upon.

Most government officials, while pleased to provide general information, will not give an opinion that can be relied upon without having all the facts *in writing*.

Information obtained informally is not binding and therefore should not be relied upon.

22.6.2. CUSTOMS BROKER

A good Customs Broker can be an excellent source of information with respect to import transactions, Customs matters, and, in some cases, the requirements of other agencies. Many Customs Brokers are also Freight Forwarders, Truckers and NVOs and therefore can also be a good source of practical information and services regarding the logistics of both imports and exports. Be aware that Customs Brokers are paid to provide 'best efforts', which is not a warranty of correctness. While many are extremely knowledgeable and experienced, consider consulting Customs Counsel when planning a major program which will have substantial long term impact or when more than ministerial problems arise.

Customs Today is a magazine published by U.S. Customs and Border Protection, formerly the U.S. Customs Service. It being unusual for the magazine to include articles from the private sector, this article, published in 1973 appeared with the note "(The author is a licensed Broker..., President of Leading Forwarders, Inc. in New York, and President of the National Customs Brokers & Forwarders Association of America, Inc. *He wrote this article at the editor's request.*)". It remains one of the most accurate descriptions of what a Customs Broker is and what services they perform.

- Continued on next page –

THE CUSTOMS BROKER

by Leonard M. Shayne

A Customhouse broker is an individual or company licensed by the Treasury Department under Sec. 6411 of the Tariff Act to render service to importers and exporters.

For over 100 years, Customhouse brokers have been performing and expanding this role. Thus, legislation recently sponsored by Treasury recommended that the name be changed from "Customhouse broker" to "Customs broker," "to reflect the changing character of the industry brokers no longer conduct business exclusively from offices at Customhouses, but now deal with Customs wherever imported cargo is handled." [Finally passed as the Customs Brokers Act in 1984]

There are about 3,000 [today there are about 12,500] individually licensed Customs brokers. Each is an American citizen who has passed an examination to prove his competence and fitness. Whatever their formal education may be, most have learned what they know largely through apprenticeship.

Most brokers do not practice as individuals, but are officers, partners or employees of companies which act as Customs brokers [of which there are about 4,600]. Some of these companies have branches in many ports. Some Customs brokerage operations are divisions of large transport companies.

Generally, however, the average Customs brokerage firm [with the exception of few very large Customs Brokers many of which are owned or tied into carriers or couriers] is small, consisting of about 10 employees. The turnover of these employees is low, and, as in the Customs Service itself, involvement with the intricacies, and perhaps the romance, of trade tends to capture the individual for life.

Most firms also perform other services which have little to do with Customs. For example, they may be export ocean freight forwarders, and as such, licensed by the Federal Maritime Commission. They may handle air freight exports by acting as air freight sales agents for airlines.

Some are international air freight consolidators who, under Civil Aeronautics Board authorization, act as indirect carriers for the air transport of goods. Some are rail or truck forwarders under Interstate Commerce Commission jurisdiction.

These are the major and more common activities. In addition, depending upon the local circumstances, brokers may also be insurance brokers, local truckman, warehouseman, packers, coopers, weighers, vessel agents, carriers' agents, travel agents, messenger services, and much more.

In addition to serving importers, Customs brokers also perform valuable services for the Customs Service. The most obvious benefit to the Service derives from the fact that most importers use Customs brokers. Thus, the people in the Customs Service have to deal with fewer people in the public sector.

If there were no Customs brokers, the Service might have to deal with 100 times as many individual importers. The administrative burden of coping with increased phone calls, mail and personal visits, would undoubtedly be beyond the capacity of the Service's facilities or personnel.

There are many ways unseen by Customs that brokers relieve the Service of burdensome demands from the public. There are countless prospective importers, and prospective exporters to the United States, who call upon brokers to given them information on how to import and how to clear an imported item through Customs.

As brokers know, the clearance through Customs of a particular import may involve far more than is apparent to the prospective importer. In fact, some of the most important questions on this subject are often those which he doesn't ask.

He usually will want to know the rate of duty – but he may not know that some physical characteristic of the item or some other factor may change that rate substantially. These may or may not be called to his attention when he directs his questions to someone in the Service who may not realize the extent of his ignorance.

The problems of valuation for duty assessment purposes as well as the existence of such impediments as quotas, dumping duties, licensing, trademark restrictions. Department of Agriculture controls, special marking requirements and other considerations may not be anticipated by the novice importer. It is rare that he knows how to get this information directly, authoritatively and all from one source in the Service, and if he does, the tax on the patience, the knowledge, and the time of the official involved must be enormous.

In any event, the Customs broker supplements this activity of the Customs Service, and adds advice and information about new restrictions which are not yet in effect but might be applicable at the time of importation. In a nutshell, the amount of information dispensed by Customs brokers to new importers has such a character that the Service could not easily dispense it and a volume beyond estimate.

Information and advice of a similar character, but at a different level of expertise, is supplied by brokers to experienced importers. At times the broker may know and supply the answers. But, sometimes the broker's most valuable contribution to both the importer and the Service is to direct the importer to the right Customs official. In other instances, he may refer the inquirer to another Government agency altogether, or to an attorney who specializes in the matter.

The "recognition of important problems" is unfortunately not a skill which can be tested in the written examination for a Customs broker's license. It is one acquired only in the hard school of experience. But the ability to analyze a problem, and knowledge of where to go for the answers, make up the hallmark of the good Customs broker.

Part the broker's time is spent as interpreter – yes, interpreting to importers the "officialese" of directives, regulations and laws. It all may be perfectly clear to those who live with it every day (although I doubt it), but it isn't so clear to the public; so, the broker has to translate for his clients.

A case in point was the recent dollar devaluation. It would be interesting to know how many man-hours Customs officials gave to importers and to brokers explaining the implications of the devaluation – and how many hundreds of times as many man-hours brokers and attorneys have spent explaining to importers what the Customs officials meant.

No offense intended! It is just a very technical subject. Besides, emotions get involved when the unexpected hits us, and not the least of the Customs broker's job is to tame the tigers on both sides of the forest.

Obviously, in order to do his job well, the broker must know how the Customs Service is organized, what makes it tick, and who does what job. And if he wants cooperation, he must know how to give it. The result is that brokers do many things to facilitate the jobs of individual Customs employees.

Members of the Customs Service find the chief evidence of the broker's existence in the Customs documents which the brokers prepare. And some, like some members of the public, think of brokers as "form fillers." That is a misconception.

Brokers devote less than 50 percent [with advent of automation and direct government interfaces today it is less than 30 percent] of their time and effort, in most Customs brokerage businesses to the actual preparation and handling of Customs documents. They spend many man-hours dealing with importers, banks, air lines, steamship companies, truckmen, railroads, and others involved in the trade process, who have their own requirements and in fact, their own language and their own mystique.

Brokers give a substantial amount of their time to obtaining and receiving documents so that shipments can be cleared. Often they provide much assistance to help importers route their shipments via the best ways.

This may involve recommending foreign forwarders in many areas of the world to handle the shipping details and documentation for export from these countries to the United States.

Brokers may arrange temporary warehousing abroad, or assembly of goods from many sources of supply, or consolidation with shipments of other importers to save costs. Then, of course, there would be the need to deconsolidate both documents and freight upon arrival in the U.S.A.

Brokers also help importers choose carriers. This is a complicated problem involving many considerations of timing and costs, and it requires the analysis of much data to which shipper, foreign forwarders, carriers, Customs broker and importer may all contribute their expertise.

For some products, it means deciding first whether to ship via air or vessel, and via what ports. Then, the decision may lie between containerization or not. The next choice may be whether to use one line rather than another, etc. These decisions are constantly being made and reviewed.

There are other details of planning for an import which the broker may give advice about, or actually arrange. These include estimates of landed cost; payment for goods through draft, C.O.D., or letter of credit; insurance; redelivery of cargo from U.S. point of arrival to destination; warehousing in the U.S.; distribution in the U.S.; and many other services which an importer may not wish to perform for himself.

Customs clearance forms are but pieces of paper, a means to an end. The end is, of course, compliance with the laws of the United States governing the goods tendered for admission to the nation's commerce.

Obviously, the broker cannot properly complete the forms unless he knows those laws and knows what procedures must be followed in order to comply.

Considering the vast complex of laws affecting various imports, it is a hard task for Customs, dividing its responsibilities among many experts, to keep abreast of things. But think of the burden on the small firm of Customs brokers which is expected to know so much about every item it handles!

When the broker deals with the Customs import specialist, he is expected to know all about the classification problems of every item in every entry he presents, about all the factors affecting the appraisement, about exchange rats, and about all the rules affecting the way the duty is then calculated.

When he deals with administrative officials, he is expected to be an expert on bonds, and on powers of attorney, and on other highly technical problems, as well as to be aware of all the special requirements of law for all the different kinds of merchandise he may handle.

When he deals with the Customs inspector, he is expected to know all about cargo handling problems. And when he deals with other agencies of the Government, it is expect by them that he will have the same expertise in their realm.

Retired Customs employees who go to work for brokers are uniformly amazed at how much a broker has to know and to do. For, no import transaction is "home free" until the broker has done what the Customs Service accepts as a perfect job, and until the carrier and the importer also judge it to be perfect.

There are still other tasks to which the broker devotes the rest of his energies. There is the matter of arranging for the release of the goods by the import carrier. This may involve the surrender to it of an original bill of lading, and sometime the disbursement of freight. There may be demurrage charges to pay if the Customs clearance wasn't affected, and the goods were not physically taken from the import carrier, within the free time.

Incidentally, the broker may be taken to task for this occurrence, although it may not be his fault at all. For example, documents needed for clearance are not received in time because delayed in the mail; documents presented to Customs are delayed in approval; documents otherwise approvable have be lost en route, or at the terminal; or goods are not picked up from the import carrier because of congestion or lack of facilities.

If the broker is forced to pay for the demurrage out of his own pocket, the cost may well exceed his fees for the Customs clearance. The final calamity occurs if the goods are sent to General Order for any of the foregoing reasons.

Things being as they are with cargo and with the human beings who handle it, there are claims and counterclaims for shortages, damages, delays, mishaps, and whatnot among the daily chores of every Customs broker. It is when these things happen to cargo or documents that the broker learns what the name "broker" really means.

The broker is the "middle man" who, working with all parties to a transaction, tries to bring them together, to keep order, to keep things moving, to minimize losses, to satisfy everybody, and to keep his head and his reputation so that he will still be around to handle the next crisis when it comes along tomorrow.

22.6.3. FORWARDERS

Freight Forwarders are good sources of information on the physical transportation of goods, but it is important to understand the scope of experience. Freight Forwarders fall into two classes: those licensed by the Federal Maritime Commission to handle exports, and those which are not licensed but handle only inbound or domestic movements. Outside of the United States, Freight Forwarders can also include, what we in the United States term, NVOs.

22.6.4. CARRIERS, TRUCKERS, CONSOLIDATORS

A carrier's business is to move freight. They are not generally a good source of information as to local government requirements, except as it affects their business. They are a good source of information on transportation.

22.6.5. CUSTOMS ATTORNEY

There are a relatively small number of attorneys who practice in the areas of Customs, Trade and Transportation. A number of very large law firms have a few attorneys who practice International Trade law, even fewer have attorneys who possess expertise in Customs matters, related agency issues, and other related transportation matters.

22.6.6. CONSULTANTS

There are many persons and companies who hold themselves out as consultants in various areas of International Trade. They range from the well qualified to the dangerous. Prior employment with the government is no assurance as to quality.

Although generally not licensed, they can nevertheless, in their areas of specialization, be a good source of information and advice. While a license is not generally required to act as a consultant, a license may be required in order to represent you before certain government agencies.

22.6.7. NVOCC (NVO)

Non-Vessel Operating Common Carriers can be thought of as a combination of carrier and freight forwarder with respect to the scope of their services and knowledge. Those NVOs that are essentially mini carriers may not always be a viable source of information, since their interest is mostly in selling transportation service. An NVO that provides a larger scope of services is a better source of information.

22.6.8. DECONSOLIDATORS

Deconsolidators essentially unload or segregate shipments for various consignees, although they may perform this function as part of other services they provide. While their services may be limited to deconsolidation and warehousing they may nevertheless be a good source of referral to other professionals who can be of assistance.

22.6.9. TRADE ASSOCIATION AND JOURNALS

Trade Associations can be, and usually are, an excellent source of general information about governmental requirements. Great care, however, should be taken in applying information on particular products or lines, since very often problems are fact specific, and when it comes to government compliance, the facts can mean everything.

- Balance of page intentionally left blank –

- Page intentionally left blank –

23. FREE FROM THE AUTHORS

23.1. FERRETING OUT IDENTITY THEFT IN YOUR INTERNATIONAL TRADE TRANSACTIONS

There are certain things that an importer and exporter can do to both protect themselves from identity theft and simultaneously achieve better control over their trade transactions. These reports are either free or relatively inexpensive, and only need to be requested periodically. They include:

- ✓ Making an annual request to Customs and Border Protection for a list of all entries made under your EIN.
- ✓ Making an annual request to Census for a list of all exports in which you are identified as the U.S. Principal Party in Interest.
- ✓ Protecting others is a way of protecting yourself. Asking your Customs Broker and Freight Forwarder to utilize Trade-ID identity verification systems, which is an industry tool for verifying corporate identities in international trade transactions, if they are not already doing so.
- ✓ If you have previously been a victim of corporate identity theft, adding your name to Trade-ID's Identity Theft Watch List, puts all Customs Brokers and Freight Forwarders using the system on notice should they get a request to do business under your EIN, and allows you to exercise extra caution to ensure it is actually you requesting their services.

> ***Free Offer***
>
> **If someone is using your identity for their import or export transactions they are ruining your reputation with the government and that could delay your shipments and cost you money.**
>
> **The U.S. government offers several trade related reports which, similar to a credit report, can help you identify unauthorized transactions undertaken in your name.**
>
> **We will send you model request forms and instructions on how you can get your own reports. Sign up for your instruction package at:**
>
> **ShayneLawGroup.com/IdentityTheftHelp**
>
> ***We do not charge for this.***
> ***We do not make unsolicited follow-up calls.***

The authors of *Managing Import and Export Opportunities and Risks* believe that these steps are sufficiently important:

- ✓ If you have already been the victim of corporate identity theft or believe that you are at prime risk of identity theft in your International Trade transactions, we will work with your Customs Broker or Freight Forwarder to add your details to the industry Watch List.
- ✓ With respect to your import transactions, once per year we will assist you in obtaining the ITRAC report from Customs and Border Protection. You will only be responsible for any

disbursements or charges from Customs along with any courier charges.

✓ With respect to your export transactions, once per year we will assist you in obtaining from Census copies of the Automated Export System records filed in your name. You will only be responsible for any disbursements or charges from Customs along with any postage.

23.2. SPIRAL APPROACH TO IMPLEMENTING AN INFORMED COMPLIANCE PROGRAM

There are as many ways to create an Informed Compliance Program as there are companies.

What is important is not the complexity of the program but that it addresses how your business actually functions. Creating a program does not have to be an overly burdensome task. What it has to be is ... done. Not just because it is the law, but because no company is perfect and having one will help you minimize your exposure to problems, if and when issues arise.

The Spiral Approach is the product of 40 years of experience working with both importers and exporters, helping them both create effective programs and guiding them through government reviews.

The Spiral Approach will walk you through 8 phases of program creation and maintenance. Those 8 phases start with a review of as little as one file for each type of transaction your company has. It is designed to delve progressively deeper into details, *if required*, until a complete program results.

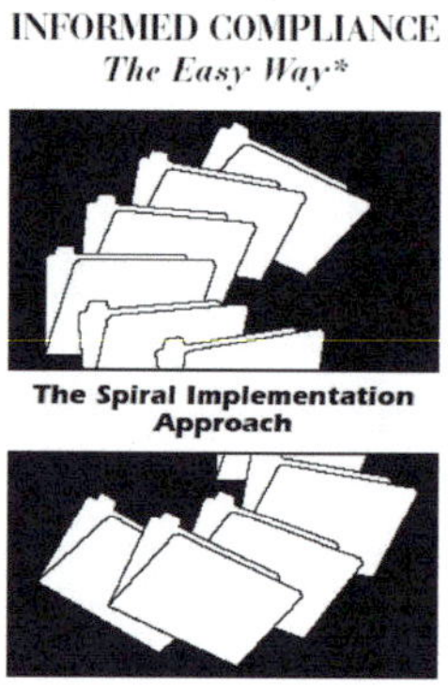

Essential to the program development is an understanding that most things a company does will, to some extent, be fully compliant. The goal is, therefore, NOT to replace your existing protocols, which only puts extra work on the plate of already over-burdened staff, and which would only be ignored anyway, but to understand the way in which your business operates so that minor, rather than major, changes can be implemented.

We can help you get your Informed Compliance program started. The package is free for the asking. But it is up to you to take the first step by asking for it.

We hope you have found MANAGING IMPORT AND EXPORT OPPORTUNITIES AND RISKS to be useful.

There will always be issues that arise that we have not covered or that you could not have anticipated or identified. If you have questions, the most important thing you can do is to make a due diligence inquiry. What you don't want to do is, through inaction, allow easy to correct errors to become institutional practices just waiting for the government to discover.

We appreciate the burden that comes from international trade compliance which is why our logo is Atlas struggling to hold up a cargo container.

While knowledge may not always identify opportunities,
it remains the best defense against risk.

William (Billie) Shayne

SHAYNE
LAW GROUP, P.C.

212 566-4949

wshayne@shaynelawgroup.com

– Page intentionally left blank –

1

2

A

B

C

D

E

R

S

T

U

V

W

CITE AS

APA

REFERENCE LIST:

Shayne, W.C. & Lazar, M.E. (2017). *Managing import and export opportunities and risks. An insider's guide for the busy executive. Business education edition.* (3rd ed.) New York, NY: International Trade Publishing Co.

IN TEXT:

(Shayne & Lazar, 2017) or (Shayne & Lazar, 2017, p24.)

MLA

WORKS CITED:

Shayne, William and Lazar, Melvin. *Managing Import and Export Opportunities and Risks*. An Insider's Guide for the Busy Executive. Business Education Edition. 3rd ed. New York: International Trade Publishing Co., 2017. Print.

IN TEXT:

(Shayne, 24)

Legal

TABLE OF AUTHORITIES:

W.C. SHAYNE & M.E. LAZAR, MANAGING IMPORT AND EXPORT OPPORTUNITIES AND RISKS. AN INSIDER'S GUIDE FOR THE BUSY EXECUTIVE. BUSINESS EDUCATION EDITION (3rd ed. 2017)

IN TEXT, INITIAL USE:

W.C. SHAYNE & M.E. LAZAR, MANAGING IMPORT AND EXPORT OPPORTUNITIES AND RISKS. AN INSIDER'S GUIDE FOR THE BUSY EXECUTIVE. BUSINESS EDUCATION EDITION [24] (3rd ed. 2017)

IN TEXT, SUBSEQUENT USE:

SHAYNE, *supra [id]* at #

20170131

Made in the USA
Las Vegas, NV
03 November 2026

57421603R00159